*Probability,
Objectivity
and Evidence*

International Library of Philosophy

Editor: Ted Honderich

A catalogue of books already published in the
International Library of Philosophy
will be found at the end of this volume

Probability, Objectivity and Evidence

F.C. Benenson
Lecturer in Philosophy
University of Birmingham

ROUTLEDGE & KEGAN PAUL
London, Boston, Melbourne and Henley

First published in 1984
by Routledge & Kegan Paul plc

39 Store Street, London WC1E 7DD, England

9 Park Street, Boston, Mass. 02108, USA

464 St Kilda Road, Melbourne,
Victoria 3004, Australia and

Broadway House, Newtown Road,
Henley-on-Thames, Oxon RG9 1EN, England
Set in Press Roman 10/12
by Columns of Reading
and printed in Great Britain
by T.J. Press (Padstow) Ltd, Padstow, Cornwall

Copyright © F.C. Benenson 1984

No part of this book may be reproduced in
any form without permission from the publisher,
except for the quotation of brief passages
in criticism

Library of Congress Cataloging in Publication Data

Benenson, F.C. (Frederick C.)
Probability, objectivity, and evidence
(International library of philosophy)
Bibliography: p.
Includes index.
1. Probabilities.   2. Relation (Philosophy)   I. Title.
II. Series.
BC141.B46   1984   121'.63   83-24538
British Library CIP data available
ISBN 0-7100-9598-8

*To my father, who first taught me
about probability*

CONTENTS

Acknowledgments ix
Introduction 1

I Problems and Aims 10
Preliminary Remarks 10
The Logical Relation Theory 13
The Requirement of Total Evidence 23
Ayer's Objection and the Problem of Induction 39
Objective and Subjective Judgments of Probability 43
Single-Case Probabilities 48

II Our Knowledge of Probabilities 52
Objective Probabilities and Realism 54
Coming to Know Objective Probabilities 59
Two Concepts 68
Subjectivism and the Logical Relation Theory 75

III Specificatory Evidence and Technology 80
The Available Specificatory Evidence 81
Decidability in Principle and Decidability in Practice 86
Objectivity and Subjectivity Again 93
Inductive Probability and Science 103
The Revision of Probability Judgments 113

Contents

IV	Revising Probability Judgments	116
	Realism and the Revision of Probability Judgments	129
	Analysis of Earlier Arguments	133
V	Statistical Probabilities	149
	Rejection Rules and Empirical Probability	151
	Confidence Intervals and Operational Definitions of Probability	161
	Statistical Evidence and the Revision of Probability Judgments	166
	Decidability in Principle and in Practice, Again	189
	A Finite Frequency Theory	196
	The Available Statistical Evidence	205
VI	The Principle of Indifference and the Classical Theory of Probability	220
	The Principle's History	221
	The Principle and Identity Conditions for Judgments of Probability	235
	Applying the Principle in Practice	243
	The Classical Theory of Probability	246
VII	Objections to the Principle of Indifference	249
	Null Evidence and Equally Balanced Evidence	251
	The Contradictions	256
	Subjectivism and the Principle of Indifference	271
	Bibliography	278
	Index	280

ACKNOWLEDGMENTS

Thanks are especially due to Crispin Wright both for the influence of his own work — in particular his writings on the philosophy of mathematics (1980) — and the advice and encouragement he has given me over a number of years for my own work. I am also indebted to my colleagues Dr C.J. Hookway and Dr H. Noonan for their interest and advice. Chapters VI and VII of the present work were, for the most part, completed in 1975 as part of my D.Phil. thesis supervised by Simon Blackburn of Pembroke College, Oxford, from whose advice I benefited and to whom part of the example with which I begin the book is due. In addition I am indebted to various friends and relations who listened more or less patiently as I groped my way towards many of the ideas in this book. Thanks also to my typist of long standing, Mrs Jill Mabbitt of Scotts Office Services, whose work made my own labours far less burdensome. Above all I am indebted to my wife, Donna, who provided the emotional environment in which I was able to finish this book; on a more practical level, my prose style, such as it is, benefited greatly from her skills and advice as a writer.

I am grateful to Cambridge University Press for permission to use quotations from S. Blackburn, *Reason and Prediction* (1973) and R.B. Braithwaite, *Scientific Explanation* (1953); also to Macmillan, London and Basingstoke, for quotations from J.M. Keynes, *A Treatise on Probability* (1921) and to Cambridge University Press (USA) for excerpts from *The Collected Writings of John Maynard Keynes,* vol. 8, The Royal Economic Society ©.

INTRODUCTION

I should begin by warning the reader that many of the views presented in this book are decidedly unfashionable; the theory of probability I defend is what has commonly come to be known as the logical relation theory, and I think it is fair to say that this theory has found little acceptance in the literature of the subject since 1960, or thereabouts. At least one of the claims I make — that this theory provides a single, correct, analysis of probability — has not been taken seriously since before the last war; since Carnap's celebrated article (1945), the most logical relation theorists have claimed is that their theory provides a correct account of an idea of inductive support central to ordinary statements on probability and statements on the acceptance of scientific hypotheses, but that the concept of probability employed *within* science is a distinct one, concerned with objective physical states. In contrast I have tried to show that the concept of probability employed in science can best be understood as that of inductive probability; to do so, it is necessary to show both how the logical relation theory of probability can be given a formulation sufficiently objective for the purposes of science, and how other attempts to explain the objective character of probability judgments are unsatisfactory. These and related questions occupy the first five chapters of the book. (The last two chapters contain more or less independent material on the principle of indifference.) I might add that, though the thesis that there exists only one genuine concept of probability has been out of fashion for a long time, the account of the objectivity of probability statements I give has been influenced by recent discussions on the nature of objectivity in mathematics and its

Introduction

relation to realist and anti-realist conceptions of mathematics. In essence, I believe that the logical relation theory alone can explain how we have objective knowledge of probabilities, and so it alone provides a viable systematization of the concept of probability used in science.

The current discussion of realist and anti-realist accounts of the meaning of mathematical terms also led me to consider what general assumptions on meaning underlie various rival theories of probability, a concern curiously absent in most recent discussions of probability theory. Although a number of logical positivists (e.g. Reichenbach, Von Mises and Carnap), as well as those influenced by their work (e.g. C.I. Lewis and R.B. Braithwaite), discussed the analysis of probability statements in the light of general considerations about meaning, their arguments were often sketchy and inconclusive; as interest in the propensity theory and subjectivist theories of probability increased, probability theorists paid even less attention to such general considerations, becoming more and more absorbed in the details specific to those theories. However, some of the philosophers who did discuss the analysis of probability statements within the context of general considerations in the theory of meaning saw that an adequate account of the concept of probability should fulfil a condition of finite decidability. In a somewhat halfhearted – and, to my mind, most unsatisfactory way – Reichenbach tried to explain how the frequency theory fulfilled a condition of finite attainability, and I discuss his views on this at some length in Chapter V. Although less explicit about the matter, Braithwaite's attempt to give rules for rejecting statements on 'statistical' probability in the light of finite observations of repeated trials was probably motivated by a similar concern. C.I. Lewis, whose work on probability seems to me unjustly neglected, also argued forcefully that any adequate analysis of probability must fulfil a condition of finite decidability; my own earlier neglect of his work meant that I only came across his views after I had formulated my own, and so, as I will indicate in more detail below, I have not drawn as much on his work as I might have.

In any case it does not seem to me that a satisfactory account of the meaning of probability statements was given by Reichenbach, Braithwaite or Lewis, and to give such an account I have drawn on Dummett's characterization of the intuitionist's explanation of mathematical terms as a paradigm of an explanation of the meaning of a class of statements in terms of finitely ascertainable assertion conditions for those statements. In effect, I conclude that the logical

Introduction

relation theory of Keynes and Carnap provides an anti-realist explanation of probability statements, along the lines suggested by Dummett.

This much said, however, let me add that since anti-realism in general — and the kind of anti-realist account of meaning envisioned by Dummett in particular — are currently the subject of much controversy, I have, wherever possible, tried to formulate the arguments of this book without appeal to anti-realist assumptions (though I doubt the reader will form that impression from the first few sections of Chapter I). In general in Chapters II-V I have tried to separate out material on realism and anti-realism from a discussion of other topics by use of appropriate section headings; more specifically, in Chapters IV and V (which, to my mind, are the most important parts of the book) I have been at pains to begin by presenting my views in an intuitive fashion (i.e. pp. 116-28 and pp. 149-89), only later in those chapters turning to a discussion of anti-realism and finite decidability. In fact, throughout most of the book I have only adopted an anti-realist viewpoint in order to have a convenient general framework within which to present a defence of the logical relation theory, which of course I believe to be viable in its own right — that is, without specific anti-realist assumptions.

None the less, there seem to me quite good reasons for using an anti-realist framework to express a number of arguments, particularly the crucial argument of Chapter V concerning the notion of 'statistical' probability, and the reader might find it helpful if I were to sketch here the main lines of that argument and its relation to the realist—anti-realist dispute. For me, the most intriguing aspect of the concept of statistical probability is the way in which judgments of statistical probability are usually held to be indefinitely revisable — that is, always open to subsequent correction. There is little doubt that such a conception of probability has some grounding in our intuitive way of thinking on probability — we commonly speak of probability statements as 'estimates', indicating our willingness to revise them. Since it appears that any probability statement is open to revision in such a way — and so can only constitute an estimate of probability — we readily conceive of probability statements forming an infinite series of ever-fallible estimates, an idea wholly in accord with the various explicatations put forward for the concept of statistical probability by philosophers of science. Moreover — and this indicates my concern with the objectivity of probability statements — the conception of an infinite series of probability estimates, each amenable to subsequent revision, seems inevitable if we regard probability statements as objectively true or

Introduction

false, as there seems to be no way to ensure that any judgment of probability we actually make on the basis of a finite amount of observation is, objectively speaking, the correct one.

But though natural enough in various ways, the idea of an objective, statistical, probability — of which we can only form a series of ever-fallible estimates — seems to me fraught with difficulties. Indeed it is such a strange conception that no agreement has ever been reached on just what such an objective statistical probability would be, with frequency theorists disagreeing with propensity theorists and propensity theorists disagreeing amongst themselves as to the exact nature of such an objective probability. I also believe — and try to establish at the start of Chapters II and V — that no finitely decidable criteria of application can be given for such a concept. But if we reject theories of objective, statistical, probability, how are we to make sense of the intuitive idea of an infinite series of probability estimates?

The answer — or at least the answer I present in Chapters IV and V — lies in the logical relation theory of probability and its analysis of ordinary statements of probability not explicitly mentioning evidence. According to the logical relation theory, probability statements are always relative to evidence, and when we ordinarily speak of the probability of a given phenomenon without specification of evidence, we have in mind the total relevant evidence available. However, the total statistical evidence available concerning a given phenomenon — the total available data on the observed frequency in repeated trials up to a particular time — is not a fixed amount, but increases with the time allotted in which the repeated observations can be made. Thus what we mean when we speak of the probability of a given phenomenon — without specification of a particular body of evidence — will vary and change over time as more and more statistical evidence can be known, and this to my mind is the origin of the idea of an estimate of probability. More exactly, the idea that any given statement of probability (by which is meant any given statement of probability not explicitly mentioning evidence) is always open to revision only reflects the fact that such statements are always relative to evidence, and thus their truth value will change as the body of evidence in relation to which they are taken changes.

It is then easy to explain the conception of an infinite series of ever-fallible probability estimates by reference to the indefinitely extendable, or potentially infinite, series of observations of repeated trials we can make over time. The potentially infinite series of

Introduction

observations of repeated instances of a given phenomenon we can make over time takes the form of a succession of ever-increasing finite totalities of observations, made at successive times. Each successive finite totality constitutes an increased body of observational evidence, and if we make a series of statements on the probability of a given phenomenon — each omitting mention of evidence — we will tacitly adopt, successively, each such totality as the second term for our judgments on the probability of the phenomenon in question; these judgments will then form an infinite series of ever-revised statements on probability, if different relative probabilities obtain in relation to the successive bodies of evidence.

Readers familiar with the intuitionist's treatment of infinity will recognize this characterization of the infinite series of observations we can make of a given phenomenon — the intuitionists claim that the only concept of infinity admissible into mathematics is that of a succession of ever-increasing finite totalities. Readers familiar with Dummett's treatment of anti-realism as a generalization of the intuitionist view of mathematics will begin to see why I rely on his characterization of anti-realist theories of meaning, for the successive finite totalities of observational evidence referred to above may plausibly be thought of as the assertion conditions for our ordinary judgments of probability.

Unfortunately, although such an analysis of probability will do as an account of our intuitive notion of a probability estimate, it does not, as it stands, shed much light on the concept of statistical probability apparently used by scientists. Scientists and statisticians have developed quite specific, and mathematically exact, techniques for estimating probability on the basis of observations of small samples and, on the surface at least, the idea of a probability estimate implicit in the use of these techniques is quite different from that described in the above paragraph. Moreover, it is natural to think that these techniques provide finitely decidable criteria for statements on objective, statistical, probability, and so allow one to give an account of the notion of an objective probability acceptable to the anti-realist. At the start of Chapter V I try to explain why these techniques cannot be so interpreted, and then try to demonstrate that such techniques can, and should, be understood within the general framework I sketched in the above paragraph. Although this is the part of the book which took the longest amount of time to complete, the basic line of argument turns out to be surprisingly simple: the statistical techniques used by scientists and statisticians to estimate probabilities are, of course, based on the binomial law and Bernoulli's Law of Large Numbers and, as interpreted within the logical relation theory, these laws refer to probability relations between hypotheses concerning the frequency in samples of a given size and information on the frequency in very large parent populations from which the samples are drawn.

In my view, each of the successively larger finite totalities of observational evidence we obtain when we carry out repeated observations of a given phenomenon over time should be thought of as a parent population from which the small samples scientists usually use as the basis of their judgments of probability are drawn. Accordingly, scientists' procedures for estimating probabilities can be thought of as techniques for estimating how accurately probability values based on the evidence of small samples approximate the values which we would obtain if we spent more time (and trouble) observing more repeated instances of the same basic phenomenon. The degree of probability, or confidence, we have in our estimates just reflects the probability relations which obtain between the larger bodies of evidence we would obtain in this way and the smaller ones we actually observe. On such a view, what we are estimating when we use the statistical techniques in question is not an objective, statistical, probability (which is the realist's way of viewing the matter) but, rather, what we would come to know of probability if we carried out more observations than we have already done, which seems to me a view admirably in accord with anti-realism. The reason we regard an estimate of probability as indefinitely revisable is that what we could come to know of the probability of a given phenomenon if we made more observations — what we are estimating — is not one thing, but an indefinite succession of different things, i.e. the probabilities relative to the information on the results in *each* of the successively larger finite populations which form the indefinitely extendible sequence of observations we can make of the phenomenon in question.

Well, perhaps, the argument is not, as I have suggested, surprisingly simple — it takes two-thirds of Chapter V (the longest chapter of the book) to work it out in detail, and the sketchy remarks I have just made can therefore do little more than convey something of the motivation behind the discussion in earlier chapters of realism and anti-realism. Though I believe this discussion of statistical probability is novel, I can take some comfort in the fact that my argument has certain points in common with other, earlier, discussions of statistical

Introduction

probability. Kyburg, whose theory I mention in passing in several places, exploited the same relations of epistemic probability between parent populations and samples to develop his theory on the relationship of statistical probability to epistemic probability. His theory differs in a number of ways from mine and it might have been illuminating to compare our two theories at greater length than I have. In many respects his theory can be thought of as a modification of Reichenbach's formulation of a finite frequency theory, which I discuss at length in Chapter V, and it suffers from the same essential defect. Specifically, neither theory can make sense of the intuition that probability estimates are indefinitely revisable, for both attempt to explain the notion of statistical probability by reference to the frequency which obtains in one very large, but fixed, finite class of observations. In this regard, my theory is closer to Braithwaite's account of statistical probability, which has the very considerable merit of explaining the indefinite revisability of probability statements in terms of the potentially infinite series of observations of a given phenomenon we can make over time. As may be obvious from Chapter V, his theory was the largest single influence on mine, but, in the end, the contrast between our two theories could not be greater, which, again, should be obvious from Chapter V.

The other writer whose views seem closest to mine is C.I. Lewis, though his treatment of statistical techniques is quite different from mine and is, to my mind, quite unsatisfactory. The main point of similarity is his criticism of objective theories of probability, particularly his claim that such theories are not finitely decidable, but there are also points of similarity in our treatment of the 'a priori' probabilities associated with the principle of indifference. Although he had a certain sympathy for the principle (like many other logical relation theorists), he did not, to my mind, appreciate the true nature of the relationship between the logical relation theory and the principle of indifference, which I attempt to clarify in Chapters VI and VII. Had I myself been familiar with his views earlier, it might have been possible (and desirable) to devote more space to discussing them.

It might be appropriate here to indicate other areas which have not received as much attention as they perhaps deserve. I have said very little in the book about theories of subjective or personalist probability, although there are numerous affinities between the logical relation theory and such theories, which it might have been worthwhile to explore in detail. I have not examined such theories at length because

Introduction

I do not believe — nor think their advocates believe — they provide an adequate account of how we have *objective* knowledge of probabilities, one of my main concerns throughout the book.

A perhaps more serious shortcoming of the book is that I have not investigated in any detail several not altogether unrelated technical problems which bear directly on the logical relation theory as I have formulated it. The first is the well-known problem concerning the confirmation of universal hypotheses. Although various solutions have been proposed to this problem — from Carnap's instance criterion of confirmation to Hintikka's suggestion to choose measure functions outside the λ continuum — I do not try to defend any of these solutions in the book, nor discuss the problem of the confirmation of universal hypotheses at any length. Partly this is because the issue is still a highly technical one for which there is no agreed solution, partly because my primary concern in the book is to show how the logical relation theory provides an adequate account of the concept of probability employed *within* science itself, and thus I have more or less taken it for granted that it provides an adequate account of the inductive probability enjoyed by scientific hypotheses. I believe — and explain at length — that the concept of probability employed within science can be understood in terms of the notion of inductive probability with $\lambda = 0$ as measure function. Although this requires a somewhat lengthy reply to criticisms raised by Carnap (towards the end of Chapter III), I do not go further and advocate the choice of this, or any other measure function, as a solution to the problem of the confirmation of universal hypotheses. At present I believe it is possible to resolve this problem without abandoning use of the $\lambda = 0$ measure function, though no doubt this must appear at first glance most unlikely. An approach which seems to me promising here is to adopt a holistic view of the confirmation of scientific hypotheses, along the lines suggested by Quine. The universal hypotheses required for the purpose of science — and thus the ones which pose the most serious problem for the inductivist — could be regarded as at the interior of a complex conceptual system, and there would be no direct confirmation or disconfirmation of these hypotheses. Instead our acceptance of them would depend on their links to observational statements at the exterior of the system, which would invariably be statistical in form. Obviously, a great deal of detailed investigation — far beyond the scope of the present work — would be necessary to establish such a view, and so, in the present work, I have more or less ignored these problems.

Introduction

Another inportant question I have more or less ignored in the main body of this work concerns the concept of relevance — throughout most of the book I simply assume various bodies of evidence are relevant to hypotheses concerning the future, without explaining how this is to be established. The logical relation theorist has no real difficulty in explaining the notion of relevance in terms of logical probabilities — once a measure function is chosen, judgments of relevance follow easily — but there remains the question of how to explain the actual techniques used by scientists and statisticians to determine relevance — for example the Chi Square test — in terms of this conception of probability. I believe this can be done, but, again, a detailed demonstration of this would go well beyond the scope of the present work. Any examination of the Chi Square test necessarily involves, *inter alia*, an analysis of the concept of randomness and random selection used by statisticians, and though I believe the logical relation theory can shed a good deal of light on these matters, the details of this analysis seem to me at present rather complicated and of secondary importance to the main concerns of the book. Moreover — and this may be a fitting point at which to end these introductory remarks — I believe that a proper understanding of the statistical procedures for establishing randomness, as well as those used to validate scientific theories involving universal hypotheses, can only be achieved once it is recognized that the concept of probability employed by statisticians and scientists is one of inductive probability, which is perhaps the main point I wish to establish in the current work.

I
PROBLEMS AND AIMS

PRELIMINARY REMARKS

What Augustine said of time seems to be true of probability: we all know what it is until we are asked to define it. When it comes to giving a systematic account of our intuitive concept of probability, even the simplest examples challenge the theoretician. Think of a gambler in the following situations: (a) an ordinary deck of cards is shuffled and placed face down with the gambler to wager whether the top card is red; (b) a roulette wheel is spun, the ball thrown, and the gambler is to place his bet on red or black before the croupier cries 'Rien ne va plus'; (c) an ordinary coin is held by an impartial participant who will toss it in the ordinary manner after the gambler has wagered on 'heads' or 'tails'. Presumably, in each case the gambler will believe that the probability for the relevant alternatives is 1/2, and indeed one could hardly think of more straightforward examples of probability judgments.

But is the probability *really* 1/2 in each case? In the circumstances described in (a) the deck of cards has already been shuffled and placed face down, so that it is completely determined if the top card is red. As regards (b), it is reasonable to think that once the wheel and ball have been spun, the final position of the ball is also wholly determined, although, unlike (a), the physical process in question has yet to be completed. In (c), however, there is little reason to regard the matter as determinate, for the coin has yet to be tossed, and the force with which it is to be tossed cannot be predicted with sufficient accuracy to determine the outcome.

A currently fashionable move here would be to say that the probability is indeed 1/2 in each case, but, in each case, the gambler has in mind a different concept of probability. In (a), the probability value of 1/2 might thus be thought of as based on the degree of partial certainty afforded the hypothesis that the top card is red by the evidence known to the gambler, i.e. that there are 52 cards, 26 black and 26 red, that the shuffle has been thorough, etc. In (c) the probability of 1/2 might be understood in terms of a long-run frequency, or even more fashionably, a propensity to produce this frequency: depending on what theory one favoured, one could say the 1/2 probability of heads with this coin was the coin's propensity to produce a 50 per cent frequency of heads, or was the actual frequency exhibited by ordinary coins in repeated trials. If, like Carnap, one believed there were only two concepts of probability, case (b) could be subsumed under the frequency/propensity account of probability, or the 'evidential' conception used to explain (a), depending on one's preferences; alternatively, one might regard (b) as exhibiting yet another concept of probability.

But, as the aficionado of probability theory knows, each concept of probability adduced by theoreticians to explain apparently straightforward examples has been found suspect by others working in the field: how can we explain case (c) in terms of long-run frequency in repeated trials if, by definition, no individual trial like that described in (c) can have a long-run frequency? An appeal to propensities might be of help here, but it is essential to formulate the propensity theory correctly for, as Mellor [1971, pp. 66-9] notes, Hacking's propensity theory suffers from an analogous problem. Mellor's own propensity theory, while not suffering from such a defect, has in turn, been found to involve an 'obscure' and perhaps even 'fantastic' concept of probability by Mackie [1973, pp. 183-4].

Similarly the explanation of case (a) as a probability judgment expressing the partial certainty warranted by the evidence known to the gambler can easily be faulted. Since the colour of the top card is wholly determined, the partial degree of certainty warranted by the evidence known to the gambler reflects, at least in part, his ignorance of the true state of affairs. Such ignorance may be a wholly subjective matter: assume there is another gambler who has caught a look at the bottom card and has observed it to be red. Relative to what the second gambler knows, the probability of the top card being red is 25/51. Which, then, is the correct probability value? Obviously the gambler who has glimpsed the bottom card is at an advantage and, if such trials were repeated, would stand to make a profit in the long run;

accordingly it would appear that his assessment of the probability is preferable. But is it in any sense the correct one? Like the gambler who takes the value to be 1/2, his assessment reflects his personal knowledge of the situation and this knowledge falls far short of the total amount which could be known in the circumstances. Indeed any probability judgment (other than the assignment of a probability of 1 or 0 to the hypothesis based on the 'evidence' of what the colour of the top card *actually* is) will appear mistaken once additional information is produced.

Thus, if we believe that probability judgments are objective, and always subject to revision if based on purely personal knowledge of a given situation, it is difficult to see how the analysis of probability initially suggested by case (a) can be sustained — that probability judgments reflect degrees of certainty warranted by known evidence. As we will see in detail later on, these and related considerations have led such diverse writers as Von Mises, Popper, Ayer, Blackburn, Lucas and Mellor (to mention a few) to reject a conception of probability which makes judgments of probability reflect degrees of certainty warranted by evidence. But if it turns out to be problematic to analyse case (c) as involving a frequency or propensity concept of probability, and problematic to analyse case (a) as involving degrees of certainty warranted by evidence, we are in a very poor position indeed, for these examples were among the simplest possible and the explanations canvassed seemed at first sight wholly natural.

In fact, like many probability theorists, I believe that the problems indicated above — and for that matter many more to be found in the literature of probability theory — can be resolved by a proper analysis of probability — that is, the one I favour. Contrary to the fashion noted above, I do not believe we need distinguish a variety of probability concepts; in fact I believe that, if it is properly elaborated, the concept of degree of certainty warranted by evidence suffices to account for the totality of our intuitions on probability, and I hope to offer such an elaboration in later chapters.

In this chapter I want to present a number of problems with our concept of probability, which I regard as particularly interesting, and indicate how they bear on rival theories of probability. As the title of this book suggests, one crucial question we will be concerned with is the objectivity of probability judgments. Philosophers working in quite diverse fields (for example ethics and the philosophy of mathematics) have become increasingly interested in the tension between 'objective' and 'subjective' features of the concepts with which they deal; this tension is nowhere more apparent than in the study of probability. The concept of probability as a degree of partial certainty afforded by evidence is one of two that have become known as 'subjective' concepts — for reasons that began to emerge above — and the rival conceptions of probability as frequency or propensity to produce frequency have often been championed as 'objective'. Among other things, I hope to come to some understanding of the sense in which a theory of probability is 'subjective' or 'objective', and see what consequences follow from adopting a subjective or objective theory of probability. One significant — though perhaps obvious — conclusion I reach is that 'objective' theories of probability are highly realist in character; furthermore there seems to be no satisfactory way in which these theories can be modified so as to remove realist presuppositions. In Chapter II, I will explain what I think is wrong with such realist accounts of probability, and the discussion there will lead on to a criticism of Carnap's thesis that there exist two distinct concepts of probability. My overall position is that, in contrast to realist theories of objective probability, the definition of probability as degree of certainty afforded by evidence is admirably suited to an anti-realist conception of meaning — as I will show shortly — and I believe this theory can be articulated in such a way as to explain all the apparently 'objective' aspects of our concept of probability. (The demonstration of this will carry us into later chapters.)

Obviously a number of very general questions on meaning, realism, objectivity, and the nature of empirical knowledge will obtrude on our study of probability, but I will try to limit my investigation of these matters to those problems most immediately relevant to probability theory. To begin these investigations, however, we require a statement of the theory of probability I wish to defend, and this will then lead to a discussion of the relationship of probability theory to more general issues on meaning, realism and objectivity.

THE LOGICAL RELATION THEORY

The theory of probability that I wish to elaborate and contrast to so-called objective theories can be traced back as far as Keynes, and possibly further; it is the view that probability judgments are always relative to evidence, and in fact merely indicate the degree of certainty a particular body of evidence gives to the hypothesis we are concerned with. Considerable attention has been given in recent years to developing this conception of probability under the name of the Logical Relation Theory of Probability, which, in Carnap's work, has become the basis of contemporary inductive logic. Where Keynes had been concerned to develop a system of comparative probability based on relations of equality and inequality of evidential support, Carnap worked to develop the quantitative theory of probability based on a quantitative inductive logic. Since many of the philosophical issues arising in connection with comparative and quantitative relations of evidential support are identical, it will be convenient to classify Keynes's and Carnap's theories as versions of the logical relation theory — which I will hereafter abbreviate as the l.r.t.

The most prominent feature of the l.r.t. is that, on it, no hypothesis can be regarded as probable in its own right; rather, it is a hypothesis coupled with some body of evidence that alone can be said to be 'probable'. An immediate objection to such a 'relational' view of probability is that most judgments of probability — whether made by gamblers, scientists or the ordinary layman — rarely, if ever, mention the body of evidence which, allegedly, is a necessary part of any judgment of probability. The reply to this objection — that such judgments are elliptical for two-term relational judgments involving some body of evidence (indeed, one usually said to be the total amount known or available) — is familiar, but warrants a good deal of attention: in my opinion, many of the most interesting philosophical issues in probability theories turn on the question of how evidence is used as the basis for ordinary probability statements which omit mention of evidence. Indeed, even a preliminary analysis of how such ordinary statements of probability are decided on the basis of evidence brings us directly to central philosophical issues on the meaning and practical role of probability statements — and then to complex questions on realism and objectivity — and so we would do well to consider straight away how evidence is used as the basis for ordinary statements on probability.

Recognizing the Truth of Probability Statements

As I remarked earlier, the claim that probability is a logical relation between bodies of evidence and hypothesis is quite congenial to a general anti-realist position in philosophy, and the basic reason for this must be obvious: the anti-realist in giving his explanation of meaning only appeals to entities which are at least in principle knowable, and both the evidence relevant to a given hypothesis and the logical relation between such evidence and the hypothesis are most readily 'knowable', indeed paradigmatically so. The term 'evidence' just refers to empirical statements which are known, or envisioned as known (as in the case of 'evidence' we can come to know), and logical relations between evidence and hypothesis are known immediately and with complete certainty, if the l.r.t. is to be believed. Thus, when an anti-realist wishes to explain what we mean when we say a certain event or hypothesis[†] has a particular probability, it will be quite natural for him to say that probability statements assert logical relations between bodies of evidence and hypotheses about the outcome of events.

In fact, I believe that one of the great advantages of the l.r.t. is that it so naturally yields an anti-realist explanation of the meaning of probability statements, though I am not sure this has been specifically recognized by others writing within this school. To put more precisely the connection between the l.r.t. and the anti-realist's general position, we should first consider how we come to know the truth of explicitly relational probability statements. Although less common in ordinary usage than those which do not mention evidence, such statements are nevertheless made with some frequency: both the scientist and ordinary layman will make statements of the form that 'given so and so, the probability of this outcome is ...', where the assumption on which the statement is premised contains a particular body of information relevant to the outcome in question. It seems to me quite plausible to maintain that we determine the truth of such explicitly relational statements by reflecting on the logical relations of partial entailment between the evidence and the hypothesis in question. The existence of such logical relations, our immediate access to them and, crucially, their use in determining numerical values of probability, are all familiar features of the l.r.t.; once accepted, they readily yield, on an anti-realist theory of meaning, the l.r.t.'s central contention that the meaning of probability statements is to assert such logical relations of partial entailment. The means by which we determine numerical probabilities are

---

[†]Throughout the book I will treat statements describing a probability to an event (or, as I will sometimes say, the outcome of an event) as strictly equivalent to statements ascribing a probability to a hypothesis stating the occurrence of that event. In this I follow most l.r. theorists, who have held that the difference between probability statements concerning events and those concerning hypotheses is a merely technical one, of no great importance.

obviously the same as the means by which we determine the truth of statements on numerical probability, and, if we accept that a statement's meaning is fixed by the means by which we determine its truth, we are driven to accept that relational probability statements assert the logical relations of partial entailment by which we determine their truth.

Of course it would hopelessly prejudice the case in favour of the l.r.t. to insist from the start that the only genuine probability statements for which we require a theory of meaning are two-term relational statements, and so the demonstration that the l.r.t. provides a plausible anti-realist theory of meaning for explicitly relational probability statements may appear of limited interest. Indeed the objection we began considering on p. 14 was to the effect that the l.r.t. with its relational account of probability could not explain the class of probability statements most central to our intuitive concept of probability, those which do not explicitly mention evidence. In fact I believe the l.r.t.'s analysis of such ordinary statements as instances of two-term relational statements *itself constitutes* an anti-realist explanation of the meaning of this important class of statements.

To see this, let us say we are, to begin with, presented with a statement to the effect that 'the probability of a given phenomenon is so and so', without any body of evidence mentioned. How do we determine its truth? What kinds of things do we use to recognize its truth? Leaving aside for the moment the question of logical relations between evidence and hypotheses, one thing seems to me perfectly clear: in determining the truth of such a probability statement, we would consider, or examine, bodies of empirical evidence, i.e. statements on the existence of various physical factors associated with the event and/or the frequency of similar events in the past. (As I will explain in Chapter II, these represent two different kinds of evidence, specificatory and statistical, both of which are highly important in determining probabilities.) That such evidence plays an important part in the way we recognize the truth of ordinary probability statements can hardly be denied; indeed I cannot imagine how we could set about trying to determine the truth of such statements of probability save by examining, in the first instance, empirical evidence on associated physical attributes and past frequencies. (The difficult question of how, if at all, we are to decide the truth of such statements when there exists no relevant empirical evidence at all will be discussed at length in connection with the principle of indifference in Chapters VI and VII.)

To put this point in a way that makes its relevance to realist—

Problems and Aims

anti-realist disputes more apparent, we may say that no matter what we take the truth conditions of statements on the probability of a given phenomenon not explicitly mentioning evidence to be — limits of relative frequency, physical propensities, what have you — the only way we can *recognize* the truth of such statements is by examining finite bodies of evidence on associated physical attributes and past frequencies. In the next chapter I will argue that objectivist accounts of probability do not offer a plausible explanation of how finite amounts of evidence can warrant conclusions on the truth of probability statements and, since such evidence must play a crucial part in determining their truth, this is a most serious problem for such objectivist theories of probability.

In contrast — and this returns us to the logical relations postulated by the l.r.t. — there is no mystery whatsoever as to how finite bodies of evidence on associated physical attributes and observed frequencies allow us to determine the truth of ordinary probability statements, as construed on the l.r.t. According to the theory, it is not merely such evidence which permits us to know the truth of ordinary probability statements, but such evidence combined with the logical relation of partial entailment it bears to the hypothesis we are concerned with. Indeed — and this is a matter I will return to later — any finite body of evidence, combined with a single logical relation to the hypothesis in question, provides us with an effective method for determining the truth of a statement on the probability of that hypothesis — we simply perform the finite task of contemplating that evidence, and then, to determine the truth of the statement, effectively compute the degree of logical probability the evidence gives the hypothesis.

We are now only a small step away from the analysis of ordinary statements as elliptical for two-term L-true relational statements (which is the essence of the l.r.t.'s claims about this important class of probability statements), and the short passage is accomplished by an anti-realist theory of meaning. Indeed, as may be obvious, if we adopt an anti-realist position and explain the meaning of a statement in terms of the effective conditions by which we come to know or recognize its truth, the l.r. theorist's account of ordinary probability statements follows immediately from the above considerations; the evidence and its logical relation to the hypothesis we are concerned with, which I said constitute the full meaning of these ordinary statements, *are* the means by which we come to know the truth of these ordinary statements. Thus the l.r.t.'s account of our ordinary judgments of probability can be understood as an example of an anti-realist theory of meaning: proceeding from the observation that we come to know the truth of ordinary judgments on probability by considering evidence and its relationship to the hypothesis we are concerned with, the l.r. theorist concludes that these ordinary judgments are actually equivalent in meaning to − elliptical for − a two-term judgment on the relationship between evidence and the hypothesis in question. Indeed, on this view, ordinary statements of probability are in no significant way different from explicitly relational statements, though their outward form differs: ordinary statements not explicitly mentioning evidence are simply relational probability statements, which, however, omit mention of evidence.

For future reference it will be useful to state explicitly how the anti-realist explanation of meaning I see provided by the l.r.t. relates to a crucial aspect of our ordinary discourse on probability − the fact that we often make several apparently conflicting ordinary statements on the probability of a given phenomenon, at different times or in different contexts. Thus at one time we may say that 'the probability of rain on 10 June is p' and at another time that 'the probability of rain on 10 June is q' ($\neq p$). Although I will devote a good deal of attention to this phenomenon in later chapters − and explain how such a practice can easily be misconstrued as counting against the l.r.t. as an explanation of our ordinary concept of probability − it is important from the outset to see how these different ordinary judgments of probability are to be understood within the framework of the anti-realist theory of meaning which I see the l.r.t. as providing.

For the l.r. theorist, the different ordinary judgments of probability made on different occasions are of course readily explicable − each is just part of a different two-term L-true statement, and the two different L-true statements involve two different bodies of evidence as their respective second terms. That is to say, on the different occasions we use different bodies of evidence to decide the truth of ordinary statements on the probability of rain on 10 June, and so in fact decide that two different ordinary statements are true on the different occasions. Since the means by which we decide what ordinary statement is true is different on the two occasions, we may, as anti-realists, say that the two ordinary statements made on the different occasions have a different meaning. This is precisely what is said by the l.r.t. − the full meaning of the ordinary statements on the two different occasions are two *different* L-true statements. Put simply, if bodies of evidence (and their attendant logical relations) are the means by which we decide the truth of ordinary statements of probability, the use of different bodies of evidence to decide what ordinary statement of probability on a given phenomenon is true will, for the anti-realist, be reflected in a difference in the meaning of the ordinary statements made. This is captured admirably by the l.r.t.'s analysis of ordinary probability statements as relative to the body of evidence used as the basis of the probability statement.

One point of clarification needs to be made concerning my defence of the l.r.t. as providing an anti-realist theory of the meaning of ordinary probability statements: in claiming that ordinary probability statements are always short in meaning for some two-term relational statements, I (like other l.r. theorists) become committed to the view that no ordinary statement can be true or false in its own right, but rather will only be true or false (and L-true or L-false at that), relative to a body of evidence. This is a view I will elaborate at length in Chapter IV, but at the moment what concerns us is that it seems to conflict with my contention that bodies of evidence, and their associated logical relations, constitute the means by which we come to know the truth of ordinary probability statements (and so for the anti-realist constitute their meaning). How can anything – logical relations, evidence, etc. – be the means by which we recognize the truth of ordinary probability statements if, strictly speaking, such ordinary statements can be neither true nor false?

This, however, is a purely verbal quibble. The anti-realist claims that the meaning of a concept is to be explained solely in terms of those things we consider when we determine the truth of statements involving that concept – specifically, for the anti-realist, there is no entity in the world independent of what we take note of when we try to verify statements involving that concept which constitutes the meaning of these statements. Now, there is no doubt that our intuitive concept of probability – which any adequate theory of probability must make sense of – manifests itself in what I have called ordinary probability statements, i.e. those not mentioning evidence explicitly, and so it is incumbent on the probability theorist to explain such statements. It is also clear that we determine the truth of such ordinary statements by examining bodies of evidence and, if the l.r.t. is to be believed, reflecting on the logical relations between such evidence and the hypothesis in question. *The primary question facing the philosopher who wishes to provide an account of our intuitive concept of probability*, then, is how to make sense of our method of determining the truth of ordinary probability statements within a systematic theory on the meaning of probability statements. The l.r.t., as I construe it, provides such a systematic account by claiming that an ordinary statement is actually just part of a two-term relational statement which we have neglected to mention one term of: our consideration of a body of evidence, and subsequent computation of the logical relation of partial entailment between it and the hypotheses we are concerned with, in order to determine the truth of ordinary statements of probability, are to be understood as the act of attending to the second term of a genuine relational probability statement, followed by the act of computing the degree of logical probability obtaining between the two terms. In effect, by claiming that the ordinary statement is elliptical for an L-true statement, we explain our ordinary action of determining its truth by examining evidence and computing a degree of logical probability as the act of verifying a genuine probability statement, which for the l.r. theorist is a two-term relational statement concerning a degree of partial entailment.

Thus, rather than conflicting with our practice of deciding the truth of ordinary probability statements by reference to bodies of evidence and logical relation (as suggested above), the l.r.t.'s claim that such ordinary statements are short in meaning for L-true relational statements is an essential part of the explanation of this practice within a general theory of the meaning of probability statements; namely, the practice is explained as the act of attending to the other term and logical relation necesssary to the verification of a genuine (that is, L-true relational), statement of probability. Moreover, it is obvious (I hope) that this explanation of our practice of ascertaining the truth of ordinary statements of probability only appeals to entities we come to have knowledge of during the very process of determining the truth of the ordinary statement (i.e. bodies of evidence and logical relations), and so is admirably suited as an anti-realist explanation of the meaning of those ordinary statements. This of course is just what I wished to convey above when I claimed – in a more compact way – that the l.r.t.'s view of ordinary probability statements as elliptical for two-term L-true statements could be seen as an instance of an anti-realist explanation of meaning, proceeding from the observation that we come to know the truth of ordinary probability statements by examining bodies of evidence and their logical relations to the hypothesis in question.

As a matter of more substance, it might, at this stage, be objected that my contention that the l.r.t. can be seen as providing an anti-realist explanation of the meaning of ordinary probability statements overlooks the fact that the logical relations of partial entailment, which are a major part of the means by which we come to recognize the truth of ordinary probability judgments, are themselves *probability relations.* This might be thought to introduce an unacceptable circularity: it might be thought that we are only entitled to explain the meaning of ordinary judgments of probability by reference to the means by which we come to know their truth if we can give an independent specification of those means, that is, a specification not including any concept of probability. But Dummett, whose account of anti-realist theories of meaning I follow here, makes it clear [1978, p. 157] that it is not an adequacy condition on anti-realist explanations of meaning that the means by which we are said to come to know the truth of a certain class of statements be specifiable independently of the concept whose meaning we seek to explain. The proof conditions, which for the intuitionist constitute the meaning of the mathematical proposition, are, as Dummett points out, only specifiable as conditions for the proof of the proposition whose meaning is in question, and this, he concludes, holds generally for the anti-realist theories of meaning.

Still, two aspects of the exaplanation of the meaning of ordinary probability statements which I believe is provided by the l.r.t. are at first glance disconcerting, and we might well pay some attention to them: on an anti-realist view of the kind I have put forward, an ordinary statement to the effect that 'the probability of so and so is' is not *about* anything save the empirical evidence and attendant logical relations by which we recognize the truth of the ordinary statement. For the anti-realist, there are no facts about probability which obtain in the world independently of our evidence of gathering and evaluating evidence to determine the truth of ordinary probability statements. To use a familiar metaphor, this enterprise itself creates, or brings into being, the facts which constitute the probability of the phenomenon in question; that is to say, what we ordinarily mean when we speak of the probability of a phenomenon is, on the l.r.t., the evidence and logical relations by which we determine the truth of our ordinary statement.

While it is perhaps somewhat disconcerting to explain ordinary statements on the probability of a phenomenon in such a way that there exists nothing in the world which, independently of our cognitive capacities, constitutes this probability, this is by now a familiar feature of the anti-realist position. A second feature of the explanation of the meaning of ordinary probability statements provided by the l.r.t. is less familiar: on it, there is no one thing – either in the world or in our cognition – which constitutes the probability of a phenomenon. On the l.r.t., the probability of a phenomenon is many different things, varying with the evidence which serves as second term of the full statement. Of course, once one accepts an anti-realist's point of view and sees that ordinary probability statements are not about something in the world but rather are about things we know, this too becomes plausible: our epistemic states – what we know – are not one thing, but many, depending on, *inter alia*, the available technology and the choices we have made about using this technology; thus our judgments on probability, as reflecting these states of knowledge, will vary.

Although the anti-realist explanation of the meaning of ordinary probability statements which I see as being provided by the l.r.t. may at first seem disconcerting in these respects, the theory of probability on which it is based is hardly new or radical: it is just what many probability theorists have maintained for well over fifty years. All I have tried to do above is indicate how the l.r.t. can, indeed should, be construed as an instance of an anti-realist explanation of meaning, both for the case of explicitly relational probability statements and ordinary statements not mentioning evidence. Indeed, if I am wrong that it can, and should, be construed in this way, or, more generally, if anti-realist explanations of meaning were to turn out not to be viable, then the l.r.t. and its explanation of the meaning of probability statements would be none the worse for that; other, quite independent, arguments which l.r. theorists have produced would still stand in its favour. However, on the more positive side, I believe that the interpretation of the l.r.t. I have just argued for does permit one to become clear about certain crucial issues in probability theory, and in later chapters I will spell these matters out in considerable detail.

My primary concern in those chapters will be the relationship of the meaning of probability statements to their practical role and the bearing this has on the objectivity of probability statements and a preliminary indication of my approach to these matters can be given on the basis of the above discussion of anti-realism and the l.r.t. When we speak ordinarily of *the* probability of a phenomenon without specifying the evidence we have in mind, the presence of the definite article betokens our belief in the existence of a single, uniquely correct value of probability. Now as I will explain, it is possible (and practically speaking, highly desirable) to single out one relational probability from the many different ones sanctioned by the l.r.t. as most desirable for the purpose of action *at a given time in given circumstances,* and this is the single value we have in mind when we ordinarily speak of the probability of a phenomenon. As long as it is recognized that such a single value only represents the probability value relative to a body of evidence singled out in the circumstances in question as most desirable for the purpose of action, no harm is done. It is easy to demonstrate — as I will do in Chapters III and IV — that the value most desirable from the point of view of action will vary over time and from circumstance to circumstance, and so must be construed, as the l.r.t. does construe it, as relational. However, if we do not adopt the anti-realist viewpoint which leads to the interpretation of such statements as relational, but instead adopt a realist standpoint, we are easily led to think of this single probability as a real entity, existing in the world independently of our cognitive capacity.

Just this seems to me to be the intuitive origin of so-called objective theories of probability, and I will argue explicitly in Chapters IV and V that these theories derive their appeal from a misunderstanding of the way evidence is used to determine the truth of ordinary statements of probability; indeed I believe such theories involve a deep confusion concerning the way we use evidence to determine the single probability values we so often need for the purpose of action. In order to sort this matter out properly, we will have to concentrate our attention on a feature of the l.r.t.'s analysis of ordinary probability statements that has been glossed over so far — that the relational probability we have in mind when we ordinarily speak of probability is the logical probability relative to the total evidence known or available, and it will be good to begin a preliminary consideration of this now. (Just how the total *known* evidence differs from the total *available* evidence is a complex question, which I will discuss at greater length in later chapters; however, since at least one eminent l.r. theorist — Carnap — has actually equated the total evidence available with the total evidence known, we may at this preliminary stage speak somewhat vaguely of the total evidence available — leaving open the possibility that this may simply be the total known evidence.)

THE REQUIREMENT OF TOTAL EVIDENCE

First we should note that l.r. theorists not only claim that the relational probability we implicitly have in mind when we ordinarily speak of probability is the one relative to the total relevant evidence available, but also that this relative probability is the most desirable one to be adopted for the purpose of action. If, as Bishop Butler remarked, probability is 'the very guide to life', any adequate account of probability must at some stage take into consideration the fact that the practical demands of our life often require us to determine a single probability value in order to make decisions in the face of uncertainty. Those who define probability as relative to evidence have, on the whole, maintained that the probability value relative to the total relevant evidence available is the one to be used for this purpose. This is usually formulated as the 'requirement of total evidence', which enjoins us to take the probability value relative to the total relevant evidence available when deciding on a course of action. The requirement of total evidence dovetails nicely with the claim that ordinary judgments of probability, i.e. those which do not mention evidence, are to be understood as elliptical for a two-term judgment involving, as second term, the total relevant evidence available at the time the judgment is made, and it is for this reason that I have introduced the requirement of total evidence in the context of the l.r.t.'s analysis of ordinary statements of probability: our ordinary discourse on probability, in which we speak of *the* probability of a hypothesis or event without mentioning evidence, is thus understood to be about the probability value preferred for the purpose of action. That is, as might be expected, our ordinary discourse on probability is about the (relational) probability value which is of the greatest practical significance to us.

This, as I said, is the usual position of l.r. theorists and, on the whole, I agree with it, and I will try to put it in a more general philosophical perspective shortly. However, in fairness to critics of the l.r.t., we should note that it is possible at this juncture to begin to have doubts on the suitability of the l.r.t. as an analysis of ordinary probability judgments: if these judgments are about the single value of probability so often needed to guide our actions, how can they be construed as relational in character? A relational account of probability can only serve as a reconstruction of a concept used to determine numerous different probabilities, and it is admitted that our ordinary discourse usually concerns single, or unique, values of probability. This would appear to be a point Mellor wishes to make (1971, pp. 53-4), though his criticism of the l.r.t. over this matter is extremely brief. Ayer's objection to the l.r.t., which we will examine in detail shortly, appears to have been motivated by similar concerns (1972, p. 55).

Problems and Aims

But it is quite mistaken to think that our practice of determining a single unique value of probability cannot be systematized within a relational theory of probability. The unique probability values we so often require for the purpose of action are only unique at a given time and in given circumstances. As we will see in Chapter III, the single value of probability by which we guide our actions over even one event will vary depending on the context in which we have occasion to act. Perhaps more importantly, as we will see in Chapters IV and V, the unique probability by which we guide our action over a given event will vary over time; this is an inevitable consequence of the fact that the single probability value by which we guide our action is the value relative to the total evidence *available* concerning that event, and no matter how we define such totalities, they will change over time. As the single probability value by which we guide our action varies with these changes in the total evidence available, it is wholly natural to systematize our practice in determining these values by a theory of probability which makes them relative to the evidence on which, at different times and in different contexts, we determine different probability values to guide our action.

However, one substantial doubt may still linger: even though the variability of the single value of probability used to guide our action naturally lends itself to systematization within a relational account of probability, it is not altogether clear that the l.r.t. as a logical theory of inductive probability is the right account for this purpose. As such a theory, the l.r.t. affirms the existence of genuine probability relations between the hypotheses of a language and all possible evidence statements of that language, and explicates these relations in an abstract and formal fashion. Using terminology derived from Carnap's work, we may call this logical theory of induction 'the l.r.t. proper' (cf. Salmon, 1967, p. 92). However, as the above discussion indicates, our ordinary statements on the single probability value usually required for action do not concern probability relations between the hypothesis we are concerned with and *various* bodies of evidence stateable in the language, much less all bodies of evidence stateable in the language; rather, on a given occasion, they concern the relation to one preferential body, the total then available. Even if this totality varies over time (and from context to context), it is hardly plausible to think that, at some time and in some context, each of the bodies of evidence stateable in the language will be the total available for a given hypothesis. Thus the probability relations we will appeal to in the analysis of ordinary discourse on probability will not be coextensive with the probability relations which form the subject matter of the logical theory of inductive probability, and, at best, are only a very small subset of the latter. Can one then claim that the logical theory of inductive probability – the l.r.t. proper – provides an adequate theory of the meaning of our intuitive concept of probability, which so often manifests itself in statements on single values of probability?†

It seems to me we can: while there is no doubt that the bodies of evidence we single out to guide our action are used to determine the truth of ordinary probability statements – and for the anti-realist this means they will play an important part in determining the meaning of such utterances – it can hardly be expected that the theory of the *meaning* of ordinary probability statements will anticipate which *particular* bodies of evidence stateable in our language will, at different times and in different contexts, be the ones singled out to guide our action. The theory which explains the meaning of our ordinary concept of probability is concerned with our general practice in determining the truth of ordinary probability statements, and it is theoretically possible that any body of evidence stateable in our language will be the total available for a given hypothesis at a given time and context. The only way to accommodate this possibility – which a theory of meaning surely must do – is to assert the existence (and explicate the precise nature) of probability relations between the hypotheses of a language and all bodies of evidence stateable in the language. The question of just what body we should single out to guide our action in a particular situation at a given time can then be treated as a separate question which, as we will see shortly, depends on a complex interplay of practical and technological factors.

The same point can be put in terms of the notion of 'possibility in principle', which is central to anti-realist explanations of meaning. On an anti-realist theory of meaning, the meaning of a particular concept is fixed by the means by which *in principle* we can recognize the truth of statements involving that concept; thus, if we think of the l.r.t. as providing an anti-realist explanation of the meaning of ordinary probability

---

†This, I take it, is the problem Mellor wishes to draw attention to when he states (1971, p. 53) that even if the l.r.t. is supplemented 'by an adequate explication of the notion of "available" evidence' to explain our practice of determining unique values of probability, 'the resulting definition of probability would then rest on other considerations than ... the logical relation holding between two propositions.'

statements, we must expect it to state, and explicate, the conditions by which we can *in principle* come to know their truth. Since it is in principle possible that any body of evidence stateable in the language would be the total amount available for a given hypothesis, an anti-realist explanation of the meaning of ordinary probability statements will allow that a given ordinary statement about the probability of an event *can* have as its full meaning any one of the full relational statements formed by combining the hypothesis in question with any body of evidence stateable in the language. This is what is accomplished by the l.r.t. proper, the theory which states the existence of, and explicates, relations of partial entailment between hypotheses of a language and all bodies of evidence stateable in that language.

The enterprise of giving a characterization of the exact nature of the single body of evidence we use to guide our actions in specific situations will, then, become part of a separate, more pragmatic, branch of study, concerned with specific exigencies of actual situations. The distinction between a theory of probability proper and the methodological study of the application of that theory for specific purposes — first drawn by Carnap, but later accepted by others, e.g. Salmon (1967, pp. 92-5) — provides a convenient way to separate the semantic study of the concept of probability from the practical matters which determine the exact identity of the body of evidence used in a given situation, and I follow this distinction throughout the book. From my point of view the most important facet of this distinction is that it allows us to separate out questions concerning the meaning of probability statements — which, for the anti-realist, concern the means by which in principle we decide their truth — from questions of a more practical kind concerning how, on a given occasion, we make and use probability statements to guide an action.

Although I will repeatedly return to this distinction in later chapters — and elaborate its significance for a wide variety of questions traditionally treated by probability theorists — one point already touched on in passing illustrates the significance of this distinction for a proper understanding of our intuitive concept of probability. The reader will recall that, while elliptical statements not mentioning evidence are the kind we most frequently make when we ordinarily speak of probability, they are not the only kind of utterance found in our ordinary discourse — explicitly relational statements, usually expressed in conditional form, are quite naturally made on a wide variety of occasions. If we regard our ordinary discourse on probability as the clearest expression of our intuitive concept of probability, any attempt to systematize this concept must not only explain ordinary elliptical statements of probability, but also the explicitly relational statements we make from time to time. To my mind, the only proper way to do this is to regard both explicitly relational statements and those not mentioning evidence as instances of the same concept of probability, differentiated by pragmatic and technological factors which prompt one or the other kind of statement. The l.r.t. proper can then be seen as providing an explanation of the meaning of probability statements of both kinds, while an account of the way this theory is applied for specific purposes in specific contexts will explain why one or the other kind of statement is made on a given occasion.

Analysis of an Example

Since, to my mind, it is only pragmatic and technological factors specific to particular occasions which distinguish explicitly relational statements from those not mentioning evidence, it will be helpful to have a specific example in mind when discussing the connection between these two kinds of statements. Paralleling a discussion in Kyburg (1970), we may take an example which might at first appear to be problematic for the l.r.t. Assume that we know e, that an individual is forty years old and smokes heavily, and that the past observed incidence of mortality in a given time-period among such individuals is 10 per cent; we then learn e', that he drinks heavily as well, and that the past observed mortality rate among forty-year-old drinkers over the same period is 4 per cent. Assume that this is the total relevant information available; specifically, that there is no information available on the mortality rate among forty-year-old men who smoke and drink heavily. What are we to say about *the* probability of this man's mortality during the period in question?

The problem here is that the precept of using the total relevant evidence available is of no help in determining a single probability value of the kind we usually require for the purpose of action, as the two parts of the total relevant evidence available are not, so to speak, comparable; i.e. they do not yield a single value when combined. (An analogous difficulty arises for the principle of maximal specificity, which is the point Kyburg wished to make in his discussion of this example.) But, actually, from the point of view of the l.r.t. there is nothing seriously problematic about such examples (which Kyburg believes to be common). Indeed even at a superficial level the example

Problems and Aims

bears out the basic theme of the l.r.t. concerning the relational character of probability — in this case there are obviously two different relational probabilities for the man's dying within a given period, one relative to e and the other relative to e'.

On deeper analysis, several points of considerable interest concerning the relationship of explicitly relational probability statements to those not mentioning evidence emerge from this example. We may note that it is exactly examples of this kind which prompt both the scientist and ordinary layman to make explicitly relational statements of the kind first described on p. 15. Moreover, both of the explicitly relational statements which would be made in the kind of circumstances described have important practical consequences: assuming we know that the observed mortality rate among forty-year-old non-smokers and non-drinkers was quite low, say 1 per cent, the relative probability values determined on e and e' would indicate that the man in question should give up smoking and drinking, advice which, in actual fact, is often proffered on the basis of just such statistics. In addition this example points up a subtle complexity in the practical functioning of probability judgments: in this example, it is easy to think of a practical need which would best be served by dividing the total available evidence into parts to form several relational probability judgments, irrespective of the import of that totality as a whole. Thus, even if we were to come to know e'', the mortality rate among forty-year-olds who both smoke and drink heavily, it would still be necessary to divide the available evidence into parts such as e and e', and make explicitly relational statements involving these bodies of evidence, in order to make the practical decision of *which* habit to give up, if the individual in question could only give up one.

In fact there are two important conclusions that can be drawn from this example as regards our practice of determining unique probability values: first, there exist certain practical needs which require us to use less than the total amount of evidence available in order to make several explicitly relational judgments of probability, each based on part of the total amount available. Secondly, even where we have practical needs which are not served by such a division (for example, the need of an insurance company to fix a single premium for the man in question in the above example), circumstances may be such that we cannot obtain a unique probability value relative to the total evidence available.

These two conclusions reveal the importance — even the necessity — of distinguishing between, on the one hand, the l.r.t. proper as a theory on the meaning of probability statements and, on the other, the methodological study of its application, if we are to give a clear account of the connection between the explicitly relational probability statements we sometimes make in ordinary discourse, and the elliptical ones we more frequently make. Once it is recognized that there exist practical needs best served by making several explicitly relational probability statements (each based on part of the total evidence available), it is easy to see ordinary probability statements on a single preferential probability value as a special case of a more general kind of probability statement, distinguished only by the character of the specific practical need prompting the judgment. Probability statements are always made to serve some practical purpose and, while these practical purposes very often require a single value of probability, this is not always the case. It is of course easy to treat those cases where our practical needs prompt us to make several explicitly relational probability statements as an application of the l.r.t. to suit those needs. Why not then treat our determination of single values in the same way, i.e. as an application of that same relational definition, but one designed to serve practical needs of a different kind. At a theoretical level this is accomplished by offering a single account of the meaning of probability statements to cover both cases, and then treating the two different kinds of statements — explicitly relational and elliptical ones — as different applications of that one definition intended to serve different kinds of practical needs. The single definition I favour is, of course, the l.r.t. — or more exactly, what I call the l.r.t. proper — and the elucidation of the kinds of practical needs which prompt different applications of the definition is what I (and others) have called the methodology of its application.

In a more complicated way, the second conclusion drawn above also indicates that explicitly relational probability statements differ from ordinary elliptical ones only in respect of pragmatic and technological factors concerning the application of a single relational definition. The second point we saw above was that even when we desire a single value of probability to guide our action, we cannot be assured of obtaining it, and that, in such circumstances, we would ordinarily make several explicitly relational statements. Now, according to the anti-realist explanation of the meaning of ordinary probability statements I argued for above, any finite body of evidence with a single relation of partial entailment to a hypothesis — such as e and e' taken separately — can in *principle* be used to decide (effectively) the truth of an ordinary

Problems and Aims

statement of probability concerning that hypothesis, i.e. one not mentioning evidence explicitly. Thus both e and e' in the above example could in principle be used to determine the truth of an ordinary statement of probability about the individual's mortality. But what does this have to do with the actual probability assertion(s) we make in the circumstances described in the example? As I have pointed out already, in the circumstances of the example we would not make an ordinary statement of probability omitting reference to evidence, but instead would make two explicitly relational statements of probability. Thus it is not initially clear how the considerations I have adduced concerning the decidability of ordinary probability statements have anything to do with this example.

However, contrary to first appearances, this example wholly bears out the points I have made concerning the decidability of ordinary probability statements; the reason we would make two explicitly relational statements of probability in the circumstances described in the example is that, in such circumstances, both the evidence e and the evidence e' are used by us to recognize the truth of ordinary statements about the probability of the individual's mortality. This suggestion may at first sight seem unusual, but, remember, on the anti-realist explanation of meaning which I believe the l.r.t. provides for ordinary statements of probability, the meaning of any ordinary statement will depend on the means by which we have established its truth, i.e. the evidence term we coupled with the ordinary statement. As I pointed out before, this entails that different ordinary statements made at different times — based on different bodies of evidence — will have different meanings, that is, will be short for two different full, two-term, L-true statements. Why not view the different probability statements made in the example described above in the same way? The two cases differ only in that in one the different probability statements make no explicit mention of evidence and are uttered successively, while in the above example they are explicitly relational and are uttered simultaneously. But the time-order is not an essential difference and, if the l.r.t.'s account of ordinary probability statements as actually relational in character is taken seriously, the difference in the apparent form of the utterances in the two cases is inessential as well. What is far more important is the common feature shared by the two cases, namely that the different probability utterances made in each case simply reflect that different bodies of evidence are used to determine the probability of the same phenomenon.

While a certain similarity between the two cases may thus be obvious, the reader may still wonder why I claimed that in the example in which we make two explicitly relational statements, we use the two bodies of evidence e and e' to decide the truth of an *ordinary* statement about the probability of the individual's mortality. As I have pointed out several times, we do not make an ordinary probability statement in such circumstances; moreover, if we did, on the anti-realist explanation of the meaning of such ordinary statements I have argued for, both the full-term relational statement involving e and the one involving e' would have to be the meaning of the ordinary statement if, as I have claimed, they are both used to decide the truth of an ordinary statement. Thus, on the account I have given, any ordinary statement of probability made in these circumstances would have to be ambiguous, that is, have two full meanings. *This* is precisely why we do not make an ordinary, elliptical, statement of probability in these circumstances but, rather, make full probability statements explicitly indicating the evidence relied upon.

To put it more clearly, my point here is that a probability statement not mentioning evidence would be ambiguous in these circumstances in a way that our ordinary utterances not mentioning evidences are not — when we ordinarily utter a probability statement without mentioning evidence, there is one body of evidence which is preferential from a practical point of view to use to decide the truth of that elliptical statement (what I have called the total available), and so there is only one full meaning for that elliptical statement. Just because there is no one body of evidence with a single relation to the hypothesis we are concerned with which is in the same way preferential for the purpose of action in the above example — for the total available evidence consists of two incommensurable parts — there will be no one *unique* body of evidence by which we can decide the truth of an elliptical statement made in the circumstances described in the example. Therefore, from the anti-realist point of view I argued for, there would be no single meaning to an elliptical statement made in such circumstances. In fact, since the form of an elliptical statement indicates that there is a unique probability being referred to — that is, it concerns *the* probability of the phenomenon — we do not make such a statement at all and thus we make several explicitly relational statements instead.

Another way to put my position here is to say that the explicitly relational statements made in the circumstances described above are 'unsuccessful' ordinary statements. That is, for the moment we are

Problems and Aims

supposing that our primary aim is to obtain a single value of probability to guide our action in a certain way in regard to an individual's mortality, and our examination of the bodies of evidence e and e' can be thought of as an attempt to obtain the desired unique value of probability. To be successful in obtaining a single value of probability in this case, or any other, the total evidence available to us must be such that there exists a single logical relation of probability between it and the hypothesis we are concerned with. Unfortunately, this is not always the case, but this cannot be known to us at the outset when we begin examining the evidence available to us in detail in the hopes of obtaining a single probability value to guide our action, and so there will be cases in which we set out to identify a single probability value to guide our action but do not succeed in obtaining one – the above example is one such case. However, in such cases we use what is qualitatively the same procedure to determine the truth of the probability statement which is intended to guide our action as we do in the cases in which that intention is successfully achieved – we examine evidence and judge the logical relation of partial entailment that the evidence we have examined bears to the hypothesis in question. When it turns out that there is no one unique body of evidence with a single logical relation which is preferential for the purpose of guiding our action – when the total available evidence forms two incommensurable parts – we can only make several, so to speak, equally valid decisions on the truth of the probability statement which was to guide our action. We must then abandon the form of speech which presupposes that there is a unique probability to guide our action, and thus we utter several explicitly relational statements of probability, each of which makes clear how we have decided the truth of the statement intended to guide our action.

Contrary to appearances, the first conclusion drawn from our analysis of this example supports this view of the relationship between elliptical statements of probability and explicitly relational statements. That conclusion was to the effect that there often exist practical needs which require us to make several different explicitly relational probability statements rather than a single one indicating some one preferred value, and that one's purpose in making explicitly relational probability statements was to serve practical needs of this kind. However, I have just suggested that explicitly relational probability statements made in the circumstances described in the above example may be thought of as 'unsuccessful' statements intended to guide our actions by providing us with a unique probability value. Do explicitly relational statements serve such diverse — and even contrary — purposes as to guide our action when we require several probability values for the purpose of action, and also when we desire, but cannot obtain, a single value of probability? Not really. The practical purposes which I suggested were best served by making several explicitly relational statements of probability are ones which actually require a single, unique, probability value in certain possible, but as of yet not actual, circumstances. Thus, the forty-year-old individual who wishes to know the mortality rate of forty-year-old smokers versus forty-year-old drinkers in order to decide which habit to give up in effect wishes to know what the single, unique, probability of his mortality would be if he gave up one rather than the other habit.

Thus the analysis given several paragraphs above of explicitly relational statements of probability — that they represent several decisions on the truth of ordinary probability statements intended to guide our action by singling out a unique probability value — also applies to explicitly relational statements made for the purposes described earlier. In such cases the separate decisions are not prompted by our *inability* to make a single decision on the truth of an ordinary probability judgment — as they were in the case most recently discussed — but, rather, are prompted by the need to know what ordinary statements, expressing a single value of probability, would obtain in various circumstances, more or less within our control. The basic point, then, which emerges from our overall analysis of this example is that ordinary elliptical statements of probability differ from explicitly relational statements only in virtue of the number of bodies of evidence we have in mind when we determine probabilities, and so such statements should be viewed as instances of the same concept manifested in explicitly relational statements, differing only in respect of the number of bodies of evidence relied upon.

A Theory of Meaning and a Theory of Methodology

Even if this characterization of the difference between explicitly relational statements of probability and the elliptical statements we ordinarily make is accepted, the reader may still find himself wondering why I attributed the difference between these kinds of statements to 'pragmatic and technological factors' to be elucidated by a theory of methodology. Surely, on the explanation I have just given, the difference between the two kinds of statements depends as much on brute facts as anything else. That is, even if one of the considerations which prompts us to make explicitly relational statements of probability is directly tied to the exact character of our practical needs — whether we need to know a single probability value which obtains in current circumstances or several distinct probability values which would be the unique value of probability in different circumstances — the other main consideration which prompts us to make explicitly relational probability statements apparently only depends on brute facts, namely whether the evidence available actually allows us to determine a unique value of probability when we desire one. But this brings us face to face with a serious shortcoming with this initial discussion of the requirement of total evidence, already mentioned in passing. So far no exact explication of the idea of 'available' evidence has been given, and while it may appear that the evidence available for a particular hypothesis is a brute fact independent of pragmatic and technological considerations, this is not actually the case. In fact, on any explication, the evidence 'available' for a given hypothesis depends on a complex interplay of technological constraints and practical needs, and it is the study of this interplay with which the methodology of probability theory is primarily concerned.

This is quite clear if we identify the available evidence with the known evidence (which, in effect, I did when discussing the above example). It is manifest that the evidence we actually know concerning a given hypothesis depends to a large extent on decisions we have made about how much evidence to gather. In discussing just such issues, Salmon (1967, pp. 92-4) points out that 'very down to earth practical considerations play an important role' in determining how much evidence we use in actually determining values of probability. Presumably he has in mind questions such as cost of gathering evidence, the importance which attaches to the decisions we make on the basis of probability judgments, etc., and in this he is surely correct.

Even if we expand our definition of 'available' evidence to include evidence which is some sense could, or should be, obtained by an individual making a judgment of probability, these same pragmatic issues again play an important part in determining what evidence is available concerning a given hypothesis. In Chapter III we will see that the most plausible way to explain the idea of the evidence which we can obtain concerning a given hypothesis is to identify it with the evidence which can be obtained by existing technology. This imposes some objective contraints on the evidence available to us — and ones I will be at pain to analyse in Chapter III — but it also incorporates a strong pragmatic component, for the technology that can be brought to bear on a particular problem at a given time depends at least in part on decisions we have already made (and continue to make) on the importance of the problem at hand. For example, while evidence concerning the surface of a distant star is not presently available to us due to technological limitations beyond our control, the fact that evidence concerning the surface of Mars is now available to us depends on decisions made in the past concerning the viability, desirability and cost of space exploration.

This means that when we cannot determine a single probability value on the evidence available in a given situation — one problem to which the above example was addressed — we may simply decide to gather more evidence, postponing any judgment of probability until we can determine the single value we desire. Alternatively, since explicitly relational probability statements serve some of our practical needs, we may decide to make such judgments on the basis of the evidence currently available. From the above remarks, it must be obvious that it thus is only an interplay — though no doubt a complex one — between practical and technological issues, such as the importance of the decision, the risks involved in delay, the cost of gathering more evidence, the time and cost required to adopt existing technology, etc., which will determine whether we settle for a number of different relational values, or attempt to gather more evidence to determine a single value of probability. Since it is only the complex interplay between pragmatic and technological factors which determines whether we make several explicitly relational statements of probability or a single elliptical one, there seems every reason to put forward a single relational definition of probability to cover both cases, and then treat ordinary statements on single values of probability as instances of this definition made when there is a suitable alignment of our practical needs and existing technology. This, in effect, is the position I outlined earlier, when I argued that the l.r.t. proper should be accepted as a correct account of the meaning of probability statements — both explicitly relational and elliptical — and that the admittedly important practice of deciding single values of probability (which is what allows us to omit mention of the evidence on the basis of which the decision is made) should be regarded as an application of this definition carried out in specific circumstances on the basis of specific practical needs.

To put the matter generally, we may say that the practical issues which affect our choice of evidence when making probability judgments

— whether we use one or several bodies, whether it is worth our while to gather more, etc. — do not in any way determine the basic character of probability statements: any genuine statement of probability will be explicitly or implicitly relational, and its meaning will be to assert the existence of a relation of partial entailment. The practical issues we have been discussing do not change or effect this in any way; rather, they only pertain to which genuine probability statement, or statements, we make in order to fulfil specific practical purposes. The main question of course is just which body, or bodies of evidence, to use to guide our actions in a given situation and the distinction between, on the one hand, inductive logic proper as a formal and semantic study of logical relations of partial entailment and, on the other, the methodology of applying inductive logic, simply allows us to locate practical questions on what, and how much, evidence we should use in making probability judgments in a non-formal branch of study different from the logic of inductive probability proper.

It may be useful to restate this conclusion in general terms concerning the anti-realist character of the l.r.t., although no doubt some of the points I will make in this regard will already be clear from earlier remarks. On an anti-realist theory of meaning, the meaning of a particular concept is fixed by the means by which *in principle we can* recognize the truth of statements involving that concept; thus if we think of the l.r.t. as providing an anti-realist explanation of the meaning of ordinary probability statements, we would then expect that the meaning of such statements would be equated with the conditions by which we can *in principle* come to know their truth. This, I believe, is what is accomplished by the l.r.t. proper, that is, the theory which asserts that all probability statements — including ordinary ones — are actually relational statements concerning a degree of partial entailment between evidence and hypothesis and which, furthermore, investigates such relations in a formal fashion. To repeat what by now may be all too obvious, on this theory of meaning, what we *can* mean by a statement that 'the probability of thus and such event is p' is not one thing, but a number of different things depending on what evidence we have in mind. To put the same point less obviously in terms of the anti-realist theory of meaning which I believe to be behind the l.r.t., we may say that since each body of evidence (and attendant logical relation) can *in principle* be used by us to recognize the truth of an ordinary statement of probability of this kind, such a statement about the probability of this event *can* have as its full meaning any one of the full relational statements formed by combining the hypothesis in question with any one of these bodies of evidence.

However, as befits a theory of meaning, this only concerns what we *can* mean when we speak of the probability of a given event or hypothesis without explicitly mentioning evidence — the *possible* meanings of a given ordinary probability statement — and ignores the fact that such probability statements must answer to practical purposes. When faced with actually deciding the truth of an ordinary probability statement for a particular practical purpose, the logical relation of the hypothesis asserting the outcome of the event in question to all the bodies of evidence by which in principle we could recognize the truth of the ordinary statement will be, for the most part, neither here nor there, as the range of *possible* meanings for the ordinary statement has no practical utility as such. The reason for this should be obvious: it is an essential feature of our concept of probability that the evidence we tacitly rely on as the second term when making an ordinary statement of probability to guide our action is evidence we have actually ascertained, that is, evidence which we have observed directly or indirectly, and this alone rules out a vast number of the possible meanings of a given ordinary statement as its actual meaning. (For example — to take an extreme case — no one would assert an elliptical statement of probability intended to guide action which tacitly involved as the second 'evidence' term a set of statements he believed to be false.) Moreover, as our ordinary statements of probability are intended to serve practical needs, the full meaning of any statement we actually assert will also depend to a large extent on pragmatic considerations; that is to say, as I indicated above, the exact amount of evidence we adopt as the basis for the ordinary probability judgment which will guide our action will depend on pragmatic and technological considerations.

It is the distinction between a theory of probability proper and a methodological theory of application which allows us to state precisely the relationship between the means by which in principle we can determine the truth of ordinary probability statements and these highly practical matters. The study of how practical and technological constraints affect our actual determination of the truth of ordinary probability statements is what I have called the methodology of probability theory; the study of the means by which we can in principle recognize the truth of such statements is what I have called probability theory proper, i.e. the study of the meaning of our ordinary concept of probability.

Problems and Aims

AYER'S OBJECTION AND THE PROBLEM OF INDUCTION

Despite having presented what I hope is a convincing case for the l.r.t.'s relational account of the meaning of probability statements and an indication — in outline only at present — of how a theory of methodology can explain how we can guide our actions in specific situations on the basis of knowledge of probabilities, we should note that the l.r.t., and its associated theory of methodology, have been explicitly criticized by Ayer on just one of the main points we have been considering. He claims that the theory and its methodology are incapable of explaining our practice of using a single probability value for the purpose of action. His objection is not that we would somehow be mistaken in considering the total available evidence when trying to determine a single value of probability — indeed he regards this as 'prudent' — nor that there can be no distinction between a theory of the meaning of probability statements and a methodological theory explaining how we use such statements for specific purposes — indeed he seems in places to accept this — but, rather, that the requirement of total evidence as a methodological precept can be given no justification in terms of the l.r.t.'s explanation of the meaning of probability statements. Specifically, at one point he restates an objection he had formulated earlier by saying:

> Neither can one escape the argument by talking of the principle of maximizing evidence as a methodological principle. For a methodological principle is not selected by caprice: it is supposed to have some utility. Its justification is that by adopting it we shall achieve better results. But what are the better results in this case? The obvious answer is 'better estimates of what is likely to happen'. But this is just the answer which we have seen that the logical theory is debarred from giving. (1972, p. 57)

In fact, this passage and related passages are a bit difficult for the l.r. theorist to make sense of: it involves the idea of an estimate of probability or, as Ayer says earlier on, an 'estimate of chances'. The idea of an estimate of probability or chance is that of a provisional assessment, capable of subsequent revision, of some intrinsically true probability value; however, for the l.r.t. all probability judgments are L-true relational statements, and so it remains to be seen if the idea of an estimate of probability can be made sense of in terms of the l.r.t. (In fact this is a matter I will investigate at greater length in subsequent chapters, particularly Chapter V.) In a similar way, Ayer requests that the requirement of total evidence be justified in terms of its utility in determining 'what is likely to happen'. According to the l.r.t., what is *likely* to happen is either a number of different things, corresponding to different probabilities relative to different bodies of evidence, or, if it is to be one thing, it can only be that outcome most probable relative to the total relevant evidence available, for this is how the l.r. theorist interprets unique probabilities. But, then, it is hardly in order to ask if the probability relative to the total available evidence is the best estimate of the outcome most likely relative to the total available evidence, as it trivially must be.

Perhaps the point of Ayer's objection is that the l.r.t. can make no sense of the question 'What is the best estimate of what is likely to happen?', but one would have hoped that his objection could be formulated in a way that permitted a meaningful and informative answer. It might then have succeeded by knowing that no useful answer along the desired lines was forthcoming — as things stand now it seems to me that Ayer's objection is often not even formulated in a way to which the l.r. theorist can reply.

However, let us be a bit more charitable — what Ayer seems to be getting at, in this and other passages, is that the l.r.t. cannot explain what subsequent concrete gains accrue to the person who adopts the requirement of total evidence as his maxim for determining the unique probabilities required for the purpose of action. This is a sensible point, and I believe it is true that the l.r. theorist cannot demonstrate that concrete gains accrue to a person adopting this policy, as any demonstration along the desired lines would involve a circularity. As far as I can see, there could be no way of demonstrating that a particular maxim of action was *certain* to lead to concrete gains when future events unveil themselves: the future is uncertain, and any practical precept can fail to succeed in its intended purpose because of the actual developments. We are, then, forced to justify practical maxims by reference to their probable success. But this can hardly be expected of a maxim which is claimed to be constitutive of what 'probable success' is, and that is just what the requirement of total evidence is for the l.r. theorist. When we ordinarily speak of 'probable success' — success given what is likely to happen — we assume that there is a unique set of probability values for possible outcomes. These unique probabilities for different outcomes are, for the l.r. theorist, the probability values for the outcomes relative to the total available relevant evidence. Thus, if

Problems and Aims

what we mean by 'the probable success' of a policy is its success in the light of probability values relative to the total available evidence, we can hardly proffer 'the probable success' of the policy of using the total available evidence as a justification of that policy.

Indeed, more generally, if Hume was correct, any attempt to justify fundamental features of inductive reasoning by reference to future success must founder on circularity: the justification lies in future events, but, as these at present cannot be directly observed, we can only have inductive knowledge of them. We inevitably, then, become involved in circular reasoning when we try to justify, by reference to future success, the procedures by which we arrive at inductive knowledge. In this case the procedure at issue is our selection of one of a number of different inductive probabilities, based on different bodies of observations, as the most desirable one for the purposes of action. Initially, one might think that the selection of one inductive probability, rather than another, as the basis for action could have some practical justification in terms of future successes — this seems to be what prompted Ayer's criticism — but there is just no way to show that one inductive probability, rather than another, is a better indication of what will happen in the future. Thus, in the same way that it is impossible to justify, by reference to the future, a choice between rival inductive inferences projecting different primitive predicates from one set of observations — which is the moral of Goodman's New Riddle of Induction — it is impossible to justify, by reference to the future, a choice between similar inductive inferences, based on different sets of observations, which is the problem Ayer has drawn attention to.

But then Ayer's objection here to the l.r.t. simply turns out to be a reworking of the fundamental problem posed by Hume for justifying induction (indeed, Salmon, who accepts Ayer's objection, comes very close to acknowledging this [1967, p. 95]). In case the reader thought otherwise, let me state clearly that I do not propose in this book to solve Hume's problem of induction, or any related reworkings of it. Some l.r. theorists have, of course, attempted to justify induction in various complicated ways (e.g. Keynes's appeal to the limited variety of nature), but I see no reason why the l.r. theorist need do this. Justified or not, we certainly do make inductive inferences. It is equally certain that we base our actions on the inferences we make, and, to my mind, a large part of such inductive reasoning involves use of probabilities. If this is correct, the l.r. theorist has an important task which is quite independent of any question concerning the justification of induction:

this is to explicate and systematize our inductive reasoning on probabilities, and elucidate — or codify — the connection of this reasoning to our actions concerning future events. What I have called the l.r.t. proper is what accomplishes the former task of systematization and explication of inductive reasoning, while the methodology of its application is concerned with the latter task of relating inductive reasoning to action.

From this perspective, it is possible to say two things by way of 'justifying' the requirement of total evidence. If, as Carnap proposed, we construe the evidence available to an individual as the evidence he knows, it is an analytic truth that *'rational action'* in the face of uncertainty involves a consideration of the total evidence available. Any agent who determines probability values for an action on less evidence than the totality known to him would be regarded as extremely irrational. Since the methodology of probability theory is only intended to elucidate and codify our practices in using inductive probabilities to guide our action, there is little more we can do to 'justify' the requirement of total evidence than point to the fact that what we mean by rational action by an individual is action taken on the basis of a consideration of all the evidence known to him.

A more difficult question arises if we do not equate the evidence available to an individual with the evidence known to him, but, rather, take the available evidence to comprise evidence which can or should be known. In fact Ayer's main objection to the l.r.t. seems to be with the requirement of total evidence construed in this way. However, to my knowledge, no clear explication of such a sense of available evidence has been given by any probability theorist, though, as indicated already, I hope to remedy this situation in Chapters III and V. Unfortunately, until such an explication is given, it is rather difficult to say a great deal by way of justification for the requirement that we take all the evidence available when making a judgment of probability; however, enough has been said so far to be able to give a preliminary indication of the main findings of those chapters.

The main point that will emerge in Chapters III and V is that probability judgments based on less than the total evidence available — in the sense of the total we can or should know — will fail to be objective. The explanation of this will not constitute justification of the requirement of total evidence by reference to its success in practice (which I acknowledged to be impossible), but, rather, will constitute an elucidation of its role in our complex thinking on probabilities and their relation to action. Specifically, I will argue that the probability judgments that can

Problems and Aims

be regarded as objectively valid are those which conform to the requirement of total evidence in this form, i.e. those which involve all the evidence it is *possible* to obtain. This, admittedly, will be an account of the objectively of probability judgments from an anti-realist point of view, for the objectivity of probability judgments will not be traced to their conformity with some fact obtaining in the world independently of our capacities of knowledge, but rather will conform in the conformity of those judgments to the most exact standards which *can* be obtained by humans in the circumstances in which the judgment is made. Other, realist, conceptions of the objectivity of probability judgments will be found to be illusory — indeed I will go to great lengths in Chapters IV and V to explain the origin of the illusion — and I will try to show that this anti-realist account of the objectivity of probability judgments is sufficient to explain scientific discourse on probability.

Obviously all of this will depend on a careful analysis of the idea of the total evidence it is *possible* to obtain in a given circumstance, and an equally careful consideration of the notions of objectivity and subjectivity as regards judgments of probability. Although these are matters I will investigate in detail in later chapters, it will be useful to begin here a preliminary consideration of them, particularly as regards questions on the objectivity and subjectivity of probability judgments.

OBJECTIVE AND SUBJECTIVE JUDGMENTS OF PROBABILITY

> The concept of probability is an unusually slippery and puzzling one. For one thing, it seems to hover uncertainly between objectivity and subjectivity. Talk about something being probable or likely seems to reflect some mixture of knowledge and ignorance — if there were an omniscient god, it is hard to imagine that he would regard anything as merely probable — and yet most of our probability statements seem to claim some objective or at least interpersonal validity. (Mackie, 1973, p. 154)

Mackie is not alone in regarding our concept of probability as a curious mixture of objective and subjective aspects. Blackburn remarks (1973, p. 98) that philosophers writing on probability have long felt a conflict between the objective and subjective aspects of the concept, and in recent times this conflict among philosophers has been paralleled by scientific controversy over the exact nature of Heisenberg's uncertainty relations. On one interpretation, these relations reflect objective physical facts, i.e. that certain physical parameters do not have precise values; on the other, more 'subjective', interpretation, the uncertainty relations simply reflect our inability to know these parameters precisely. As I am not concerned with foundations of quantum mechanics, I will not consider this scientific controversy directly, but instead will try to come to an understanding of the issues involved in the conflict between 'objectivists' and 'subjectivists', and in later chapters will argue that the l.r.t. — and the l.r.t. alone — can account for both objective and subjective aspects of our concept of probability.

As I understand the term, 'subjective' judgments of probability are those which reflect merely personal assessments of the probability of some outcome. As with so much in probability theory, it is easier to illustrate what people have in mind when they speak of 'subjective' judgments of probability than to identify one agreed definition of subjectivity. However, the example of two gamblers possessing different information about a deck of cards with which we began this chapter illustrates well how a certain 'subjectivity' in making probability judgments can arise from different individuals' assessments of a particular situation: one, knowing nothing more than that he is dealing with a regular deck of cards, naturally judges the probability of the first card being red to be 1/2; the other, knowing the bottom card to be red, judges it to be 25/51. This example crystallizes a feature common to most actual card games: the different players in the game are usually given different information about the distribution of cards through the use of 'down cards' whose identity is known to one player only, and so each player's assessment of the chance of a particular outcome will usually differ slightly. More generally, in any situation in which individuals are obliged to make judgments of probability on different information, their judgments will, to a large degree, express merely personal assessments of the situation, and so inevitably will contain a subjective component.

Broadly speaking there are two different ways in which probability theorists have attempted to systematize personal, or 'subjective', judgments of probability. The first is the l.r.t., which defines probability in terms of logical relations between known propositions and hypotheses stating possible outcomes. On this theory, probability judgments express degrees of belief which individuals are warranted to have in certain outcomes, with the 'warrant' depending on logical relations between the evidence known and the hypotheses stating the outcome.

Problems and Aims

Depending on the different evidence known to different individuals, different degrees of belief in a particular hypothesis may be warranted.

The other main approach which tries to systematize subjective judgments of probability is that cluster of theories known loosely, but appropriately, as theories of subjective, or personal, probability. In the first formulation of these theories, given by Ramsey (1926), probability was defined as degree of belief (as with Keynes's version of the l.r.t.), but without the further qualification that such a degree of belief was warranted by logical relations to known propositions. For Ramsey, degree of belief was to be defined in terms of propensity to wager on commodities of given utility, rather than immediately known logical relations, and so, on his theory, the degrees of belief involved in probability judgments need only be rational in the minimal sense that the wagering pattern expressing these beliefs must conform to the axioms of probability.

Recently, a good deal of work has been done to develop theories of 'credal probability', in which probability judgments are relativized to rational corpora, that is, sets of beliefs fulfilling various rationality conditions. This approach is something of a hybrid of the l.r.t. and Ramsey's wholly subjective theory; like both these theories, it is an attempt to formalize the conditions which lead individuals to have rational degrees of belief about events whose outcome is unknown. However, on this approach the rationality of our graduated beliefs consists in more than a certain coherent betting strategy (as with Ramsey's theory), and in fact depends on these beliefs being related in a specific way to a whole network (corpus) of other beliefs about the world. Construing probability judgments, i.e. judgments about degrees of belief, as relative to such a corpus has strong affinities to the l.r.t. as formulated by Carnap − Keynes appears to be a common ancestor (Kyburg, 1961, p. 6) − but there are important differences as well.

One prominent difference, which must be noted from the start, is that many rational corpora theorists define credal probability in terms of primitive concepts which are cognate to probability. Levi, for example, employs a primitive undefined 'chance' predicate, and defines credal probabilities by direct inference from rational corpora including beliefs on chance. Kyburg defines statements of 'epistemic' probability about individual objects relative to rational corpora involving statements of frequency concerning that kind of object, with the crucial proviso that the object whose probability we are concerned with be known to be a 'random' member of the class in which the frequency is displayed. In addition Kyburg specifically argues against the possibility of reducing the 'randomness' relation to a probabilistic one.

My own feeling is that it is not particularly illuminating to define probability in terms of notions that are cognate to it. First of all, this leads to an unnecessary multiplication of entities, namely, the postulation of two distinct but related concepts where one should suffice. Secondly, since probability is defined in terms of some cognate concept such as chance or randomness, the definition of probability given by rational corporate theorists will only be as plausible as the definition they offer of the cognate concept. Unfortunately, with some rational corporate theorists (Levi in particular), the cognate concept used in defining probability is itself left undefined, and so a whole host of important questions concerning probability are, in effect, swept under the carpet. (This is not the case with Kyburg's definition, which I will have occasion to mention again in Chapter V.)

In contrast to my view of rational corpora theorists, I have virtually no sympathy with the purely subjective theories of Ramsey and his followers, and will say virtually nothing about such theories in the rest of the book: this is because I believe such theories to be non-starters. For one thing, such subjective theories can make no sense of why we regard certain individuals' assessment of probability as wrong, and others as correct (where all wager in a manner consistent with the probability calculus), but, as I hope to show, this central feature of our concept of probability can be explained on the l.r.t. Secondly, by explaining judgments of probability as propensities to wager, subjective theories of probability put the horse before the cart: all but the most naïve gamblers try to establish (by reference to the evidence available) what the correct probability of an event is − to what degree it is reasonable to expect it to occur − in order to decide how to wager; they do not blindly wager and then conclude what degree of belief they must have had in its occurrence.

In any event, rather than attempt a systematic evaluation of the subjective theory of probability or rational corpora theories, I will confine myself to demonstrating that the l.r.t. adequately systematizes the 'subjective' aspects of our concept of probability which appear to support such theories; this will not be particularly difficult for, as I have already remarked, the l.r.t. can account for subjective differences between individuals' probability judgments by appealing to different evidence known to those individuals. The more difficult task will be to demonstrate that the l.r.t. is also capable of accounting for many, if not all, of the objective features of our concept of probability that have been cited by philosophers critical of both the purely subjective theory of probability and the l.r.t., and it will, perhaps, be appropriate now to conclude this chapter by outlining various attempts philosophers have made to articulate an objective concept of probability.

Objective Theories of Probability

Broadly speaking, those favouring objective theories of probability identify probability with a material, physical (or, as they often say, empirical) property of the world. Perhaps the most extreme position in this respect is the frequency theory of Von Mises, for he claimed his theory of probability was itself an empirical theory about mass phenomena on a par with the traditional sciences of physics, chemistry, etc. Waismann and Carnap effectively criticized this claim and, following Salmon and Reichenbach, it seems preferable to regard the frequency theory as a specification of a semantic interpretation for the a priori axioms of probability in terms of an empirical property of the world, namely limit of relative frequency. No doubt, if there are such objective features of the world as limits of relative frequency, it is possible to use them to provide a model for the axioms and theorems of the probability calculus.

There are numerous objections to such a frequency account of objective or empirical probability, and we should briefly take note of the two most famous straight away: that probability conceived as a limit in an infinite sequence is not applicable to individual events, and that statements of limiting values of frequency in infinite sequences are unverifiable and irrefutable, being compatible with any frequency displayed in observable, finite initial segments. Because of the latter objection, it is necessary to supplement the frequency theory with a theory of estimation, providing rules for extrapolating to limits from finite observations. It is important to note, however, that advocates of the frequency theory still insist that probabilities are the limits of relative frequency, and that procedures of estimation only provide the means for our having knowledge — inductive or otherwise — of the objective properties of the world said to constitute probability. For example, Von Mises (1957, p. 57 and pp. 84-5) argues that all empirical sciences must employ procedures of estimating, and so the theory of probability as a study of one kind of empirical phenomena naturally has to be supplemented by rules of estimation. Similarly, Salmon (1967, pp. 84ff) treats limits statements as wholly meaningful statements about future events, with inductive inference providing the means for us to 'know' such limits. Doubts one may have over the validity of inferring limits of relative frequency are, naturally enough, subsumed under the problem of induction: Salmon notes that we observe apparent convergence to limits in finite sequences and thinks the only problem is whether we are justified in inferring that this observed convergence will continue indefinitely.

In the next chapter, I will examine the consequences of adopting various theories of estimation to supplement the frequency theory, but we should note right away that not all philosophers who believe in empirical, or objective, probabilities have been happy with the identification of probability with unobservable limits of frequency; instead they define objective probabilities as *propensities* to produce frequencies. Such a move has two main advantages: first of all, as Popper pointed out (1959), one is not required to claim that infinite sequences with limits actually exist for probabilities to obtain — the existence of a 'chance set up' or 'trial' (to use the fashionable term) with a disposition to produce 'long-run' frequencies suffices to ensure the existence of probabilities. For Popper, probability, or chance, was a propensity to produce limits of relative frequency; for Hacking (1965, pp. 6-7 and elsewhere), it was a propensity to produce certain finite frequencies; and for Mellor it was a propensity to produce the 'chance distribution', which, while involving certain actual frequencies, is not identical with them. Conceived in any of these ways, probabilities cease to be the unobservable limits of frequency they are in the theories of Reichenbach's and Von Mises, and become (allegedly) ordinary empirical properties of the world, albeit of a dispositional kind.

A second advantage claimed for propensity theories — in comparison with the standard frequency theory — concerns the other problem we noted, that of single-case probabilities. As a number of important issues arise in connection with this objection to the frequency theory, we may conclude this chapter by considering this objection — and the position of propensity theorists on it — in some detail.

SINGLE-CASE PROBABILITIES

As we have seen, the most important function of probability statements is to guide our action in the face of uncertainty and for this reason the frequency theory must give some account of single-case probabilities —

Problems and Aims

most of our practical decisions in the face of uncertainty concern individual events. Salmon and Reichenbach, in particular, were concerned to give the frequency theory application to the single case, but it is arguable whether they did so in a satisfactory manner. The primary difficulty here is all too familiar: while the relative frequency for the kind of outcome we are concerned with (say mortality) appears to provide a plausible measure of the probability of its occurrence in a single trial (this person's chance of mortality in the next year), such a measure actually yields numerous different probabilities for the same individual outcome, depending on what reference class (e.g. forty-year-old men, academics, heavy smokers, etc.) is used for determining the relative frequency. Elsewhere (Benenson, 1977), I have argued that the attempt of Reichenbach and Salmon to resolve this difficulty by an appeal to 'weights', which are fictitious or pseudo-probabilities, is unsatisfactory. As I indicated there, we may resolve this difficulty by defining a *relational* concept of probability, which makes the determination of the probability for a particular outcome relative to the reference class chosen. Such a theory has strong affinities to the l.r.t.; in particular, the choice of a reference class to determine the probability of an outcome may be regarded as a choice to use the evidence that the event in question belongs to that reference class. Since, for the purpose of action, we usually require a single or unique probability for the event, we must supplement this relational definition with a rule for selecting one reference class, the favourite principle being that of choosing the narrowest reference class for which statistics are available. As often noted, such a principle corresponds closely to the requirement of total evidence, which, we saw, was used to give the l.r.t. the unique application usually required for the purpose of action. As use of a reference class (e.g., forty-year-old men) to determine this man's mortality embodies the evidence that he is forty years old, use of progressively narrower reference classes (e.g. the sub-class of forty-year-old academics, then forty-year-old academics who smoke heavily, etc.) obviously corresponds to more and more detailed specification of the conditions that the individual instance fulfils. In using the narrowest reference class for which statistics are available we, in effect, employ the most detailed, or total, evidence available to us.

Propensity theorists are, however, known to be unhappy with such a strategem. Mellor claims (1971, p. 73) that both the l.r.t. and the reconstruction of the frequency theory just indicated break down because some limit must be set to the amount of evidence that can be employed (unless we are to take all probabilities to be either 1 or 0, as 'evidence' of the outcome in question gives this value), and yet no clear account has ever been given as to how this limit is to be set. In point of fact, I believe this problem can be solved for the l.r.t., and I will present this solution in Chapters III and IV. Nevertheless, any resolution of this problem in terms of epistemic probability differs considerably from a propensity theory designed to apply to individual events; on such a theory, the probability of an event is a dispositional property of that event which is said to be an objective feature of the world, holding independently of any evidence known about the event, or any knowledge we have of the reference classes to which the event belongs. Thus the propensity theorists need not elucidate the kind or amount of evidence to be used in making probability judgments, but rather must explain what facts of the world constitute the dispositions it identifies with objective chance. Propensity theorists usually claim that the question of what disposition obtains in a particular case, i.e. what the probability of a particular individual event is, is a scientific question, that is, one to be settled by the methods of science; Mellor, in particular, emphasizes this.

One consequence of this — and one which will emerge shortly in the next chapter as characteristic of so-called objective theories of probability — is that any judgments as to the particular propensity obtaining in an individual case is subject to revision in the way all scientific judgments about the world are: just as, say, subsequent developments showed Copernicus (and Galileo) to have been incorrect in maintaining that the planets moved in circular orbits, any earlier determination of the propensity obtaining in a particular case may have to be revised in the light of additional scientific knowledge. Putting the matter generally, Mellor remarks:

> All the probabilities I am concerned with are empirical. Apart from logical and mathematical errors, the most well-informed physicist may just be wrong in taking the half life of radium (the length of time in which the chance of a radium atom decaying is ½) to be t_1. It might in fact be t_2 ($\neq t_1$) or, pace current theory, there might be no half life at all. It is logically possible that what is chemically identified as radium simply is not, despite appearances, a radio element as currently understood. Many current assumptions about chances might be false and they could conceivably all be rejected in the light of future science. (1971, p. 25)

Problems and Aims

As a final point in this preliminary discussion of objective theories of probability, we should take note of an unnerving consequence of this aspect of propensity theories, namely that, for all we know now, no propensities genuinely exist, and thus there may be no truly chance phenomena. This would be the case if all phenomena in the universe were deterministic, and our current belief in indeterministic trials (for example, those of quantum mechanics) depended on the inadequacy of current scientific theory (as Einstein believed about quantum mechanics). Propensity theorists are aware of this possibility – as Mellor puts it, 'In a deterministic world there would be no propensities' – and so, from Peirce onwards, have argued that determinism is false. At the moment we need not concern ourselves with the intrinsic plausibility of such a denial of determinism – though I will return to related questions in Chapter IV – but, merely, should note that it follows directly from the propensity theory's attempt to provide a fully objective alternative to the frequency theory's treatment of single-case probabilities: by identifying single-case probabilities with dispositional properties which hold independently of any evidence known about that case (or what comes to much the same thing, independently of our knowledge of the reference classes the case belongs to), the propensity theory becomes committed to the existence of genuine indeterminacies in the world for probabilities to obtain. Only such indeterminacies can constitute the objective dispositions which are equated with probability by the propensity theory.

Although preferable to the claim – often made by frequency theorists – that individual events do not have genuine probabilities, the idea that a dispositional indeterminacy in the world – whose exact relationship to actual frequencies has never been agreed upon – corresponds to our ascriptions of probabilities to individual events, has struck many probability theorists as quite strange, and may well have begun to appear so to the reader. In fact I believe the peculiarity of this conception – like those of other objective theories of probability – is closely linked to epistemological issues concerning our knowledge of probabilities, as well as semantic questions on the kind of theory of meaning appropriate to a study of probabilities. In the next chapter, I hope to examine these issues and show how the general viewpoint provided by objective theories is, inevitably, unsatisfactory. The stage will then be set for demonstrating that the l.r.t. is able to explain in a far more satisfactory fashion all our discourse on probability, including that found in science, which will be done in Chapters III-V.

II
OUR KNOWLEDGE OF PROBABILITIES

It will be useful to begin our critical analysis of objective theories of probability by noting that both the frequency theory and the propensity achieve their alleged objectivity by defining concepts of probability which are not — in a sense which has already been introduced — effective. In mathematical logic, concepts are regarded as effective if, and only if, there is a procedure for determining (in a finite time) whether or not that concept applied in a particular case. Although of course in the philosophical analysis of probability we are not dealing with matters which can be exhaustively characterized in terms of the tools of mathematics and logic, it is useful to employ a notion of effectiveness analogous to that found in pure logic, and to a certain extent this has already been done in the previous chapter: to put it briefly — for I will return to this matter in greater detail later — a particular concept of probability is effective if, and only if, there exists a definite procedure for determining (in a finite time) whether a statement of probability involving that concept is true or false.

The import of this criterion of effectiveness is easily, and profitably, illustrated by examining the frequency and propensity theories, for they employ concepts of probability which are not, in this sense, effective. It should be clear that there can be no procedure for determining, in a finite time, if a limit of relative frequency exists for a sequence of events actually found in the world — indeed, as regards empirically given sequences there can be no procedure for determining if they will even continue indefinitely, and so qualify as infinite. In place of a definite procedure for determining whether a particular probability statement is true, frequency theorists offer us procedures for

Our Knowledge of Probabilities

inductively *estimating* the limits of frequency, which constitute the truth conditions for the statement of probability. Such procedures of estimation do not — and cannot — settle conclusively the truth or falsity of any probability statement (as understood by frequency theorists); rather they provide means for making a provisional assessment of the truth value of the statement, subject always to later revision.

This is particularly clear with the method of inductive estimation recommended by Reichenbach and carefully analysed by Salmon — the so-called straight rule of induction. By this rule, we are to estimate the limit of a sequence to be equal to the currently observed frequency and, as the number of observed instances increases, 'a new inference is to be made from the observed frequency in the larger sample and the earlier inference from the smaller sample is superseded' (Salmon, 1967, p. 86). Rather than being concerned by the manner in which inductive estimates of the limit of frequency require revision as new statistical evidence becomes available, both Salmon and Reichenbach commend this procedure of induction because of its 'self-correcting' character, that is, the way in which later estimates based on greater evidence replace, or supersede, earlier ones. But because inductive estimates of limits may always have to be revised in the light of new evidence, this procedure of estimation does not provide a method for determining the truth value of a probability statement in a finite time. Thus, supplementing the frequency theory with rules for inductive estimation of limits of frequency does not remedy the basic difficulty in question, namely that the concept of limit of relative frequency is non-effective.

The non-effective character of most propensity theories is just as striking; rather than providing a criterion for deciding if particular statements of probability, or chance, are true, most propensity theorists treat the question of the truth value of such statements as an objective matter of fact for *scientists* to settle. Since science is an open-ended inquiry, no determination of chance, or probability, can be definitive in the manner given by a decision procedure. In particular (as the quotation from Mellor cited on p. 50 illustrates), the probability, or chance, ascribed to an individual event may have to be revised when further relevant scientific knowledge becomes available; this of course means that no decision procedure can be given for determining the probability, or chance, of an event at a given time — it is impossible to give effective rules which anticipate the course of future developments in science.

In fact, as we will see in considerable detail in later chapters, this non-effective character seems essential to the basic idea behind objective theories of probability: Blackburn, who has little sympathy for the frequency theory or related accounts of probability, stressed that the objective aspect of our concept of probability is 'an aspect of the notion which leads us to regard a probability as something to be known about or ignorant of, something of which estimates can be made and progressively rectified by more and more knowledge of circumstances' (1973, p. 106). Even the average layman will speak of probability estimates — in distinction to definitive probability judgments — thereby betraying at least a suspicion that probabilities are not susceptible to definitive determination, but may always require revision. In my view, any concept of probability which entails that all genuine probability statements are amenable to revision is non-effective in character.

What are we to make of such non-effective conceptions of probability? As the reader may have begun to suspect on his own, such conceptions are the mirror opposite of the l.r.t.: whereas that theory (which has been criticized as subjectivist but, nevertheless, is effective in character) can be viewed as providing an anti-realist explanation of the meaning of probability statements based on quite valid observations on how we come to know the truth of those statements, non-effective objectivist conceptions of probability are highly realist in character, and can provide little in the way of an explanation of how we can know the truth of probability statements on the basis of finite bodies of evidence. Although this may be obvious, and was hinted at in the previous chapter, these are matters of sufficient importance for us to examine in some detail, and indeed the demonstration that such non-effective conceptions of probability are incapable of plausibly explaining how we come to know the truth of probability statements on the basis of finite observations can only be completed (in Chapter V) after a careful study of statistical methods for inferring probabilities.

OBJECTIVE PROBABILITIES AND REALISM

One's first impression of the frequency and propensity theories is that they are of course realist in character, as they seek to define probability in terms of an allegedly objective, or empirical, property of the world, rather than anything we know of the world. They are alike in equating probability with properties which, allegedly, obtain in the world quite independently of our knowledge. The frequency theory involves an extreme form of realism, for the limits of relative frequency which are said to constitute probabilities are, in principle, never observable.

I must admit that I am not wholly clear as to the degree, or variety, of realism propensity theorists are committed to — Mellor certainly acknowledges the realist character of his theory, and Popper's theory seems similar in this respect. (Indeed at one point (1968, p. 212) Popper characterizes his propensity theory as a theory about 'the structure of the world'.) While such a realist conception of probability does seem in keeping with the intentions of propensity theorists from Peirce onwards — for these theories usually claim that certain tendencies inherent in 'nature' constitute chance — it may be possible to formulate a propensity theory in a less overtly realist manner. Given a suitably anti-realist interpretation of dispositional concepts, it might be possible to find a formulation of it not committed to identifying probability with features of the world which obtain independently of our capacities of knowledge. In fact Braithwaite's version of the propensity theory can be thought of as an attempt to give such an anti-realist account of statistical probabilities, but it is one which I believe to be unsuccessful. In Chapter V, I will specifically address the question of whether an anti-realist account of statistical probability — on a propensity theory or any other theory — can be given, and try to show that such an enterprise is doomed to failure. Whether another form of propensity theory, not concerned with statistical probabilities, can be given an anti-realist formulation must remain an open question — I do not know of any theory along these lines and do not think such a theory could be of much interest. In any event, until I deal specifically with Braithwaite's theory in Chapter V, I will — except for occasional asides — continue to concentrate on realist versions of the propensity theory as exemplified by Mellor and Popper, and I will treat such versions as paradigmatic of propensity theories.

In fact, there is more to the matter than a superficial appearance that frequency and propensity theories are realist in character, and the deep sense in which the frequency and propensity theories are committed to realism depends on the non-effective character of those theories, just explained: specifically, Dummett, whose views on realism I have to some extent followed, has suggested that realist explanations of the meaning of a concept involve reliance on non-effective criteria for the application of that concept. To simplify Dummett's position a bit — as some further elaboration will be required shortly — what he claims is that the means by which we come to know, or recognize, the truth value of a particular statement are analogous to the decision procedures of mathematical logic; i.e. the means by which we recognize the truth of a particular statement are procedures for deciding the truth value of the statement in a finite time. Since the anti-realist maintains that the meaning of a particular concept is to be explained by reference to the means by which we come to know, or recognize, the truth of various statements, the anti-realist will maintain that a concept can only have meaning in so far as there exists a decision procedure for determining the truth value of the statements in which it occurs. Where there is no decision procedure for determining the truth value of such statements, the concept has no meaning, and thus no question can arise as to the truth or falsity of statements involving the concept. (This of course led Dummett to a discussion of the principle of bivalence and the validity of the law of excluded middle, but these topics do not concern us directly; however, compare footnotes to pp. 166 and 175.)

The relevance of Dummett's remarks on effective decidability should be obvious: because we are always prepared to revise judgments on empirical, or objective, probability, no decision procedure exists for settling the truth value of statements involving such concepts. This, on Dummett's view, constitutes a commitment to realism, and such an analysis fully accords with the immediate impression that these theories are essentially realist in character.

Two rejoinders on behalf of objective theories of probability may seem in order here: first of all, it may be thought that any genuinely objective theory of probability must be realist in character. The l.r.t., which I have claimed is anti-realist in character, has long been criticized as subjectivist, and this might be thought to be an inevitable feature of any anti-realist account of probability. Moreover, objective theories of probability are usually put forward to systematize the concept of probability in sccience and, it might be argued, the most plausible account of scientific concepts is a realist one.

I do not propose to try to settle here the general question of whether a realist or anti-realist account of science is more plausible; nor do I think I would be able to do so if I were so inclined. I will instead confine myself to specific arguments about our concept of probability, which seems to me a special case, and I will try to see if all accounts suitable for explaining the objective character of the probability judgments made in science require highly realist assumptions. In fact what I propose to do is present a formulation of the l.r.t. that is both anti-realist in character and yet wholly objective. Thus the question of whether an objective formulation of a theory of probability must be realist in character is premature; I suggest the reader keep an open mind on this issue, and later judge for himself whether the avowedly anti-realist formulation I give to the l.r.t. in Chapters III and V is sufficiently objective to serve as an analysis of a scientific conception of probability.

A second, quite different, rejoinder to my claim that objective theories of probability, such as the frequency and propensity theories, are realist in character is possible: namely that I am mistaken, having taken too simplistic a view of how the realist/anti-realist dispute applies to probability theory. No doubt the explanation just given of the realist character of the frequency and propensity theories has been simplified (as I hinted), but not, I hope, mistaken. One of my basic contentions has been that objective theories of probability employ non-effective concepts of probability, namely ones for which the truth or falsity of a probability statement cannot be settled *with certainty* in a finite time. But it might be thought this involves too narrow a characterization of the notion of effectiveness appropriate for context outside mathematics and pure logic. Dummett himself has indicated that the anti-realist need not treat empirical statements as capable of being verified (or falsified) with certainty:

> There may indeed be some empirical statements whose truth can never be known with certainty, for which there cannot be any wholly conclusive evidence. For such statements there will, for the anti-realist, be no question of there being anything in virtue of which *they are (definitively) true, but only of things in virtue of which they are probably true*; the notion of absolute truth simply will not apply to such statements. But, though the realist must hold fast to the conception of an absolute truth value as attaching to every statement, the anti-realist does not need to. For him the meaning of a statement is intrinsically connected with that which we count as evidence for or against the statement; and there is nothing to prevent a statement being so used that we do not treat anything as conclusively verifying it. The use of inductive arguments as establishing, either conclusively or as subject to the possibility of revision, the truth of a statement thus becomes for the anti-realist an intrinsic feature of the meaning of that statement. (1978, p. 162, my italics)

In other words, an anti-realist need only explain the meaning of a concept in terms of the conditions for its justified assertion, and there is nothing to prevent the assertion of a statement as being justified at one time, in the light of certain evidence, and its negation justified later in the light of different evidence. What we require — and what Dummett has in mind — is a notion of effectiveness which makes a concept ϕ effective if, and only if, we have a procedure, terminating in a finite time, which determines if we are justified then in asserting a statement involving ϕ. To put it in terms of our coming to know the truth of statements involving ϕ, our concept of ϕ will be effective if, and only if, there exists a procedure, terminating in a finite time, which allows us to know the truth of these statements with at least a high degree of probability, though not necessarily with full certainty.

I suspect that for most contexts outside of logic and mathematics, this notion of effectiveness is the one appropriate to anti-realist explanations of meaning, and, at first glance, the concept (or concepts) of probability adumbrated by objective theorists seem to be effective in this sense. This would suggest that objective theorists could provide an anti-realist account of probability (if they chose to) simply by explaining the meaning of probability in terms of the conditions that led to the justified assertion of probability statements, the conditions in virtue of which we could know such statements to *'probably'* be true.

The problem with such a programme is, however, the recurrence (italicized here and above) of the concept of probability. Although the anti-realist may explain the meaning of a variety of concepts in terms of conditions in virtue of which we established the *probable* truth of statements involving that concept, such an explanation for our concept of probability must be examined very carefully to see that no circularity or equivocation is involved. In fact in the next two sections of this chapter I hope to show that objective theories of probability cannot be formulated along anti-realist lines without introducing an unacceptable circularity, or unnecessary multiplication of concepts. The arguments I wish to present seem to me significant in their own right, and transcend any dispute between realists and anti-realists; indeed my interest in demonstrating that theories of objective probability are realist in character and, moreover, cannot be reconstructed along anti-realist lines, stems from a deeper interest in what I might call the epistemology of probability theory. Specifically, what I will be concerned with is whether objective theories of probability can give a plausible account of how we come to know the truth of probability statements and, to some extent, the relation of this epistemological question to the questions on realism and anti-realism should be obvious: if objective theories of probability can give a plausible account of how we come to know the truth of probability statements — can plausibly give a specification of the conditions which, when known, constitute valid grounds for asserting statements of probability — it should be possible to reconstruct these theories along anti-realist lines. To do so, we need only equate the conditions specified as justifying the assertion of the probability statement with its meaning. Conversely, if objective theories of probability do not yield a plausible account of how we come to know the truth of probability statements, the prospects for an anti-realist version of these theories are decidedly dim: there simply will not be any conditions which, when known, justify the assertion of statements of probability and, of course, an anti-realist explanation of probability presupposes the existence of such conditions. No doubt most proponents of objective theories of probability believe that they have given a plausible account of how we come to know the truth of probability statements — or at least believe that some such account compatible with their theory could be given, for, in many cases, objective theorists are quite sketchy about the details of how we come to know the truth of probability statements — but we should now begin to investigate this question in some detail.

COMING TO KNOW OBJECTIVE PROBABILITIES

The basic difficulty facing objective theories of probability is that, on them, probability statements become ordinary empirical statements, incapable of being known with certainty. Obviously the a priori methods of logic and mathematics cannot alone afford knowledge of these empirical matters — for knowledge obtained purely through them is certain — and so such theories require supplementation by some account of how we obtain our less than certain knowledge of empirical probability statements. The most natural — and common — move here is to treat objective probabilities as empirical magnitudes analogous to, say, length. The problem of how we can know the truth of numerical probability statements, then, can be treated as a problem of estimating one kind of empirical magnitude. To begin with, this presents no particular problem for theories of empirical probability: all empirical magnitudes require estimation, and so the estimation of empirical probabilities may be treated as one instance of a general theory of estimation (see Mellor, 1971, pp. 101-4). But now we cannot overlook the fact that scientists, statisticians and ordinary laymen all characteristically assign degrees, comparative or quantitative, of what they call 'plausibility', 'confirmation', 'acceptability' or indeed 'probability' to estimates of empirical magnitudes. The same of course goes for estimates of probability. In order not to prejudge the crucial question of whether the less than certain knowledge embodied in our 'estimate' of probabilities can, or indeed must, itself be treated as probabilistic knowledge, we require a neutral term to designate the degree, or quantity, of uncertainty ascribed to probability estimates: until further discrimination becomes appropriate I will use the term 'degree of credence' for this purpose.

The basic dilemma — as I see it — facing theories of empirical, or objective, probability is that they must either identify the degree of credence given to estimates of probability with degree of probability (as explicated by their theory), or treat it as a distinct concept. Both approaches can be found in the literature, but neither is satisfactory. Identifying the degree of credence ascribed to estimates of probability with a degree of probability for those estimates is viciously circular, generating an infinite regress. On the other hand, treating this degree of credence as a distinct concept leads to an unnecessary multiplication of concepts.

Let us first consider the infinite regress generated by treating the degree of credence ascribed to estimates of empirical probability as itself an empirical probability. I will illustrate the problem in terms of the frequency theory's explication of empirical probability, but shortly will generalize the argument to other theories of empirical probability. Let us say (to use an example closely following one of Von Mises (1957, p. 7)), that on the basis of 100,000 observations of forty-year-old men, we estimate the probability of mortality of forty-year-old men, i.e. the limit of the rate of mortality in an infinite sequence of forty-year-old men, to be 0.011. This would be based on an observation of 1,100 deaths in a given year. We can call this an estimate of the empirical probability at level 1, the basic probability we are concerned with. How are we to determine the degree of credence which attaches to this estimate of the level 1 probability? If it is said that the only rational degree of credence that can be attached to this estimate is the degree of probability it enjoys, we must say that this is the limit of frequency with which similar estimates turn out to be correct, for only the empirical fact of a limit in an appropriate sequence will constitute a probability. Such a probability, if it exists, can be called a second-level probability.

But even if we can define an appropriate reference class, say, of estimates of mortality rates based on 10,000 or more observations, and also have data to the effect that a proportion, say, 85 per cent of these have so far been successful, we can still only estimate that the second level of probability is 85 per cent. (By a 'successful' estimate we might mean one that turns out to be correct — within a specified margin of error — for all subsequent observations.†) Since, then, our figure of 85 per cent can only be an estimate of the appropriate second level of probability, we may ask what degree of credence to attach to it as an estimate. Even if we could identify some reference class in which a limit of frequency would give us a plausible value for the degree of credence to ascribe to this estimate of the second level of probability (as we did for estimates of first-level probabilities), we again could only estimate this figure on the basis of some finite body of observation. It is obvious that we are here drawn into an infinite regress, and equally obvious that the regress has been generated by identifying the degree of credence given to estimates of empirical probability (here a limit) with an empirical probability (again here a limit), which in turn can only be estimated.

Lest it be though that the proposal to identify degrees of credence in estimates of empirical probability with empirical probabilities is too implausible to be taken seriously, we may note that Reichenbach put forward a theory very similar to the one just outlined (1949, sections 90 and 91). Characteristically, Reichenbach wavered on whether the degree of credence he attributed to a particular estimate of probability could be called a probability, for such a probability would be a probability for a single case. In the end he termed this degree of credence the 'weight' of an appraised posit, for this was the

---

†The reader may have noted that the task of assigning degrees of credence to estimates of probability is doubly fraught for frequency theorists. Besides the infinite regress which I hope to exhibit in the above argument, there is the further problem that we can never know that one estimate of frequency has been correct, much less that a certain proportion of a kind of estimate are correct: to know that an estimate has been correct we would have to know the actual limit of the frequency we are concerned with and this, of course, is impossible. I ignore this added complication because it seems to me simply another instance of the basic problem of how we are to come to know limits of frequency.

term he generally adopted for single-case probabilities. 'Posits' are what I have been calling estimates, and the weight of a particular posit, in Reichenbach's theory, is determined by a limit of relative frequency in a suitable reference class (1949, p. 465). As such, the weight of an initial posit of course can itself only be posited. This second posit in turn has a weight, determined by a limit in a suitable reference class. This limit again can only be posited, and so on *ad infinitum*. Although — or perhaps because — Reichenbach recognized that this method of positing probabilities would lead to an 'infinite hierarchy of posits', he insisted that this regress be stopped at some finite level. This was to be done by use of a 'blind' or 'anticipative' posit, that is, an estimate of a limit whose weight (i.e. degree of credence) cannot be known or even estimated, despite the fact that such a weight may objectively obtain if there is a limit to the percentage of success in the class of similar estimates.

Such a move does prevent the infinite regress described above, but at the cost of undermining the entire enterprise of ascribing degrees of credence (or weight) to estimates of probability. First of all we should note that the whole idea of a blind posit whose weight, or degree of credence, cannot even be estimated is somewhat unusual: throughout the history of probability theory there has been considerable controversy as to whether or not there could be 'unknown' probabilities (cf. Keynes, 1921, p. 372, and Carnap, 1962, p. 171). Of course the empirical probabilities of the propensity theory and frequency theory can be wholly unknown, but the conception of a blind posit is far more unusual than that of an unknown probability. A blind posit of the kind we are considering is a second estimate of a probability to be assigned to another estimate although its own probability cannot even be estimated. Such a blind posit is a truly wild estimate, in the sense that we have no idea *whatsoever* how accurate it is.

The objection to introducing such an unusual conception is that it is difficult to see why we would go in for the enterprise of estimating empirical magnitudes, then ascribing — even provisionally — degrees of credence to those estimates if, in the end, we cannot attribute any degree of credence to an estimate crucial to the whole chain so far constructed. In terms of our example of mortality statistics, what would be the point of estimating (on the basis of 100,000 observations) that the mortality rate of forty-year-old men was 0.011, and then qualifying this estimate by saying it had an 85 per cent probability of success, when we had to acknowledge that the figure of 85 per cent

Our Knowledge of Probabilities

was itself only an estimate whose credibility we were *quite unable* to assess. If the figure of 85 per cent were wildly out, with the real frequency of success of similar estimates a mere 2 per cent, it would hardly make sense to regard the original estimate of the mortality as very sound. And the problem is that, although we do not know the figure of 85 per cent (or whatever figure we make a blind posit of) to be wildly off, we do not know, nor even are able to estimate, anything about how much credence to attach to the figure of 85 per cent.†

At this juncture one might be tempted to object that the infinite regress at the heart of the problem we are considering is not vicious.

†In all fairness we should note that Reichenbach introduced the idea of a blind posit at a finite level in the hierarchy of posits as part of an extended treatment of the problem of induction: his reply to the above objection was that the policy of forming a hierarchy of posits with a blind posit closing it at a particular level to avoid an infinite regress has the justification of being known to be the best one for achieving success in estimating limits of frequency (if those limits of frequency exist). But this simply ignores the basic problem motivating our present line of enquiry, that is, whether the explication of probability as limit of frequency can satisfactorily explain how we come to know probabilities. Reichenbach's theory, complete with its pragmatic justification of induction, only tells us that if probabilities are identified with limits of frequency we can form estimates of those probabilities from finite data, even if we cannot know them with certainty. The degrees of credence we attach to estimates of probability are, on this theory, taken to be weights determined by other limits of relative frequency. When we object that this leads to an infinite regress, we are told that an end can be put to the regress by refusing to assign any weight to certain estimates of probability. If we object that this means we cannot ascribe any degree of credence to an estimate underpinning all previous ones, we are told that such a policy has the justification of being known to be the best one for estimating probabilities and degrees of credence *if they are identified with limits of frequency*. So much the worse, we must conclude, for identifying probabilities and degrees of credence with limits of frequency – with such an identification the best policy of estimating probabilities we can devise is one which, by an independent standard, is most unsatisfactory. I might also add here that Reichenbach's purported pragmatic justification of induction is suspect on other grounds: even if a method of induction is justified by its 'pragmatic' success in estimating limits of frequency, such a method has no real practical use for its adherents. As critics of the frequency theory have long pointed out, any individual will be dead long before convergence to a limit need occur, and so there is no assurance correct estimates of limits of frequency will provide any concrete gain to an individual.

Our Knowledge of Probabilities

It may be that my intuitions on what distinguishes a vicious regress from an innocuous one are less developed than they should be, but the regress in question does seem to me vicious. One kind of vicious regress found in philosophical analysis — though there may be others — takes the form of appealing to a second judgment of a disputed kind in order to resolve one's original dispute. As regards the proposal to identify probability with limits of frequency, our original question is how can we have even probabilistic knowledge of such unverifiable empirical phenomena. We are told that we do so by estimating the limits of frequency, and that we may assign weights to these estimates (i.e. probabilities for single cases) in virtue of different limits of frequency in classes of repeated estimates. But these limits, which constitute the objective weight of the estimate, can themselves only be estimated: hence we can only have *genuine* probabilistic knowledge of the original limit if we have *correctly* estimated a second kind of limit. Of course we can never be certain we have correctly estimated the second limit, and so can only appeal to the high probability of having done so in order to claim that we have probabilistic knowledge of the original limit. But this third probability is itself a limit that can only be estimated, and our estimate of it must be correct for us to have genuine probabilistic knowledge of the second limit, and so on *ad infinitum*. Put generally, the difficulty is that in order to explain how we have probabilistic knowledge of our original probability (the first limit), we must show we have probabilistic knowledge of a second limit. This is a problem identical with our original one, and so can only be resolved by appealing to probabilistic knowledge of our new third limit, a problem again identical with the original. Such a regress is clearly vicious.

Although I have formulated this objection specifically against the frequency theory, it seems to me to hold generally as an objection to one way of explaining the possibility of knowing objective probabilities that are treated as empirical phenomena or magnitudes. We cannot have certain knowledge of such empirical phenomena or magnitudes, and if we say that our knowledge of such empirical probabilities is itself probabilistic, in the same sense of probability, we generate the vicious regress just explained. Put intuitively, once we introduce the idea of a probability that an original judgment or estimate of probability is correct, there is no end to the matter; treating this second level judgment of probability, like the original judgment, to be a judgment about an empirical feature of the world, and so inherently uncertain, we may ask

Our Knowledge of Probabilities

how probable is it that this second level judgment is correct, and so on *ad infinitum*.

It is easy to reformulate this objection in terms of my claim that empirical theories of probability involve non-effective criteria of application: lacking definitive, i.e. effective, criteria for application of the concept of empirical probability, we fall back on the expedient of saying such probabilities are capable of being estimated with varying degrees of credence. But then the idea of the degree of credence attached to such estimates is itself given non-effective criteria of application by identification with an empirical probability, generating the regress just indicated.

Such a regress does not arise on the l.r.t., nor could it if, as I have claimed, the l.r.t. provides an anti-realist explanation of the meaning of probability statements. The regress in question arises when we attempt to explain our knowledge of probabilities in terms of probabilistic knowledge of empirical phenomena. However, it should by now be obvious that the l.r.t. can readily explain our knowledge of probabilities without generating such a regress; the l.r. theorist claims that we know the truth of full (two-term) probability statements by our immediate intuitive apprehension of logical relations of partial entailment between the two terms in question. In claiming that we can know these relations of partial entailment with full — indeed logical — certainty, the l.r. theorist prevents the regress involved in asserting that we only have probabilistic knowledge of the truth of probability statements. We should also note that, while a regress similar to the one generated by objective theories would arise for the l.r.t., if there were something further we needed to know to have certain knowledge of relations of partial entailment, this is precluded by the l.r. theorist's claim that our knowledge of logical relations of partial certainty is immediate and intuitive.

It may be thought that this explanation lets the l.r. theorist off too easily — the problem posed for objective theorists was not how to explain our knowledge of explicitly relational probability statements — which, in any case, are not the primary concern of such theories — but, rather, how to explain our knowledge of those statements in which we speak, *without specification of evidence*, of the probability of a given phenomenon. Thus, to claim any real advantage for the l.r.t., we must articulate it in such a way as to explain, without regress, how we come to know the truth of such statements, as well as how we come to know the truth of explicitly relational statements.

But this is in effect just what I did early on in Chapter I (specifically, see pp. 16-20), where I pointed out that, for the l.r. theorist, the means by which we come to know the truth of, i.e. decide, ordinary probability statements are our observations of finite bodies of evidence and apprehension of decidable relations of partial entailment. Thus, every time we affirm an ordinary probability statement we, so to speak, register an (effective) decision on the probability of the phenomenon in question. Since on this analysis, there is nothing further to be done — no further facts to be ascertained — to complete our decision on its truth, a regress of the kind generated by objective theories of probability in explaining how we decide the truth of such a statement does not, and cannot, arise.†

Finally, I should add that the above argument concerning the regress generated by objective (realist) theories of probability provides a deep, and thoroughgoing, rationale for adopting an anti-realist definition of probability. If — in a realist fashion — we identify probabilities with entities which obtain in the world independently of our cognitive capacities, the question arises as to how we know when a given entity of this kind obtains, and, by answering that we have probabilistic knowledge of this, a vicious regress is generated. In contrast, if we do not identify probabilities with entities obtaining in the world but, rather, identify them with that by which we recognize the truth of probability statements — evidence and logical relations — we entirely avoid postulating the existence of a separate — so to speak real — entity, knowledge of which we must then explain. This prevents any regress of the kind we have just been considering.

† It seems to me of considerable significance to the theory of knowledge that it is possible, on the l.r.t., to provide effective criteria for determining the truth of probability statements. The important consequences which the l.r.t. has (to my mind) on complex issues concerning fallibilism, foundationalism and the ultimate basis of empirical knowledge cannot be examined here in any detail; I can only indicate in outline how I believe the l.r.t. as explained above relates to the important question of whether there exists a sheet anchor to our knowledge of empirical matters, i.e. whether there is something of which in the end we may be certain in regard to empirical matters. Here it is natural to think that the concept of probability provides the firm basis for all the rest of our knowledge — we may not be certain of our judgments on a whole host of things but, surely, it is natural, and plausible, to think we can be certain as to how probable such judgments are. And it is, for me, the primary merit of the l.r.t. that, on it, we can indeed be certain of the truth value of probability judgments.

Our Knowledge of Probabilities

There are several interesting reasons why the regress which I believe to be generated by objective theories of probability — but not the anti-realist l.r.t. — has not been widely noted and taken as a decisive drawback to these theories. First of all — and this seems to be the viewpoint adopted implicitly by most practising scientists and statisticians — there exist mathematical techniques for estimating degrees of probability, which appear to resolve this problem in a straightforward and convincing manner. These are statistical methods for testing binomial hypotheses, for example the Neyman-Pearson method of confidence interval testing. By use of this, or similar methods, one estimates probabilities from small samples of data on frequencies and, crucially, the pure probability calculus alone suffices to determine a second-order degree of probability, or confidence,† in the estimate being correct within a specified margin of error. The degree of confidence, or probability, that we have in the estimate is *not* itself estimated, but, rather, is known with mathematical certainty, and this blocks the regress considered above.

Such a theory of statistical estimation is complicated and interesting in its own right, but I must defer discussion of it to a separate chapter on statistical probability. In that chapter I will also consider Braithwaite's variant of the Neyman-Pearson theory of statistical testing of probability hypotheses, and will try to show how neither it, nor the original Neyman-Pearson theory, can serve as the basis for a satisfactory definition of objective, statistical, probability. At the moment, we should consider what in fact I believe is the more common way objectivists have managed to avoid falling into the regress we have been discussing, and this is the expedient, already alluded to, of multiplying different senses for the concept of probability.

---

†Some, e.g. Mellor, have suggested that Neyman may not have intended his confidence coefficient to be interpreted probabilistically, but this is how it is usually interpreted in statistics, and such an interpretation appears in accord with Neyman's own words (Compare Mellor, 1971, p. 104 and Neyman, 1952, p. 235). Indeed, as far as I can see, since this technique is based on the pure probability calculus, it only allows us to infer confidence coefficients which are second-order probabilities of precisely the same kind as the (first-order) probabilities we wish to estimate; thus no other interpretation of the confidence coefficient would, formally, speaking, be valid.

TWO CONCEPTS

It is notable that even Carnap, the most influential recent proponent of the l.r.t., claimed that there exist two distinct concepts of probability — probability$_1$, or epistemic probability (historically given various explicata including Carnap's own version of the l.r.t.), and probability$_2$, statistical or objective probability (whose explicata we have just been critically considering). Carnap's claim has been widely accepted and, once accepted, allows proponents of objective theories of probability to avoid the regress just discussed. The basic question at issue is how objective theories of probability can explain our knowledge of probability, and any attempt to treat the degree of credence characteristically assigned to estimates of probability as itself a probability (in the same sense as the original 'objective' definition of probability), leads to the regress examined above. Clearly the regress is avoided if one postulates a distinct concept of rational credence, which is said to be the means by which we come to have knowledge of empirical probabilities, and Carnap's distinction between probability$_2$ — as objective probability — and probability$_1$ — as epistemic probability — serves this purpose nicely.

In fact many proponents of objective theories of probability reject Carnap's idea of inductive probability — Popper is a notable example — and instead claim that a non-probabilistic concept of confirmation, or corroboration, best explains our knowledge of all empirical matters. Our knowledge of empirical probabilities can then be explained as highly confirmed, but non-probabilistic, knowledge of one kind of empirical phenomenon or magnitude.

As regards our regress, the effect of adducing a non-probabilistic concept of confirmation as an explicatum for what I have neutrally called 'degree of credence' is much the same as adducing a second probabilistic concept, such as Carnap's probability$_1$ — either way the regress is blocked. But either way there is a cost to such a move, which is, specifically, a loss in conceptual economy. Certainly, the idioms which we naturally use to speak of the plausibility, credibility, or acceptance of hypotheses on empirical phenomena bear a noticeable similarity to the language of probability. If possible, in the interests of conceptual economy, one should try to define one concept, naturally called probability, that covers a variety of judgments from single statements about games of chance, to more elaborate statements on the probabilistic phenomena studied by natural science, as well as statements about the degree of credence of scientific hypotheses themselves. In any event, a concept of inductive probability seems required in a reconstruction of empirical knowledge — though a certain minority of philosophers, e.g. Popper and his followers, might deny this — and so a considerable conceptual economy can be achieved by explaining all these superficially similar idioms in terms of the concept of inductive probability. As already indicated, I hope to show in later stages of the book how this can be done.†

---

†It will be useful to contrast my position here in regard to the regress described above with that of C. I. Lewis, the only writer I know to have raised a similar objection to objective, or empirical, theories of probability. Lewis (1946, pp. 288-90) argues that the frequency theory is drawn into an infinite regress when it attempts to explain our knowledge — inevitably less than certain — of the limits of frequencies, which are said to constitute objective probabilities. In this respect his argument is identical to the one I presented on pp. 60-5, though (as I indicated in the Introduction) I was not aware of its existence when I first formulated my own views on this matter. However, there are two vital differences between Lewis's position over this matter and my own: first of all Lewis did not, apparently, appreciate that this regress can be blocked by introducing a second distinct concept of rational credence — which may be explained probabilistically or non-probabilistically — which is said to be the one involved in our less than certain knowledge of the objective probability in question. This may seem to be a relatively minor difference between our two theories, but in fact it is only by appealing to such a second distinct (indeed, also a third distinct) concept of probability that Lewis's own theory of epistemic probability manages to avoid a similar regress.

Lewis's theory of epistemic probability (which he thought of as a version of the l.r.t.) required the introduction of additional distinct concepts of probability to avoid a similar regress because he found it necessary to distinguish between hypothetical probability statements and what he called 'categorical' probability statements. The former are, as far as I can see, what I take to be statements of logical probability, while the exact nature of the latter remains somewhat obscure to me; their presence in Lewis's theory marks the second major difference in our two positions. (Other l.r. theorists, e.g. Hempel (1965, p. 384), have also found this distinction alien to the conception of logical probability.) Without going into the details of his definition of categorical probability statements, suffice it to say that such statements can only be asserted when we have established, *to a high degree of probability*, the truth of the evidence statement which figures as one term of the categorical statement. As Lewis readily appreciates (1946, p. 333), this can generate an infinite regress, as we need to be able to know the truth of some evidence statement in order to assert cate-

Our Knowledge of Probabilities

From the point of view of an anti-realist theory of meaning, there is another decisive objection to introducing a second concept of rational credence to block the regress generated by objective theories of probability. The second concept is introduced to explain how we come to know the truth of statements of objective probability; the second concept thus constitutes the means by which we come to know the truth of statements involving the first. But of course, on an anti-realist theory of meaning, the means by which we come to know the truth of statements involving a given concept constitute that concept's meaning; hence, the suggestion that there exists a second *distinct* concept of rational credence, which explains how we come to know the truth of statements of objective probability, is quite unacceptable. Thus, if our distinct concept of rational credence is explained probabilistically — for example, in terms of the epistemic probability provided by inductive evidence for objective probabilities — the concept of objective probability would, for the anti-realist, reduce in meaning to that of the allegedly distinct concept of epistemic probability. From the point of view of an anti-realist theory of meaning, the second possibility we have considered — that the concept of rational credence by which we come to know the truth of statements about objective probability is *non-probabilistic* in character — is worse. If this were so, we

gorically the underlined 'high' probability required to assert our original categorical probability statement, and so on *ad infinitum*.

Lewis blocked this regress — and so prevented the whole edifice of empirical knowledge from 'tumbling down' (ibid.) — by a complicated two-part theory involving the 'prima-facie' probability of memories, and the increase in probability afforded by the logical relation of congruence among memories. Such a move is simply a variant of the strategy discussed above. The possible regress generated by introducing a concept of probability — here Lewis's concept of a categorical probability statement — which requires us to make other further judgments of probability is blocked by introducing a distinct concept (or concepts) of probability to answer this need, here the prima-facie probability of memories and the logical (but non-inductive) probability due to congruence among memories.

On my view — as explained at pp. 65ff. — the single logical relation of inductive support is sufficient to explain our knowledge of probability. Lewis, I suspect, was unable to see this because of his general 'fallibilist' standpoint, a standpoint which sits ill with the l.r.t. The question — which may have been what prompted Lewis to offer his fallibilist theory of probability — of how the l.r. theorist is to explain revisions to probability judgments will be examined in length in Chapter IV.)

could be committed to the view that, by definition, our concept of objective probability was non-probabilistic in character, whatever that might mean.

Of course, many philosophers who distinguish between a concept of (objective) probability and a concept of rational credence (e.g. Popper) would not be inclined to accept an anti-realist theory of meaning, and this argument would carry no weight with them. Since we will be concerned throughout much of the remainder of the book with the question of whether there exists a viable anti-realist concept of objective probability distinct from that of inductive probability, we need not at present consider any further whether there are two distinct concepts of probability of the kind Carnap postulated. However, since there does exist at least one prominent school in the philosophy of science which would accept neither an anti-realist theory of meaning, nor the existence of a viable concept of inductive probability — namely, that of Popper and his followers — we should consider here whether there are good independent grounds for accepting the existence of a non-probabilistic concept of rational credence. (Such a concept will then of course be distinct from any concept of probability used in scientific discourse.) Specially, we should consider Popper's claim that a non-probabilistic concept of corroboration is at the heart of all our knowledge of empirical matters, which of course, for Popper, would include knowledge of the probabilities scientists are concerned with.

Probability and Confirmation

Anyone with even the least familiarity with the work of Popper and Carnap will know of the longstanding, and sometimes bitter, controversy over the relationship between inductive probability and confirmation. I do not wish to rehearse the details of this controversy here, nor do I wish to digress very far into what has become known as confirmation theory. What I should like to do is indicate, in outline, how Popper's central claims about the concept of corroboration, or confirmation, can be explained within the terms of the l.r.t., as well as indicate (more by passing reference than anything else) how the central aspects of confirmation theory can be brought into accord with the l.r.t.

Popper's fundamental argument against identifying 'corroboration' with probability is that the degree of corroboration attaching to a theory depends on the severity of the tests it has passed, and this, Popper claims, varies inversely with the logical probability of the theory.

Thus we find:

> I may perhaps say here that I regard the doctrine that *degree of corroboration or acceptibility cannot be a probability* as one of the more interesting findings of the philosophy of knowledge. It can be put very simply like this. A report of the result of testing a theory can be summed up by an appraisal. This can take the form of assigning some degree of corroboration to the theory. But it can never take the form of assigning to it a degree of probability; for the probability of a statement (given some test statements) simply does not express an appraisal of the severity of the tests a theory has passed, or of the manner in which it has passed these tests. The main reason for this is that the content of a theory — which is the same as its improbability — determines its testability and its corroborability. (1968, pp. 397-8)

Let us denote the probability of a theory relative to an existing body of empirical data as $P(A,B)$, with B designating the theory and A designating the empirical data. The probability of that theory on the existing empirical data and the result of a new test C, severe or otherwise, can be designated by $P(A.C,B)$. Now one branch of the l.r.t., the so-called theory of relevance (Carnap, 1962, Chapter VI) formulates a measure of the degree of relevance of new data to a hypothesis, given existing data. This is the so-called relevance quotient $\frac{P(A.C,B)}{P(A,B)}$, which obviously provides a measure of the increase in B's probability by C, relative to existing knowledge A. It has been argued that such a quotient is the most plausible measure of the degree of confirmation of B by C, when A is already known (Swinburne, 1973, Chapters I and III; Mackie, 1969).

Whether or not this is correct depends, I believe, largely on what one means by the confirmation of B by C, given A. If we are concerned with the effect the *addition* of the observation C makes to the credence we have in the hypothesis B when A is known, this ratio is a highly plausible measure of confirmation. If we are concerned with the effect of C and A together on B, then $P(A.C,B)$ is the obvious measure of the confirmation of C by B when A is known. What *Popper* appears to mean by corroboration of a hypothesis by an observation is the degree to which a new test *adds* to the credence of the hypothesis when some knowledge is already known — for example, in the passage quoted above, Popper speaks of an appraisal of a theory taking the form of a 'report of the result of testing' the theory.

Thus, if, as just suggested, the measure of the effect of such additions to knowledge is taken as the quotient $\frac{P(A.C.B)}{P(A,B)}$, Popper's basic argument against identifying corroboration, or confirmation, with probability is readily understood, and put into context. By division on the second equality of the general multiplication theorem — $P(A.B.C) = P(A,B) \times P(A.B,C) = P(A,C) \times P(A.C,B)$ — this ratio equals $\frac{P(A.B,C)}{P(A,C)}$ where $P(A,C) \neq 0$. Since Popper is concerned with hypothetico-deductive systems in which an observation C is generally deduced by strict logic from a theory B, $P(A.B,C)$ will usually equal 1 when B is tested by an observation C. The ratio $\frac{P(A.C,B)}{P(A,B)}$ measuring the effect of adding C then depends only on the value $P(A,C)$, and is inversely proportional to this.

This explains why Popper insists that the degree of corroborability, or testability, of a theory depends on the theory's improbability, and its actual corroboration depends on the severity of the tests it has passed. If we take the not implausible view that a theoretical set of laws forming a hypothetico-deductive system has no meaning in itself, but depends for its meaning on derived observational consequences, the probability of a theory B depends on the probability $P(A,C)$ of all observational consequences C of B. Since, as we have seen, the degree to which B can be confirmed by derived observations varies *inversely* with $P(A,C)$, we may say its corroborability or testability is determined by the improbability of the theory, that is, how improbable its deductive consequences C are, on the data which is already known, A. Similarly, any particular test C confirms B in inverse proportion to the probability of C on A alone, that is, in proportion to how unlikely that deductive consequence C was, given what is already known. This can be expressed by saying that the more severe the test of B (the more unlikely it is that this particular consequence of it will be found to obtain), the better the theory is confirmed when the consequence turns out to obtain.

Now it would be rather optimistic to think that the above sketch of an account of Popper's theory of corroboration will settle the myriad controversies over the relationship between probability and confirmation or corroboration, nor do I regard this sketch as altogether novel. Salmon (1967, pp. 114-22) and Mackie (1969) have pointed out the similarity of Popper's theory with various probabilistic measures of confirmation, though neither has claimed that Popper's position is identical with one in which the relevance quotient is regarded as the measure of corroboration. What is significant is that the above considerations indicate, in outline at least, how even a Popperian theory of confirmation can be brought into accord with probability theory as explained by the l.r.t., for Popper's apparently distinct concept of corroboration can be seen as concerned not with the logical probability given to a hypothesis by an observation, when some evidence is already known, but instead with the relevance of that observation as determined by a ratio of logical probabilities.

More generally, Swinburne (1973) has attempted to provide a comprehensive account of virtually all existing confirmation theory in terms of the relevance quotient of the epistemic probabilities of the l.r.t. It would take us well beyond our main concern to try to evaluate this account of confirmation theory. What is important to note here, however, is the contrast between the l.r.t. and theories of empirical probability, in respect to confirmation theory. As we have seen, theories of empirical probability must, on pain of regress, be supplemented by separate accounts on the degree of credence to be ascribed to empirical hypotheses on the basis of observational evidence. The l.r.t., in contrast, is a theory about the degree of credence provided for hypotheses by various bodies of evidence. Even if there exist arguments, say along the lines suggested by Popper, which require us to introduce finer distinctions into probability theory, such as relevance quotients, the l.r.t. does not require us to distinguish a variety of different concepts of probability and epistemic support, as did the theories of objective probability and chance we considered earlier. Indeed, even if there remains some doubt of the eventual success to be achieved by explaining statements on the confirmation, or degree of credence, given to scientific hypotheses in terms of logical probabilities, it is at least *prima facie possible* to provide a single definition of logical probability suitable for characterizing statements of probability and such statements on confirmation or degree of credence. The same cannot be said for the theories of objective probability and chance we considered before.

In effect, the position we have arrived at is this: assuming a plausible account of discourse within science on probabilities can be given in terms of the l.r.t. − which Carnap for one did *not* believe − the l.r.t. has an immense advantage over other theories of probability and confirmation, in that it can provide a single unified account of all our discourse on the 'probability', 'plausibility' and 'acceptability', of empirical hypotheses; indeed, on the view I wish to advocate, ordinary statements of probability, statements of probability within science and statements of the degree of credence, plausibility, etc., ascribed to scientific hypotheses can all be subsumed under the concept of inductive probability. In order to establish this claim it will be necessary to show that the l.r.t. can be given a wholly objective formulation, for any theory which purports to account for scientific discourse must demonstrate that the probabilities it sanctions are at least as objective as scientific knowledge is thought to be. Although the details of this formulation can only be given later (specifically, in Chapters III and V), it will be appropriate to conclude this chapter by examining this matter in the context of the discussion of objectivity and subjectivity given in the previous chapter. Specifically, we should now consider the objection, referred to earlier in passing, that the l.r.t. is essentially subjectivist in character.

SUBJECTIVISM AND THE LOGICAL RELATION THEORY

One immediate difficulty which faces us is that there exists no clear agreement as to whether the logical relation theory is objective or subjective in character. Popper and Von Mises actually call the l.r.t. 'the subjective' theory of probability, and the exposition I gave of it earlier suggested some justification to this view. On the other hand, Keynes and Carnap were keen to point out the objective character of their theory, and even Mellor, a propensity theorist, has accepted this claim (1971, p. 19).

The failure of different writers to agree on this matter can be traced to the fact that there are two quite different ways in which a theory of probability can be subjective in character. Once we distinguish the two, it will be relatively easy to state the conditions which must be fulfilled if the l.r.t. is to be given a wholly objective formulation. In fact the two sources of subjectivism in probability theory correspond to the distinction made earlier between a theory of probability proper — as a theory of meaning — and the methodology of applying that theory with particular practical aims in mind.

As we noted from the start, one prominent feature of the l.r.t. is its insistence that the degree of probability which obtains between a given hypothesis and a particular body of evidence depends solely on logical relations between the two propositions; thus the degree of probability obtaining between a hypothesis and a particular body of evidence does not, for the l.r. theorist, depend in the least on anyone's belief about the degree of probability afforded the hypotheses by that evidence — rather, it is wholly determined by a measure function to be chosen a priori.

It was precisely because the degree of probability obtaining between pairs of evidence and hypotheses would not depend on individuals' beliefs that Carnap (1962, p. 43ff) claimed that the l.r.t. was an objective account of probability. This is not an implausible claim and it is significant that most authors who defend the objectivity of the l.r.t. point out that the degree of probability obtaining between pairs of evidence and hypotheses is determined by objective logical relations, rather than actual beliefs. To have a convenient, if not all together elegant, phrase to describe a theory which determines the degree of probability between evidence and hypotheses on objective grounds, rather than by personal beliefs, we may say that such a theory is free from subjectivism 'in the theory proper', or that 'the theory proper' is objective.

Unfortunately, as Carnap himself came to recognize, it is one thing to assert that the logical relation of partial entailment between evidence and hypothesis is an objective matter not dependent on individuals beliefs, and another to explicate this relation in such a way that nothing is left to individual, subjective beliefs. Carnap himself believed that there existed a continuum of measure functions — the positive values of λ excluding $\lambda = 0$ and $\lambda = \infty$ — suitable for this purpose, and there is no doubt once a measure function is chosen, the degree of probability between a hypothesis and body of evidence does not depend on any individual's beliefs.

The problem, though, is how to choose a measure function; as we will see in more detail later, Carnap believed the different values of λ corresponded to different weightings of logical factors in relation to empirical data, but he was never able to find an objective way to determine what weighting to use. Within certain (very wide) bounds the only grounds for choosing a weight of this kind seems to be personal preference and, as Carnap saw, this introduced a subjective element into his theory (Jeffrey, 1980, p. 112). In Chapters III and VII I will argue that the only way to remedy this — and so remove any taint of subjectivism in the l.r.t. proper — will be to adopt the $\lambda = 0$ measure function. Specifically, in Chapter VII I will argue that Carnap's conception of a weight to be attached to logical factors is spurious, and so any choice of such a weight can only be arbitrary and subjective; by adopting the $\lambda = 0$ measure function we attach no weight to this factor (which seems most appropriate if it is indeed spurious).

In any case quite independent of any subjectivism in the l.r.t. proper, there is another way in which the l.r.t. may fail to be objective, and this depends on the way it is applied in practice to determine the unique probabilities required for the purpose of action. All along it has been admitted that any theory of probability as a relation of evidential support must provide some account of our practice of deciding on a course of action on the basis of a single probability value identified as uniquely correct, or preferential. I indicated how the requirement of total evidence was used for this purpose, but no elaboration of the requirement was given, and in fact its formulation was deliberately left sufficiently vague to permit a number of different interpretations (see p. 23 and pp. 35-6). Carnap construed the requirement of total evidence in such a way that the evidence available to a person is the evidence he is actually aware of; the requirement to take the total evidence available then reduces to the rather weak requirement that one should consider all the information one is aware of at the time of making a judgment of probability (1962, p. 211).

As should be obvious from earlier discussions, such a formulation of the requirement of total evidence allows the l.r.t. to systematize subjective aspects of our concept of probability, for on this formulation the l.r.t. can readily account for the way in which different people arrive at different judgments on the unique, or preferential, probability for the same hypothesis. If, as Carnap suggests, we explain judgments on the unique, or preferential, probability value required for action as the probability relative to the total information *known* to the individual making the judgment, such judgments may well differ from individual to individual.

But just because it is suitable for characterizing the way in which different people make different judgments on the unique, or preferential, probability of one and the same hypothesis, Carnap's version of the l.r.t. — *coupled with his formulation of the requirement of total evidence* — is subjectivist. Judgments on the probability value for a hypothesis required for the purpose of action will only be 'unique' for a particular individual at a particular time, for the probability determined on the basis of the requirement of total evidence, as Carnap understands it, will actually vary subjectively from person to person, depending on what evidence that person happens to know. Although minimally sufficient for the purpose of determining a course of action — an individual required to make a decision in the face of an uncertainty can easily do so if he has determined what is for him, at that time, a single preferred value out of numerous relational ones — such an account cannot explain our belief that there is a correct, or preferred, value of probability for a given hypothesis that does not depend on what a particular individual happens to know, and this seems vital to our idea that probability judgments have some form of objective validity.

Indeed one writer, Lucas, takes Carnap to task over precisely this point: he argues (1970, p. 54) that if probability judgments arrived at by the l.r.t. involve as first term the evidence known to the person making the judgment, this theory 'readily leads to subjectivism'. This variety of subjectivism may appropriately be called subjectivism in the application of the l.r.t., as it is obvious that it arises not in the theory proper (see above), but instead from using a weak formulation of the requirement of total evidence as the rule for determining the unique probabilities required for the purpose of action.

It is important to see that such subjectivism in the application of l.r.t. can be avoided entirely if we give a sufficiently strong formulation to the requirement of total evidence: we will not arrive at different unique, or preferential, values of probability for different people if we specify that the unique probability to be used for the purpose of action is one involving the total evidence *available*, in the strong sense of that evidence which can, or should, be known to the individual making the judgment, rather than that which he happens to know. (This was the possibility first canvassed on p. 43).

The main difficulty involved in fixing such a sense of available evidence is that of setting a non-arbitrary limit on the amount of evidence available to a person making a judgment of probability. Carnap's identification of available evidence with known evidence certainly puts a limit, and arguably a non-arbitrary one, on the evidence available to someone making a judgment of probability, but the limit is clearly too low, and leads to the subjectivism just noted. On the other hand, it would be grossly implausible to identify the evidence available about an event with the totality of true propositions concerning that event: presumably there are a vast number of true propositions concerning, say, material bodies in distant regions in space that are not in any real sense available to us. Moreover, if we equate available evidence

Our Knowledge of Probabilities

with the totality of the true propositions concerning an event, it would be difficult to avoid the unwelcome conclusion that the probability of most events is 1 or 0 relative to the available evidence.

In fact this problem is sufficiently complex to require separate treatment, and I will begin attacking it in the next chapter, finally concluding my discussion of it in Chapter V.

III
SPECIFICATORY EVIDENCE AND TECHNOLOGY

Although few probability theorists have explicitly drawn the distinction, there are in fact two quite different kinds of evidence used in making probability judgments, what may be called 'specificatory' and 'statistical' evidence. These terms are drawn from Ayers (1968, pp. 43-4), who explicitly discusses the two kinds of evidence, but the distinction seems implicit elsewhere, e.g. Mackie, 1973, pp. 164ff.

Specificatory evidence, roughly speaking, is evidence of the material properties relevant to the outcome of a certain event – for example, evidence of the weight and shape of a coin when we are concerned with the chance of it landing heads on a particular occasion. Statistical evidence is evidence of observed frequencies of the phenomenon we are concerned with – for example, evidence of the percentage of times this or other coins have landed heads in previous trials. Both kinds of evidence are important in determining probabilities and important connections obtain between them – for example, evidence of the shape of the coin would be relevant only if past trials showed a difference in frequency among coins with different shapes.

These two different kinds of evidence pose different philosophical problems and it will be convenient to treat these problems separately. In this chapter I will begin by giving an explication of the idea of 'available' specificatory evidence, turning in Chapter V to the case of statistical evidence. Thus until – and unless – I specifically mention statistical evidence, I will, in this chapter, understand by 'evidence' specificatory evidence.

Specificatory Evidence and Technology

THE AVAILABLE SPECIFICATORY EVIDENCE

The only explication of the idea of available evidence we have come across so far is Carnap's identification of the available evidence with the known evidence. Although such an explication may have some validity in the case of statistical evidence (which is what Carnap probably had in mind), it is far from satisfactory in the case of specificatory evidence: as noted at the end of the last chapter, the l.r.t. leads to a subjectivist conception of probability if it is applied on the basis of the requirement of total evidence, with 'available' evidence understood in this way. As also noted there, the remedy for this is to define available evidence in such a way that the available evidence becomes the evidence one could or should know, rather than the evidence that one merely happens to know; the problem is that in philosophy it is notoriously difficult to give accounts of modal concepts such as 'could' and 'should', and it is for this reason, I suspect, that probability theorists have never given an adequate explication of the idea of available evidence.

However, to give the desired account for specificatory evidence, we need only appeal to the concept of an effective procedure introduced in the last chapters. As before, we will need to employ this concept in connection with fields other than pure logic and mathematics. For this purpose, I regard an effective procedure for determining some result as a procedure which yields that result in a finite time. We may then say that a piece of specificatory evidence which could or should be known to a person making a probability judgment — specificatory evidence available to him — is evidence which is, or would be, obtained by implementing some particular effective procedure.

This seems to me a wholly natural way to explain the idea of 'evidence which can be known' since, so defined, a particular piece of evidence can be known if, and only if, there is an extant procedure which if implemented would yield that information in a finite time. Moreover — and this is how it relates to the normative question of the evidence which should be known — such a proposal answers precisely to our need to find an objective sense of available evidence, one in which the evidence available to a person depends on objective matters rather than what the person happens to know. If we regard evidence as available if, and only if, there exists an effective procedure for determining that evidence, the relevant evidence available for a particular hypothesis depends on what procedures there are for determining evidence and not on the evidence actually known to a particular person. If a particular individual fails to implement an extant procedure for determining evidence, then of course he will not know that evidence, though, in the sense defined, the evidence is available to him.

To take a trivial example of the way in which effective procedures are used to ascertain empirical evidence relevant to probability judgments, there exists at least one effective procedure for ascertaining whether or not it is raining at present — you simply step outside and see if it is (any similar action which yields a result in a finite time would suffice as well). Such procedures are crucial to the correct analysis of the role evidence plays in probability judgments, and virtually all examples of probability judgments involve use of such procedures to determine the evidence used as the basis for the judgment. Thus, for example, when an insurance company wishes to decide if a particular person is worth the 'risk' of insuring, it will gather evidence by implementing a number of known procedures, each yielding a result in a finite time — that is, it would carry out a number of standard medical tests. The rational gambler wagering on a horse-race will do much the same, though in a more informal way — he will take steps to ascertain the horses' blood lines, the condition of the track, etc. A scientist embarked on any empirical enquiry behaves in a similar way, that is, he implements certain known procedures in order to ascertain in a finite time the information relevant to his enquiry. In general, no matter what the subject matter in question, there will exist a set of known procedures which, when implemented, will yield in a finite time evidence which is relevant to assessing the probability of a particular outcome.

One other condition needs to be mentioned concerning the procedures which ascertain specificatory evidence relevant to a probability statement: a procedure which will determine evidence relevant to a statement on the probability of a certain outcome cannot require, for its implementation, knowledge of the result of the outcome. The need for this condition is obvious: otherwise one would permit information on the outcome of an event to form part of the evidence relevant to determining the probability of the outcome and, as far as I can see, this would mean that all probabilities would be 1 or 0. (The condition that the evidence relevant to an outcome be logically independent of that outcome is, as it stands, a bit vague but this will not prevent us from giving, quite shortly, an exact characterization of the desired notion of available evidence.)

Here it is particularly important to note that only a finite number of

Specificatory Evidence and Technology

procedures for ascertaining evidence relevant to a particular probability statement will exist at a given point in time. Although new procedures for ascertaining relevant evidence are constantly discovered in the physical sciences and may, for all we know, continue to be so discovered indefinitely, the number of scientific experiments that will have been carried out at a particular time must always be finite and this alone ensures that the number of procedures which, at one time, determine parameters relevant in a particular field of enquiry is also finite. Similarly, at any one time only a finite number of procedures will exist which yield evidence relevant to the less exact fields of study in which probability judgments figure prominently, e.g. horse-racing, speculation or prudent investment in financial matters, or economic forecasting at the macroeconomic level.

Since the number of procedures which yield evidence relevant to a particular field of study is always finite, it is in principle possible to give an exhaustive specification of all the procedures relevant at any one time for any given field of study. Obviously researchers familiar with the field of study, rather than philosophers, are best suited for specifying what at any given time is the totality of procedures relevant to that field, and so I will make no effort to enumerate the totality of procedures extant at present in any field of study. For our purposes, all that matters is that it is possible to enumerate all the procedures relevant to any field and there seems little doubt that this is so.

These considerations allow us to give quite a precise characterization of the specificatory evidence 'available' at any given time in a field of study: the available evidence is the evidence ascertainable by a certain determinate (and finite) set of procedures and the actual enumeration of these procedures will fix a definite meaning for 'the available evidence' as it pertains to any particular field of study at a given time. Because we fix meaning for the idea of available evidence by explicit enumeration of a finite set of procedures, the somewhat vague condition that these procedures be logically independent of the outcomes we are concerned with does not present any difficulty: since the actual list of procedures fixes the sense of the concept of available evidence, there is no ambiguity or vagueness in this definition.

As regards one of our main concerns, the objectivity of probability judgments, it should be clear that this explication of available evidence allows us to formulate the requirement of total evidence in such a way that the unique probabilities determined by it depend wholly on objective factors. Because the total number of procedures that yield evidence relevant for a given hypothesis is finite, it is always possible to ascertain the total available evidence relevant to any hypothesis: one simply implements each procedure and waits the time required for that procedure to yield its evidence. After every such procedure has been so implemented one is, perforce, cognizant of the total available evidence. Anyone wishing to make a probability judgment which employs as one term the total evidence available must therefore meet certain quite objective standards: he must know all the evidence which can be ascertained by implementing all extant, relevant, procedures. Put another way, if we require the unique or preferential probability used for the purpose of action to be the probability relative to the total available evidence, the above explication makes it a wholly objective matter what this unique or preferential probability is to be − it is that which is relative to all the evidence ascertainable by implementing a particular finite set of procedures.

Since it is an objective matter what the unique or preferential probability of a given hypothesis is, any individual who makes a statement about such a value may or may not be mistaken. This of course means that the l.r. theorist can explain how an ordinary statement of probability − not explicitly mentioning evidence − can, objectively speaking, be said to be correct or incorrect, for, on his theory, such statements are to be understood as tacitly relative to the total evidence available. In fact there are three ways in which an individual can be mistaken in his ordinary statement. First of all, he may be aware of the total available relevant evidence but have failed to evaluate its import correctly. He may, so to speak, have misapprehended the logical relation which exists between this body of evidence and the hypothesis in question. Such an error can be compared to making a mistake in deductive reasoning, and would indeed be an error in inductive reasoning. Secondly, he may have omitted to implement some extant procedure for determining relevant evidence − out of negligence, laziness, the mistaken belief that the evidence he would have ascertained is irrelevant, etc. − and correctly computed the logical probability of the hypothesis relative to a body of evidence which is less than the total amount objectively available. And thirdly, he may of course have made some error in ascertaining the total evidence available, namely come to believe that some fact obtains, which in reality does not. The second and third form of error do not reflect on his ability to determine logical, i.e. inductive, probabilities, but rather on the application he has made of this ability to guide his action: instead

Specificatory Evidence and Technology

of determining a logical probability relative to the body of evidence most desirable as the basis for action, he relies on a different body and so may be said to have erred in the application he has given to l.r.t. in guiding his action for specific practical purposes.

This explication also provides effective (as well as objective) criteria for the truth of judgments on unique or preferential probability. Judgments of a unique or preferential probability are judgments of the probability of a hypothesis relative to the total evidence available; if the l.r.t. is formulated so as to provide effective rules for determining the degree of probability between observational evidence and hypotheses on the outcome of particular events (as it usually is), we only require an effective means for determining the total relevant evidence available for a hypothesis in order to have effective criteria for judgments on the unique or preferential probability of that hypothesis. And this is just what the above explication of available evidence gives us: the total relevant evidence available for any hypothesis can be ascertained by implementing each of a finite set of procedures and each procedure terminates in a finite time. As the number of procedures which ascertain available evidence is finite, and each procedure yields its evidence in a finite time, we have, through this process, an effective means of coming to know the total relevant evidence available for any given hypothesis in a finite time. To form or assess a judgment on the unique or preferential probability of a hypothesis, we need then only implement the effective rules given by inductive logic for determining the degree of probability between a particular body of evidence and a specific hypothesis.†

---

†I should emphasize that my proposed explication of the specificatory evidence available only yields effective criteria for the truth of probability statements on the assumption that there exists an effective inductive logic for determining the degree of probability on the basis of a finite body of observational evidence. In point of fact, several authors — notably Putnam and Hintikka — have questioned whether any effective inductive logic can be satisfactory. I can only say that I believe Carnap has answered Putnam's criticisms (in Schilpp, 1963) decisively and that Hintikka's objections only pertain to the (admittedly difficult) problem of inductive support for universal generalizations, a problem which I acknowledged to be beyond the scope of the current work. Thus in what follows I will ignore — save for passing reference — the questions posed by these critics of effective inductive logics and will assume that we have available to us an effective inductive logic. From my point of view, a more relevant problem is that all effective inductive logics rely on statistical evidence as well as specificatory evidence and

So much was, of course, to be expected from what I said in Chapters I and II concerning the l.r.t. and the realist/anti-realist dispute as characterized by Dummett — indeed my remarks there demand that I give an explanation of the unique or preferential probability of a hypothesis that makes it possible to decide effectively whether or not a particular statement about this probability is true. In fact I claimed from the outset (see pp. 16-20) that finite bodies of evidence combined with their logical relation to the hypothesis in question were the means by which we could in principle decide the truth of ordinary statements of probability; to guide our action in a specific situation — that is, given particular practical needs at a particular time — we relied on the total relevant evidence *then* available for this purpose. Of course at that stage, no explication of the idea of available evidence had been given, but in claiming that we use the total evidence available to decide, effectively, the truth of this particularly important kind of probability statement, I became committed (at the very least) to providing an explication of the notion of the total evidence available which made it possible to use such evidence in this way. As indicated in the above paragraph, I believe this to have been accomplished by the argument so far.

DECIDABILITY IN PRINCIPLE AND DECIDABILITY IN PRACTICE

It is notable that when mathematicians and logicians speak of a proposition which is effectively decidable, they mean a proposition that it is in principle possible to decide; that is, one which is decidable by a procedure which terminates after *some* finite time, though there is no specific limit on how long this time is. Indeed it is possible that the recursive procedure which decides a given proposition may, in reality, take thousands of years to terminate on a given computing device. Following the customary usage (introduced in Chapter I), we may say that while such a proposition is in principle decidable, it is not in practice decidable by the machine, with it understood that decidability in practice means decidability within time-spans reasonably convenient for human activities. I might also add that, to some extent, the distinction between

so the effective criteria I have just given presuppose — as does much in this chapter — that we have a satisfactory account of the way statistical evidence figures in statements of inductive probability. As indicated before, I hope to give such an account in Chapter V.

Specificatory Evidence and Technology

decidability in practice depends on the extant state of technology: there exist problems (e.g. the four-colour problem) which, though decidable in principle, would not be decidable in practice without the aid of sophisticated computers.

Here, however, we are primarily concerned with the distinction between decidability in principle and decidability in practice as it pertains to probability theory, rather than pure mathematics and deductive logic. Following the suggestions of Dummett, I have tried to extend the idea of effectively decidable properties to statements of probability, in particular what I have called ordinary probability statements; as we have just seen, it is possible to explicate the idea of available evidence in such a way that ordinary probability statements become effectively decidable on the basis of the total specificatory evidence available, though only in a sense analogical to that in which propositions are effectively decidable in mathematics and logic. While the rules of inductive logic for determining the degree of probability of a hypothesis relative to a given finite body of evidence are effective in the strict mathematical sense of being computable, the rules just given for determining the unique or preferential probability of a hypothesis on the basis of the total available specificatory evidence are 'effective' only in the extended, or analogical sense, of terminating in a finite time. The analogy depends on the inherent similarity between an experimental or technological procedure for determining an empirical parameter in a finite time and a general recursive function; the notion of effective decidability is then extended to ordinary probability statements by noting that the degree of probability between a finite body of observational evidence and a given hypothesis is computable and that the number of empirical or technological procedures used in deciding a given ordinary probability statement at any one time is finite.

One point of singular interest for probability theory emerges from this extension: in so far as ordinary probability statements are in principle decidable at a given time on the basis of the total evidence then available, they are also (a) decidable by technology existing then, and (b) decidable by this technology within relatively short periods of time. Taken together these mean that such propositions are not merely decidable in principle on the basis of the total evidence available, but also, in any sense that matters to probability theory, decidable in practice on that basis. Though this may be immediately obvious, it is a matter of sufficient importance for me to explain it in some detail.

Specificatory Evidence and Technology

Condition (a) follows on the above proposal if we assume that it is technologically possible to gather all the statistical evidence relevant to a particular ordinary probability statement (a matter I will investigate in detail in Chapter V): the total available specificatory evidence, which is the other part of the evidence by which the statement is decided, is by (my) definition a body determinable by extant technology; indeed it is the maximum amount which can be obtained this way. Condition (b) is established by a slightly more extended, but similar, argument. First of all we should note that the technological or empirical procedures which determine specificatory evidence relevant to probability statements are, unlike recursive procedures, designed to terminate in reasonably short times. No scientist would seriously propose a procedure for identifying a physical magnitude which would take, say, 200 years to carry out. Nor, to press the disanalogy to recursive procedures further, would a scientist consider using a procedure for identifying a physical magnitude which was such that he knew it would terminate, positively or negatively, in some finite time (perhaps 10^{10} years, perhaps 5 million), though there would be no way of knowing in advance when it would so terminate. To forestall such possibilities, the technological procedures used to discover empirical information relevant to probability statements one and all terminate in reasonably short periods of time, usually much less than a year.

Similarly, the number of different empirical procedures which ascertain evidence relevant to a particular statement of probability is not only finite but (up to the present day) relatively small at that. The characteristics of a coin known to be relevant to the outcome 'heads' or 'tails' surely are nothing more than weight, balance, initial position, force acting on the coin and (just possibly) atmospheric conditions then obtaining; it is obvious that few technological procedures are involved in ascertaining such evidence. Similarly, the physical characteristics currently known to affect human mortality are relatively small in number — certainly less than 10^5 and probably less than 10^3 — and so the technological procedures which determine evidence relevant to a person's mortality will be relatively small in number.

The upshot of this is that on the assumption that it is technologically possible to gather all the statistical evidence relevant to a particular hypothesis in a relatively short period of time and, on the weaker assumption, that it is technologically possible to compute the degree of probability between the total relevant evidence (statistical and specificatory) available for a given hypothesis in a relatively short period of time, the account just given of the total specificatory evidence available at a given time makes these statements technologically decidable in a relatively short period of time.

This conclusion seems to me the only possible one concerning the ordinary probability statements that are our primary concern; probability is meant to be 'the very guide to life' and thus it cannot take inordinate amounts of time to decide the truth of those probability statements which are most important from the practical point of view (i.e. those on a unique or preferential value); nor can this require technology not currently extant. Life will not wait so long for decisions to be made, or stay its course pending the development of new technology. This is as true of the concept of probability used by scientists as that used by everyone else: probability values for the success rate of different drugs in treating a specific illness must be determined within relatively short periods of time or they will be of little use for practical purposes. Even in the more theoretical sciences, probability values must be determined within relatively short periods of time for they form an important part of a complex network of statements which are *continually* being tested and revised; without knowledge of the probability values for the decay of various particles, all sorts of tests in physics and other sciences become impossible, e.g. testing of time dilation in special relativity via particle acceleration. Given such practical needs, our concept of probability is, and must be, of such kind that we can determine the truth of probability statements which are to guide our action within the periods of time required by the press of our practical affairs.

Admittedly the 'press of practical affairs' is a vague and somewhat pliable conception and the amount of time appropriate to decisions in one area of science, e.g. the testing of a new drug, will not be the same as the time appropriate for others, e.g. the testing of relativity theory. However, this does not seem to me to affect the main point, namely that probability judgments in science, like probability judgments in everyday life, must be made within relatively short timespans − certainly no more than 10^3 years and arguably never as long as 10^2 years − and so the means we employ to determine their truth must yield their results within such relatively short periods of time. The explication of the concept of available evidence and the requirement of total evidence which I have just given obviously yields a concept of probability which fulfils this demand: the part of the

Specificatory Evidence and Technology

means by which we recognize the truth of ordinary statements on the unique or preferential probability of an event or hypothesis with which we are presently concerned is specificatory evidence obtainable by existing technological procedures, and these procedures (both singly and collectively) yield their results within the relatively short periods of time required for practical decisions.

Put simply, the total evidence available provides a means for deciding in practice the truth of ordinary statements on a unique or preferential value of probability. This of course is not to say we invariably *do* in practice decide the truth of these statements on the basis of this body of evidence, but merely that it is in practice *possible* to do so. As we saw earlier, there are various reasons why an individual might fail to decide a given ordinary statement on the basis of this body of evidence, e.g. negligence or error in ascertaining evidence. This of course is why, on my account, these statements can be regarded as objectively valid: they are relative to all the evidence we *can* in practice ascertain by existing technology, and only if we have correctly determined this relational probability will our ordinary statement about the probability of the phenomenon be, objectively speaking, correct. Indeed, when I speak subsequently of an ordinary judgment of logical probability being objectively valid, I will mean just this: that the ordinary judgment has actually (or, as I will often say, has in practice) been decided on the basis of all the evidence it is possible to ascertain by existing technology.

Of course the more one reflects on it, the more it appears that the notion of decidability in practice is the one which is crucial to probability theory: since probability judgments are to guide our action in practice, it would seem that we would have to be able to implement criteria for their truth in the time-spans necessary for action, i.e. implement them in practice. Why then even bother to introduce the notion of decidability in principle into the discussion of probabilities?

Actually, in my view it is essential to distinguish between decisions we can in practice make on the truth of probability statements and those we can in principle make, and some of the reasons why this is so have already been indicated in Chapter I. There I pointed out that although at a given time (and in a given context) we may use just one body of evidence to decide the truth of an ordinary probability statement not mentioning evidence (namely the total relevant evidence then available), this body can change over time, for example, if new evidence later becomes available. With new evidence available, our ordinary

Specificatory Evidence and Technology

judgment on the probability of the phenomenon will change, and in Chapter I, I argued that such a change was most naturally systematized into a general theory on the meaning of probability statements by construing ordinary statements of probability as relative to evidence.

Now, as I just explained, the total relevant evidence available for a hypothesis at a given time is a body of evidence by which we can *in practice* decide the truth of an ordinary statement of probability about that hypothesis − that is, on the basis of it, we can actually decide the truth of it within the time-span dictated by our current practical needs. However, a body of evidence including data that has become available at a later date is obviously not something we can in practice use to decide the ordinary probability judgment at the earlier date. At the earlier date we lack the technology to ascertain the new data − that is why the data is not then available − and so we *cannot in practice* ascertain it then and use it to decide the truth of our probability statement. How, then, are we to characterize in a general way the possibility of new evidence becoming available which, later, can be used to decide the truth of our ordinary statement of probability? This question is far from idle, as nothing can be more central to a theory of meaning for probability statements than an exact and general characterization of the process by which we determine the truth of probability statements, and the possibility in question obviously is part of this process. The simplest and most obvious way to characterize this possibility is to describe it as the future possibility that we can in practice decide our probability statement by reference to this evidence − while admitting that in practice it cannot be decided earlier.

However, a far more perspicuous way to accommodate this possibility into a theory of meaning is to treat it as a possibility in principle. That is to say, while it is not in practice possible at the earlier date to decide a given ordinary statement of probability on the basis of evidence which cannot be ascertained by technology existing then, it is in principle possible then − and at any other time − for this body of evidence (or any other finite body with an appropriate logical relation to the hypothesis in question) to be used to decide its truth.

In point of fact, there is very little, if any, substantive difference for probability theory between characterizing the possibility of changes in our decisions on the truth of ordinary probability statements in the light of future advances in technology as a possibility in principle or a future possibility in practice. The distinction between decidability in principle and in practice which I have taken over from logic and mathematics — or the philosophy thereof — depends to a large extent on the same factors of temporal passage and technological advances and so is readily used to characterize the kind of changes in question. To see this, we need only note that any proposition in logic or mathematics that is in principle decidable can also be decided in practice given elaborate enough computing devices and/or enough time.

Of course it is not merely a (perhaps) superficial parallel between the role played by temporal passage and technological advance in the determination of probabilities and the computation of mathematical or logical problems that leads me to think a distinction between decidability in principle and decidability in practice is of considerable import to probability theory: to my mind, this distinction is intimately connected to central questions concerning the meaning and practical utility of probability statements, questions which, moreover, it is most important to keep distinct. In Chapter I, I argued that the aim of a theory on the meaning of probability statements was to explain how in general we decide the truth of statements of probability, not how one person or group of people decides them at a particular point in time given particular practical needs. The latter is the concern of a separate study I called the methodology of probability theory, while a theory on the meaning of probability statements must make sense of how, in any circumstances and at any time, we would decide the truth of probability statements. Adapting Dummett's terminology (and an anti-realist viewpoint), I expressed this by saying an adequate theory of the meaning of ordinary statements of probability would explain their meaning in terms of the conditions by which *in principle* we recognize their truth, and this, I claimed, was accomplished by the relational definition of probability expressed in the l.r.t. proper. Given the distinction between decidability in principle and decidability in practice which we have been considering, we may now say that, in contrast, the quite distinct methodological study undertaken in this chapter of what in a given situation — with specific practical needs and specific technological limitations — constitutes the relational probability value most describable for the purpose of action concerns the question of how in practice we recognize the truth of a given ordinary statement of probability.

In any event, as it is a complicated and important matter, I will return repeatedly in the next two chapters to the distinction between decidability in principle and in practice, as it pertains to probability theory; indeed, I will spell out in further detail how this distinction can

Specificatory Evidence and Technology

be used to characterize changes over time in the evidence we use to decide the truth of ordinary probability statements and I hope these discussions will illustrate the importance of this distinction to probability theory. At the moment, however, we should turn our attention to a number of less general, but still interesting, consequences of the explication I have given so far in this chapter of the notion of available evidence and the requirement of total evidence. Perhaps the most interesting concerns how this explication relates to the tension between objectivity and subjectivity we have noted to be inherent in our concept of probability. Indeed once we become clear over this matter, we will be in a position to understand the way judgments of logical probability figure in scientific discourse on probability, a topic which will bring us to the end of this chapter.

OBJECTIVITY AND SUBJECTIVITY AGAIN

In case it is not yet apparent, let me make it clear that the account I have given of how we use the total evidence available to decide ordinary probability statements is intended to explicate the procedure we actually use for this purpose, or at least would use if we were not, from time to time, negligent in this respect. There is, however, one obvious objection to this claim: while the explication I have given of this procedure makes the truth of ordinary probability statements an objective matter, our ordinary concept of probability simply is not objective in this way, as it involves at least some subjective component. This is fair comment, but only indicates that the above account must be modified somewhat to explain the way in which probability judgments 'shift' between objectivity and subjectivity.

I may begin by stating my overall view concerning this 'shift', which we noted from the outset was a puzzling feature of our concept of probability. Put simply, my view is that while probability judgments are always made on the basis of the total relevant evidence 'available', the kind and amount of specificatory evidence which we regard as 'available' varies from context to context. The explication I have just given of the specificatory evidence 'available' for judgments of probability is a correct account of the kind of evidence we use in conjunction with probability statements in *certain* contexts − primarily those occurring in science − but not at all plausible as an account of the kind of specificatory evidence relied on in others, for example, games of

Specificatory Evidence and Technology

'chance' where artificial constraints are placed on the information obtainable by players of the game. Depending on the kind of specificatory evidence relied on (which in turn depends on the context in question), the probability judgments that result from applying the l.r.t. will be objective, subjective or inter-subjective in character. Thus the apparently puzzling shift between objectivity and subjectivity found in probability judgments has as its origin nothing more puzzling than the fact that for different kinds of contexts we use different sorts of evidence as the basis for judgments of probability.

It is in fact quite easy to give examples of contexts in which the requirement of the total evidence as elucidated earlier in this chapter leads to quite implausible results. Consider, for example, the case of a horse that has a rare disease, as yet neither detected nor even suspected by its owner or trainer. This disease is known to affect running performance to a considerable extent (hence evidence of it is 'relevant' to the outcome of the race); moreover, the disease can be diagnosed quite early if the proper tests are administered (hence evidence of it is 'available' in the sense given in the previous section). But what, for the betting public, is the probability of this horse winning a given race? The requirement of total evidence tells us that the probability should be determined by reference to the total relevant evidence available and so would be quite low, if not negligible, for this horse. However, it seems to me far from clear that in such circumstances the probability of the horse winning is actually low.

Of course this example, like much else in probability theory, is somewhat complex and elusive — indeed is so for the very reasons that we are at present considering. Perhaps it is right to say that the horse's chance of winning is low and anyone who thinks otherwise is, objectively speaking, quite mistaken, despite a certain subjective justification for his judgment. Another example, drawn from Reichenbach, allows us to identify the specific issues involved here more clearly and, moreover, makes their resolution fairly straightforward. Reichenbach remarks of a game of roulette, that with

> precise observation of the initial velocity of the spinning ball, it should be possible to foretell with any degree of exactness where it will come to rest. It is only lack of technical ability that prevents us from equalling Laplace's superman. Once the velocity of the spinning ball has died down noticeably, such a computation comes into the scope of technical possibilities. This is well

known to owners of gambling places, who stop such attempts
by the croupier's call 'rien ne va plus'. (1949, p. 150)

The question for us is: what are we to take as the total evidence available just prior to the croupier's call? If this evidence — in relation to which we are to make our judgment of probability — includes precise specification of the ball's velocity, then, contrary to our ordinary assumption, the end result is not a matter of chance. If we were to accept Reichenbach's hypothesis that such precise observations are beyond our technical resources, we can deny that this 'evidence' is available to us for, by this hypothesis, there exists no scientific procedure that would yield the information. But clearly now, and presumably also at the time Reichenbach wrote, numerous scientific procedures exist which could determine the velocity with sufficient accuracy to predict the result in question. It may only be possible to carry out such procedures with elaborate and bulky equipment, but, none the less, they do exist.

Must we then conclude that evidence of the ball's initial velocity is available to us and, accordingly, that roulette is not truly a game of chance? Such a conclusion seems to me most implausible and indeed somewhat alarming: in a similar way we could conclude that a wide variety of events have outcomes which are certain (for example the horse-race mentioned in the previous example), but that, failing to consider all the available evidence, we mistakenly take them to be probabilistic. Such a view — which I will discuss explicitly shortly — often seems lurking round the corner in discussions of probability and is one which should be avoided, if at all possible.

Reichenbach's example makes it clear that we are led to such a result only because we have such a strong notion of 'available' evidence, and thus it is clear that for many contexts we require an explication of this notion far weaker than the one given earlier in this chapter. To see the general form of approach to this problem, we need only recall that our precept of using the total available evidence is only intended as a precept to guide our actions in the face of uncertainty. But as Ayer points out while discussing the requirement of total evidence:

> a methodological principle, considered simply as a guide to action, may be expected to be vague: so let us say that the principle is simply that we should always try to maximise the relevant evidence. In actual practice this could be taken too far. There are times when it is rational to act on evidence which one knows to be incomplete:

a general who refused to launch an attack until he ascertained the position of every enemy soldier would not be very successful. There may be moral as well as practical limitations. If I am trying to pick a winner on a race course, the principle of maximising evidence may be held to fall short of requiring me to attempt to bribe the stable boys. (1972, pp. 56-7)

Ayer's remarks here illustrate well the variety of circumstances in which we seek to maximize evidence, and this is crucial. Every action in the face of uncertainty involves a decision made on imperfect knowledge, that is, on knowledge which is not sufficient to predict an outcome with certainty, and on such occasions we require judgments of probability. However, the circumstances in which we thus need to make judgments of probability are many and varied: on the one hand we have occasions (rather like those facing the general) in which life and limb depend on the outcome of the trial for which complete knowledge is difficult or impossible. At the other extreme, we find occasions in which few practical consequences follow and for which we impose artificial constraints on our knowledge for the pleasure of testing our capacity for decision-making under imperfect knowledge. Card games for small stakes with imperfect disclosure are clear examples of this. In between these extremes lie a whole host of circumstances in which imperfect knowledge figures in yet different ways — decisions on stock speculation are obviously of sufficient importance to require serious efforts at attaining the maximum possible information but, in the interests of fairness, many governments enforce restrictions preventing the use of 'inside' information. In roulette the practical consequences may be little or great, and restrictions on information would be imposed in the end by casino owners.

With such a myriad of circumstances in which we either need or desire to act on the basis of probability judgments, it would be unreasonable to expect one ambiguous guide for action; in other words, any precept governing our actions in the face of imperfect knowledge will have to be sufficiently pliable to allow diverse application to very different circumstances. Since the precept of using the total available evidence is our guide to action in such circumstances, we must expect in actual practice a multiplicity, or family, of related criteria for what constitutes the available evidence, rather than a single clear criterion.

Our game of roulette provides a particularly clear illustration of this — if the total available evidence is defined to include any evidence that could be obtained at the right time by an extant scientific procedure, the ball's eventual resting place will be wholly predictable on the basis of the total available evidence. But it is rather implausible to think casino owners would permit the elaborate testing required to measure the crucial factor of the ball's initial velocity, and so, in a very real sense, such evidence is not available to gamblers.

Such restrictions on the evidence 'available' to us in various situations may, for convenience, all be termed 'practical restrictions'. However, the variety of the contexts in which we make probability judgments make it impossible to codify these restrictions in a way that yields one clear criterion of what evidence is available. Indeed I should think that any exhaustive codification of what in varying circumstances we regard as available evidence would be exceedingly complex. Accordingly I will only try to indicate briefly the broad outlines of what in different contexts constitutes the available evidence.

At one end of a continuum of criteria for what constitutes available evidence, there is the criterion we have in mind when we judge what evidence is available to a scientist engaged in research proper. Unlike the card player who cheats if he tries to obtain all possible knowledge, a scientist engaged in research is expected to take all possible steps to maximize his knowledge. Accordingly our formulation of a criterion for the evidence to be considered 'available' to a scientist should be as strong as possible. My initial explication of 'available evidence' in terms of information resulting from the implementation of extant scientific procedures suffices here and indeed was proposed with this purpose in mind. A scientist who wishes to make probability judgments on the basis of all the evidence available to him must therefore ensure that he has not overlooked any relevant evidence ascertainable by an extant procedure of his science, for such evidence is 'available' to him. This seems a wholly satisfactory conclusion. In our example of a horse with a rare, but undetected, disease, it seemed inappropriate to say that evidence of this disease was available to the average punter, as he could hardly be expected to obtain it. But a scientist attempting to confirm a physiological theory of equine motor activity would be expected to test for and uncover this disease if, for example, he were trying to explain why the horse failed to fulfil a prediction of his theory. Conversely, when attempting to predict the horse's motor activity on the basis of his theory, he would be expected to carry out this and any other relevant test, and so it is plausible to characterize such information as available to him.

One of the main points I wished to make earlier was that adopting an explication of available evidence along these lines led to an objective conception of probability. The reason for this should now be apparent: objective judgments are those which conform to the standards set by the current state of science and so probability judgments based on all the evidence which can be obtained by extant scientific procedures will be, in an important sense, objective. In the light of this, I will, in what follows, speak of the objective criterion, or objective sense, of 'available evidence'; by 'available evidence' in this objective sense I will mean that evidence which can be known by implementing any relevant extant scientific procedure.

At the furthest remove from such an objective sense of available evidence, we find that some writers have defined the evidence 'available' to a person as that of which he is consciously aware. Although this criterion is so weak as to cause the distinction between available evidence and known evidence to collapse entirely, it is worth some attention: if we understand available evidence in this weak sense, the requirement of total evidence reduces to the very weak, but not implausible, requirement that probability judgments made by a person must be relative to the total evidence known to him at the time he makes the judgment. As we noted in Chapter I, this is precisely the form of the requirement of total evidence Carnap puts forward. As we also noted, such a formulation of the requirement of total evidence allowed Carnap to systematize, quite plausibly, the so-called subjective aspects of our concept of probability, and this, at the moment, is of paramount importance. It seems quite clear that there are certain contexts in which the subjective aspect of our concept of probability predominates: most card games are examples of this for, in them, each player's assessment of his chances of winning must in part be based on information known only to him, namely the identity of his down cards. Put more exactly, the body of evidence which each player considers in making judgments of probability is one which includes information known only to him and which also excludes information which could be obtained by implementing various extant procedures. (For example, players are specifically barred from implementing the procedure of picking up the pack of cards and looking at the next card.) It seems to me natural to say that in such a context the evidence available to a player is the evidence which is known to him from playing the game according to its proper rules. Similarly, when we speak of individuals forced by the press of events to make quick decisions in the face of uncertainty, the evidence we regard as available to them is the evidence actually known to them when they have to make the decision. When the evidence available to a person is understood as that which happens to be known to him, I will say that 'available evidence' is understood in a weak, or subjective, sense, contrasting it to the objective sense explained initially. I suspect that the contexts in which we actually understand 'available evidence' in this weak, subjective, sense are limited but, in any case, this sense is significant in that it fixes a lower bound for the range of criteria we use when speaking of the evidence available to an individual. (The upper bound was fixed by the explication of 'available evidence' given initially.)

In between the extreme contexts in which available evidence would be understood in, respectively, an objective and subjective sense, there is a middle ground comprising a large variety of contexts in which the evidence we would deem 'available' to us is greater than that which we happen to know but, nevertheless, still limited by what I have called 'practical restrictions'. In such circumstances the evidence deemed available will be some proper subset of that which could be obtained by the totality of extant scientific or technological procedures; for example, the evidence 'available' in a casino is a proper subset of that available in a laboratory. Similarly, if the evidence which we regard as available in these circumstances coincides with that known by a particular person, this will only be due to his diligence in acquiring evidence, and not simply a consequence of our understanding the idea of available evidence in a subjective sense.

This latter consideration suggests one feature common to many contexts in which probability judgments are made relative to a body of evidence deemed the total available. Even when the criterion we have in mind for 'available evidence' is weaker than the objective one appropriate to the practice of science proper, it is primarily an inter-subjective criterion. By this I mean that the evidence deemed available to one person in a given situation will ordinarily be thought available to all in a similar situation. Honest gambling houses make provision to ensure no privileged information is accesible to a minority of players in board games such as roulette and, as we noted, stock markets often prohibit participation of those with 'inside' information. It seems appropriate to say that in such contexts the available evidence is understood in an inter-subjective sense, rather than the objective or subjective senses already noted.

Of course what we call these different senses of 'available evidence' does not matter a great deal. What I have tried to show is that what we regard as the evidence available for making probability judgments varies from context to context and so, obviously, will the application we give to the l.r.t. in these contexts on the basis of the requirement of total evidence. Three general points of interest emerge from this: first of all, as claimed in Chapter I, applying the l.r.t. on the basis of the requirement of total evidence does not yield a single unique probability for a given hypothesis at a given time; it only yields such a value at a given time *for a given context*. The fundamental reason for this is that uncovered in the quotation from Ayer given several pages back: the requirement of total evidence is meant to be a guide to action, determining the relational probability most desirable for the purpose of action. However, the circumstances in which we have to act are so varied that we can expect no ambiguous guide for action, and so we must distinguish a number of different senses of 'available evidence' appropriate to use in different circumstances.

These considerations underscore the importance of distinguishing between probability theory proper and the methodological theory of its application. The factors which determine whether we decide the truth of a given ordinary probability statement by reference to the total evidence available in an objective, subjective or inter-subjective sense are intensely practical. Indeed I emphasized in Chapter I that the factors which determined how much evidence we gathered in a given situation were highly practical in character and we have just now seen specific examples of the way 'practical restrictions' imposed by context limit the kind of evidence appropriate for making probability judgments. Such practical exigencies are not the concern of a theory on the meaning of probability statements, for the aim of such a theory is to explain within one definition of probability how we determine the truth of probability statements in any kind of context we encounter. For ordinary probability statements this is best accomplished by the l.r.t.'s relational definition of probability; for we do not determine the truth of even one ordinary probability statement on the basis of just one thing — one body of evidence — but a number of different things, depending on, among other factors, the context in question. The explanation of which relational probability is most appropriate for a given context is then to be treated separately in a branch of study specifically concerned with detailed practical issues — what I have called the methodology of probability theory.

Another way to put the same point is to say that the l.r.t. proper — as a theory of meaning — is concerned with how *in principle* we can recognize the truth of ordinary statements of probability — how in any context, with any kind of practical need, we would recognize the truth of such statements. On my view we can in principle use any finite body of evidence (which has a single logical relation to the hypothesis we are concerned with) to decide the truth of an ordinary probability statement, and this fact is systematized into a theory of meaning by the l.r.t.'s definition of probability as a relation between hypotheses and finite bodies of evidence. What body of evidence we use to decide the truth of a given ordinary statement with specific practical needs and specific 'practical restrictions' imposed by the context in question is a different matter, one which concerns how *in practice* we decide the truth of the ordinary statement. As I remarked just above and earlier in the chapter, the detailed practical considerations involved here are the subject matter of the methodology of probability theory.

A second point of interest to emerge from this discussion of the practical issues determining the amount and kind of evidence appropriate to different contexts concerns a perennial philosophical problem in probability theory which was briefly touched on earlier in this section. Adopting the strongest criterion of available evidence, the objective, we saw how ordinary games of 'chance', such as roulette, could easily appear not to involve genuine probabilities — if the 'available evidence' means that which a scientist using all extant procedures could obtain, the outcome in roulette is predictable with certainty on the basis of the total available evidence well before any wagers need be made. A similar point could be made about other apparently probabilistic matters; we thus would easily be led to the unhappy conclusion that for many cases ordinarily thought of as matters of chance, the 'actual probability is something near 1 or 0, but that normally we do not know which', as Blackburn puts it (1973, p. 106). (This difficulty, of course, has been discussed elsewhere, Hacking, 1965, p. 24.)

However, in the example of roulette, the reasoning to this conclusion involves the application of an objective criterion of available evidence to a situation in which this is demonstrably inappropriate. Thus, at least part of the reason why we might be led to the unhappy conclusion that probabilities were generally near 1 or 0, though we ordinarily did not know which, can now be diagnosed: this conclusion stems from a disregard of the multiplicity of criteria found in our complex pattern of practices involving probability judgments.† Contexts for which the objective criterion of available evidence is appropriate – science proper – are fastened on to and treated as paradigmatic. Application of this criterion to very different cases – ones in which our knowledge is deliberately limited for the sake of sport – leads us into the following quandary: surely roulette is a game of chance, yet surely the outcomes of roulette are predictable with certainty. The way out of the quandary is to see it as arising from treating as paradigmatic a criterion for available evidence which, in fact, is only appropriate to a limited range of cases.

Finally, and perhaps most significantly, the identification of a variety of criteria for what constitutes the 'available evidence' provides us, as promised, with a perspicuous explanation of the apparently puzzling way our concept of probability shifts from objective to subjective. This shift is not to be explained by postulating a multiplicity of concepts of probability: there is only one concept of probability, that of a relation between evidence and hypothesis, but, depending on the context in question, different kinds of evidence, taken in their totality, are tacitly relied on as the second term of our judgments of probability. In scientific contexts we tacitly rely on all the evidence which can be obtained by extant procedures for discovering physical parameters; this makes our judgments of probability objective in the important sense of not depending on the information known to any individual. In other circumstances, the evidence we rely on as second term in making a judgment of probability is the totality which happens to be known to us, yielding judgments subjective in character. In yet other circumstances, we rely on evidence inter-subjectively 'available', and so our judgments of probability have an inter-subjective character. But in each kind of judgment – for each aspect of the concept of probability – there are two common strands, namely that probability is a relation between evidence and hypothesis and that when no specific body of evidence is mentioned in the judgment of probability, there is always a specific totality of evidence tacitly pre-

---

†The analysis I give here of this problem seems to be incomplete in one important respect – it does not take into account the possibility of changes in our knowledge over time – and it will be necessary to deal with this in the next chapter, specifically on pp. 142ff.

INDUCTIVE PROBABILITY AND SCIENCE

supposed as the second term of the probability judgment. It is only the exact identity of such totalities which vary from context to context.

It is well known that frequency and propensity theorists usually justify their accounts of probability by an appeal to the probability statements found in scientific discourse — indeed their fundamental contention is that scientists, in making judgments of probability, are making judgments about an empirical phenomenon no different in principle from any other phenomenon studied by the methods of natural science. In contrast, the inductive probabilities of the l.r.t. are of course given a priori and reflect purely logical relations to various bodies of evidence. Although Carnap — and many of his followers (e.g. Kemeny in Schilpp, 1963) — accepted the claim that a distinct concept of statistical probability (or probability$_2$) was indeed the subject matter of scientific statements on probability, there seems to me no necessity to do so. Certainly scientific discourse employs the a priori concept of pure mathematics and deductive logic, and so, if there is a valid a priori concept of probability with its own (inductive) logic, there is no reason why scientists should not employ it in much the same way they do the concepts of pure mathematics and deductive logic. Having given in the first section of this chapter a formulation of the l.r.t. which makes its application objective — and thus suitable for a reconstruction of a scientific concept of probability — I will begin in this section a lengthy argument to establish that the probability statements of science are in fact purely logical statements of the kind the l.r.t. construes statements of probability to be. However, the issues raised by scientific discourse on probability are so complex and varied that the argument will only be concluded at the end of Chapter V.

As a preliminary point, let me say that if most ordinary statements on probability made outside the realm of science *do* involve logical relations between evidence and hypothesis, there is little reason to suppose that scientists use a radically different concept of probability. Barring definitive assertions by scientists to the contrary, the immediate presumption is that the concept of probability employed by them bears the same relationship to that of ordinary discourse found with other concepts (such as length, time, velocity, etc.) which figure in both scientific and non-scientific discourse: the concepts of science may have a more precise delineation, with more precise procedures for application, than those of ordinary discourse, but this will only mark a difference in the degree of precision attaching to those concepts, rather than a fundamental difference of character.

One serious objection to analysing the concept of probability employed in science in terms of logical relations between evidence and hypothesis has, I hope, been removed by the argument of the first section of this chapter: that these relational probabilities are inherently subjective in character and therefore, *a fortiori*, different from the probabilities required in science, which are objective in character. Since, in general, the probability statements made in science do not explicitly refer to evidence, the l.r. theorist must explain these statements as elliptical for ones involving reference to the total available evidence. However, as we saw, it is possible to elaborate this analysis in such a way that it is a wholly objective matter as to what constitutes this relational probability; it is the probability relative to all the evidence ascertainable by implementing the set of technological procedures used in science to discover empirical parameters. It seems wholly natural to say that such probabilities, reflecting as they do all the evidence ascertainable through currently extant techniques of science, are just the kind of objective probabilities appropriate to scientific discourse.

This of course is only a preliminary justification for my claim that the probability statements of science involve the relational probabilities we have been concerned with throughout the book so far; full justification of this claim must wait a close examination of a large number of issues, including the role of statistical data in science, which I have indicated I will discuss in Chapter V. However, even before such an examination is complete, a number of important points can be made concerning the probability statements of science and their relationship to the l.r.t. The first and most obvious point is that the actual numerical probabilities assigned to phenomena by scientists (e.g. half-life and mortality rates), are wholly in accord with an inductive conception of probability: these probabilities are based on past observations (of a sample) and so can be construed as relative to the evidence of that sample. On the whole, scientists use 'unbiased' methods of inference, and so assign numerical probabilities which are equal to the frequency observed in the sample. Obviously this is an inductive inference and, as such, it can be formally characterized in terms of the inductive probabilities of the l.r.t. In fact, the inference corresponds to the measure of the function $\lambda = 0$ of Carnap's continuum of inductive methods and it seems to me that the most natural way of regarding this inference is to see it as an instance of logical probabilities determined by a measure function chosen a priori. Of course, critics of the l.r.t. have characterized this inference in different ways: Neyman denies that there can be inductive reasoning along the lines advocated by the l.r.t., and so treats such an act of inference as inductive 'behaviour', as opposed to inductive reasoning; Reichenbach endorses the so-called straight rule of induction which leads to identical assignments of probability, but claims that this rule is only justified pragmatically in 'the limit'.

Whether or not these alternative characterizations of the inference to a probability value p from observation of a frequency p in the sample are philosophically viable need not concern us at the moment (though of course it has concerned us elsewhere in this book); what matters is that such an inference is in complete accord with the l.r.t., as it can be seen as an application of the measure function $\lambda = 0$.

One of the main reasons in favour of using this function — which I will sometimes just call the straight rule — is that it makes the numerical probability holding between a hypothesis and a body of *specificatory* evidence depend solely on empirical factors, namely the observed frequency of the kind of phenomena we are concerned with, given the presence of the physical attributes referred to by the specificatory evidence (cf. Carnap, 1952, p. 40). This seems to me to ensure that the probabilities determined by the l.r.t. are sufficiently 'empirical' in character to be used in science; conversely, the reason scientists do use unbiased techniques of the kind encapsulated in the straight rule is because such techniques make the determination of numerical probabilities, given a body of specificatory evidence, depend solely on statistical experience.

Because the straight rule links probabilities so directly to statistical experience, it will not yield values in the absence of statistical data, and this has been thought to be problematic by some writers, e.g. Carnap and Waismann. Various remedies are possible: Carnap proposed a limit convention by which the probabilities determined by the measure function $\lambda = 0$ in absence of statistical evidence was to be the limit of the probabilities determined for different values of n for λ as n approaches zero. Waismann argued that the choice of a measure function should be made by convention in absence of statistical data. In point of fact, the problem of how to assign logical probabilities in the absence of statistical evidence is a vexed one involving the notorious principle of indifference, which has been thought to provide a means of determining numerical probabilities in the absence of all relevant evidence. (Indeed Carnap's first proposal for a measure function, m^*, to determine numerical probabilities in the absence of all statistical data was based explicitly on the principle of indifference.) I discuss these matters at length in Chapters VI and VII, where I endeavour to show that there is no particular reason for an l.r. theorist to assign probabilities in the absence of the statistical data and that the principle of indifference need not be used to assign such a priori probabilities. At the moment, we need only note that the question of how to assign probabilities in the absence of statistical data is at best of theoretical interest for the probability theorist, and has no practical bearing on how scientists determine probabilities, for they invariably rely on quite extensive statistical data. And what I wish to claim is that in doing so they determine logical probabilities on the basis of the straight rule of induction.

In case there is any doubt over the matter, let me say quite explicitly that despite the central, indeed crucial, role played by statistical experience in determining probability values via the straight rule of induction, the probability values so determined are logical inductive probabilities which obtain a priori, i.e. irrespective of any (further) empirical considerations. To see this, it is crucial to recall a point made at the start of this chapter, namely that the evidence used in determining probabilities is both specificatory and *statistical*. Although there exist measure functions which determine logical probabilities for a body of specificatory evidence in the absence of any relevant statistical evidence, such probabilities are dubious at best (as we will see when we consider the principle of indifference). Carnap himself indicated in reply to an objection of Nagel that he would 'not strongly protest [if] instead of any function c in my theory [others] would use the subfunction c' restricted to the cases of factual evidence.' (Schilpp, 1963, p. 996.) This would mean applying the subfunction on the basis of specificatory evidence of certain attributes and statistical evidence of the frequency of the outcome in question already observed in the presence of such attributes. The $\lambda = 0$ measure function, however, is a function which by its very nature is restricted to cases where there exists factual evidence of a statistical kind and, so, if we were to modify Carnap's system so as to restrict ourselves to such subfunctions, $\lambda = 0$ would be the most natural choice of measure function. In any case, and this is the main point at issue at the moment, given a

Specificatory Evidence and Technology

set of physical attributes mentioned in the body of specificatory evidence and a body of factual evidence concerning the observed frequency, the probability values determined by the straight rule are wholly a priori in that they do not depend on any further empirical factors.

I should also add that the probability values determined by the $\lambda = 0$ are wholly objective, and in no way depend on individual beliefs or preferences. There are two reasons why this is so: first of all, once a measure function is chosen, the probability values between a given body of evidence and a given hypothesis are fixed quite objectively. The second, and to my mind more important, reason is a fact just cited, namely that the $\lambda = 0$ measure function does not determine probability values in the absence of all empirical information; nor does it permit any factor other than observed statistical data to weigh in the determination of the numerical value of probability. This is not so for the other measure functions of Carnap's λ system, and (as I hope to show in Chapter VII), there can be no objective way to determine probabilities in the absence of empirical information, or to balance empirical and non-empirical factors when measuring probabilities. Both these matters can only be settled by arbitrary choice, which may vary from individual to individual. In contrast, by determining probability values solely on the basis of observed frequencies, the $\lambda = 0$ measure function does not allow any leeway for individual choice, and so fixes probability values in a wholly objective way.

Carnap's Arguments against the Straight Rule

Of course, Carnap himself offered a number of specific arguments against the straight rule as a measure function, and it behoves us to consider them in some detail. Carnap's first argument was based on the fact that this measure function yields rather surprising results for very small samples, say of size 1 or 2:

> Thus, if all we know about the universe is that the only observed thing is M, then the method of straight rule leads us to assume with inductive certainty (i.e. $c_0 = 1$) that all things are M and to take the estimate of the *rf* of M in the universe to be 1. The strangeness of these results becomes especially striking when we remember that both a value of *c* with a singular predictive inference and a value of an estimate of *rf* may be interpreted as stating a fair betting quotient. Thus, on the basis of the observation of just one thing, which was found to be a black dog, the method of the straight rule declares

a betting quotient of 1 to be fair for a bet on the prediction that the next thing will again be a black dog and likewise for a bet on the prediction that all things without a single exception will turn out to be black dogs. (Carnap, 1952, p. 43)

Obviously such a result is unsatisfactory, but the fault seems to me to lie with the size of sample used, not the measure function itself: as I will explain shortly, I see nothing wrong with holding a particular hypothesis inductively certain relative to a given body of evidence, though I think using an inductive sample of size 1 is most undesirable. Indeed, concluding on the basis of the evidence of this sample that the outcome in question had a probability of 0.5, 0.999, or whatever (depending on the language used and the measure function chosen), would be no better. The difficulty here seems to me not to be the statement that relative to the evidence of this sample there is an inductive probability of 1, 0.5, 0.99, etc., but the statement *simpliciter* that there is such an (inductive) probability. As we have seen repeatedly, we ordinarily only make the transition to a probability statement not involving explicit mention of evidence, when the evidence in question is the total amount available; what Carnap's example really does is raise the question of whether we would ever treat such a sample as the total evidence available. By identifying the available evidence with the evidence actually known, Carnap readily produces a case where such a sample appears to be the total amount available ('if all we know about the universe is that the only observed thing is M then ...'), but we have already seen that such an identification for specificatory evidence leads to unacceptable consequences in most cases. The same seems to be true for statistical evidence: almost invariably the available statistical evidence will be far more extensive than a sample of one, even if that is all the statistical evidence actually known. Obviously, in order to put this point precisely I will have to offer an explication of the notion of 'available' statistical evidence and, as promised, I will do so in Chapter V. On the explication given there, small samples will never constitute the total available statistical evidence, and thus Carnap's first objection to the straight rule will not apply.

In later work (see Schilpp, 1963), Carnap modified this argument so as not to rely on the size of the sample involved: here he objected to the straight rule simply because it could yield probability values of 1 (or 0) on the basis of finite observational evidence in finite languages, irrespective of the amount of observational evidence used (Schilpp, 1963, p. 976). This more general argument seems to me weak for two reasons: first of all, all his measure functions determine probabilities of 0 (and by negation, 1) on the basis of finite observations for universal hypotheses in infinite languages — this is the problem for which he proposed the instance criterion of confirmation. I myself can see no *intuitive* reason why the values of 1 or 0 are acceptable on the basis of finite observations in infinite languages and not in finite languages: thus all of Carnap's measure functions would seem intuitively on a par with $\lambda = 0$ as regards the question of probability values of 1 or 0.

Secondly, although intuitively appealing, Carnap's rejection of probabilities 1 and 0 (except for cases of pure logical consequence) depends on a confusion between two notions of 'certainty'. Truths of mathematics and logic may be said to be *absolutely* certain in that no consideration can be adduced to make us withdraw or revise these statements.†

In contrast, if we assign a hypothesis a probability of 1 or 0 based on empirical data (on a frequency of 0 per cent or 100 per cent) measured by $\lambda = 0$, the hypothesis (or its negation) will only be *relatively* certain, in the very real sense that it is only inductively certain in relation to the data in question. Relative to different data, the hypothesis's probability could well be different, and this is crucial in understanding why we are reluctant to accept a probability of 1 or 0 for hypotheses in the light of observational data.

In essence, we are reluctant to accept such values because we think that no matter how much inductive evidence we have uncovered in favour of a given event's occurrence, the event still might not occur. And, of course, we naturally think that a hypothesis given a probability of 1 should be true — that the event described by it will occur. But this is not so if probabilities are relational: Carnap accepts the assignment of probability 1 to hypotheses which are deductively entailed by a body of evidence, and, similarly, by negation, 0. The events described by hypotheses assigned the probability 1 (or 0) in this way do not always occur (or fail to occur) and I can see no reason why this should

---

†Unless, of course, we accept arguments which purport to show that there is no such special class of truths immune from revision. Carnap, of course, did not accept such arguments — indeed Quine developed his criticisms of the analytic/synthetic distinction in opposition to Carnap. What, if any, probability value to assign to statements of mathematics and deductive logic if the analytic/synthetic distinction is rejected is an intriguing question which I have no intention of investigating here.

be the case when probabilities of 1 or 0 are assigned by the $\lambda = 0$ measure function on the basis of empirical data.

But, surely, even if the non-occurrence of an event is theoretically consistent with its being given a relational probability of 1 by some body of evidence, the non-occurrence of the event must show that one had been mistaken in thinking it certain to occur. Well, yes and no: yes, once the event has occurred we would no longer regard events of that kind as certain. But this is wholly compatible with use of the $\lambda = 0$ measure function — once we have made one observation of a negative instance, we can never again assign that kind of event a probability of 1, as the observed frequency will thereafter always remain less than 1. But, on the other hand, the subsequent non-occurrence of an event does not conflict with the event having a probability of 1 relative to the data available beforehand — indeed its occurrence or non-occurrence can have nothing to do with this relational probability.

In fact, in contemplating the future non-occurrence of one instance of a kind of event assigned a probability of 1 by the straight rule of induction on existing data, we tacitly shift the basis for our probability judgments concerning that phenomena, and this is why we think it mistaken to assign a probability of 1 to that kind of event. Instead of relying on the currently available evidence indicating a frequency of 100 per cent for the kind of phenomena in question, we rely on a body of evidence incorporating at least one instance of this kind of event's non-occurrence — *for this is just what we envision happening* — and, as indicated above, this leads us to assign a probability value of less than 1 to this kind of event.

In effect, then, the belief that the possibility of the subsequent nonoccurrence of an event precludes the assignment of a probability of 1 to that event at earlier times is an illusion engendered by a tacit change in the body of evidence relied on for probability judgments concerning that phenomena. In fact, in Chapters IV and V, I will examine in great detail the effects of adopting different bodies of evidence at different times to evaluate the probability of a single hypothesis and the illusion I believe to be at the heart of Carnap's argument here will be seen to be just one instance of a more general form of error. (The reader may wish to refer back to my argument here after completing Chapter V.)

Carnap's second objection to the straight rule is, on the surface, more powerful. It purports to show that, by a widely held standard

Specificatory Evidence and Technology

of success (the mean square error test), there always exists an identifiable measure function more successful than the straight rule. Carnap's argument is supposedly concerned with the success of estimating the relative frequency (*rf*) for Q properties in an unknown universe (whose true character is captured in the state description k_T), based on a sample from that universe of size s, whose evidence he calls e_Q. (Actually it turns out that his argument shows nothing of interest about this.) Since, for Carnap, the estimate of relative frequency determined by a measure function always equals the probability value ascribed to the kind of occurrence we are concerned with, the mean square error of the estimate of relative frequency provides a good test for the efficacy of a given measure function. Carnap, by an argument too elaborate to be reproduced here, shows that the mean square error of the estimate of relative frequency for the Q properties based on $\lambda = 0$, $m_Q^2(e_Q, k_T, s)$, is greater from *all* samples of size s than the mean square error, $m_Q^2(e', k_T, s,)$ from such samples for some identifiable 'biased' measure function e'.

Carnap goes on to explain:

> It is important to keep clearly in mind the meaning of m_Q^2 in order to interpret correct the result (24-7), $m_Q^2(e, kT, s)$ is the mean square error of the estimates of the *rf*'s of all Q's, supplied by the function e based on all samples of the fixed size s in k_T. If X, after observing the sample described in e_Q, goes on observing more and more individuals without ever forgetting any result of an observation once more, then the samples with which he will be concerned in the future form a particular sequence of samples of increasing size, each containing the preceeding one and hence all containing the one described in e_Q. The result (24-7) refers, not to this sequence of the samples of X, but to all samples of size s. Therefore, X cannot infer from this result that he will be more successful in his future estimations if he uses e' than if he uses e_Q. Whether or not this is the case depends upon which particular sequence of individuals will happen to come his way. What X learns from the result is something which concerns, not his own course of life in particular, but rather the universe as a whole and hence, so to speak the average observer. (1952, p. 78)

Carnap's argument only requires the apparently innocuous assumption that the true state of the universe k_T be non-homogeneous, namely that at least two individuals have some distinct Q properties. Carnap believes

Specificatory Evidence and Technology

that this assumption is easily met in most cases we are concerned with, as the samples we deal with are ordinarily non-homogeneous so 'obviously the universe cannot be homogeneous' (ibid., p. 76).

But Carnap here has made a subtle error. The assumption of non-homogeneity of the universe is only justified after a particular non-homogeneous sample is drawn and *then* the mean square error of *all* samples of size s is of no interest to us: all that could *then* matter to us is some measure of the success of the estimates made by the procedure e' or e_Q on the basis of *this* sample or subsequent larger samples including it. Perhaps the square of the error of estimates based on this sample would do but, as Carnap notes elsewhere (1962, p. 535ff) this cannot be known. The *estimated* square error of estimates based on this sample — another possible candidate for measuring the success of different measure functions — will not do either; as Carnap remarks, this

> ... is, so to speak, an internal affair within one system of inductive logic based upon a chosen function c; it cannot be used as a method for obtaining an external, objective judgment on the goodness of a system of inductive logic. (1962, p. 539)

Of course, prior to drawing a particular sample of size s, we may quite legitimately be concerned with the mean square error of a particular estimation technique among all samples of size s: all we then know is that some sample of size s will be drawn. However, at this stage, the assumption of non-homogeneity of the universe is totally unwarranted, particularly for an inductivist. As far as I can see, an inductivist, prior to making any observations, must either assume nothing about the order in the universe or, given his implicit belief in the uniformity of nature, anticipate complete homogeneity in the universe. Obviously we currently believe that the part of our actual universe which is as yet unobserved is not homogeneous, but this is only based on our past experience of diversity, and thus is a belief to be systematized by inductive logic, not assumed in order to justify a particular system of inductive logic.

The general problem for Carnap is that when his assumption of non-homogeneity is justified by our having observed a non-homogeneous sample, his result on the mean square error of an estimate method for *all* samples of a given size ceases to be relevant — we are then only interested in the error of estimates based on the evidence e_Q of our chosen sample. When the mean square error for all samples of size s

Specificatory Evidence and Technology

is relevant, i.e. before any one sample is chosen, the assumption of non-homogeneity is not justified.

Obviously all these replies to Carnap's objection to the straight rule are fine points of detail and are, perhaps, open to further dispute. In any case, relatively little of my argument before Chapter VII will depend on use of the $\lambda = 0$ measure function — as opposed to the ones favoured by Carnap — for reconstructing scientists' discourse on probability in terms of the l.r.t. However, because I think the $\lambda = 0$ measure function *does* provide the most plausible reconstruction of scientists' procedures in handling statistical data, I will usually assume this is the measure function employed for inductive inference, and will only indicate in passing how my argument can be extended to cover the other measure functions advocated by Carnap in his development of the l.r.t.

THE REVISION OF PROBABILITY JUDGMENTS

Before we proceed further, we should consider a radical objection to my proposed reconstruction of scientists' discourse on probability, particularly as the issues which emerge from it will turn out to be crucial to an analysis of the use of statistical data within science. The objection is that most scientists' statements on probability are probability *estimates*, i.e. statements on probability that are hedged, or qualified, as provisional and subject to subsequent correction. While Carnap has explained how statements on logical probability can be construed as estimates of relative frequency, there is, on the surface, no way an l.r. theorist can make sense of an estimate of probability, understood as a provisional statement of probability whose truth is uncertain. For the l.r. theorist all probability statements in full relational form are L-true and hence, *a fortiori*, true: how then can they also be provisional and capable of correction?

This seems to me a profound question, and one which I will discuss at length in the next chapter. In the end I think much of the conception of a probability estimate is based on a confusion which can only be remedied by coming to a correct appreciation of how the l.r.t. explains the revision of probability judgments. However, for the moment I will try to put the precise point in question as clearly as possible in terms of the analysis given earlier in this chapter of the specificatory evidence available for probability judgments. For this

Specificatory Evidence and Technology

purpose, let us assume that in making a judgment of probability we have identified the total specificatory evidence available relevant to a particular phenomenon, in the strong objective sense appropriate to scientific contexts. Further, let us assume we have gathered an appropriate body of statistical data concerning the instances of the phenomena we are concerned with; using the $\lambda = 0$ measure function we then make a judgment on the probability of a specific instance of the phenomenon — call it p_1. We will then have correctly determined the probability most desirable for the purpose of action at that time. Subsequently, perhaps years later, technological advances allow us to discover physical properties associated with the phenomena not previously identified but, in fact, highly relevant to the kind of outcome we have been concerned with. In the light of this new, highly relevant, specificatory evidence, we make a new judgment of probability, p_2, which supersedes the earlier one p_1.

I have of course referred to this kind of revision before and have indicated my belief that it is best systematized into a theory on the meaning of probability statements by the l.r.t. (cf. pp. 18 and 91-9), but it now begins to look as if the exact opposite is the case. The problem is that once new evidence becomes available, our original judgment p_1 will be regarded as a fallible (indeed failed) estimate of the unique probability we were concerned with. The kind of addition to our knowledge which prompted the revision of p_1 to p_2 could in principle occur indefinitely many times and thus, as one writer put it (Blackburn, 1973, p. 105), we are faced with the possibility of an 'endless hierarchy' of ever-fallible probability estimates, that is, a series of probability statements, none of which is ever certain to be correct. This of course is just the opposite of what I (and other l.r. theorists) claim to be the nature of probability judgments.

In fact, the more carefully we reflect on the possibility that any judgment of probability made relative to one body of evidence (even if it is the total amount objectively available) can always be superseded by another judgment made in the light of more information, the more the claims of this and the previous chapters on the logical character and objectivity of judgments of probability begin to look suspect: how can a judgment of probability be objectively valid, much less L-true, if it is always possible that it will require revision in the light of new evidence. In fact, my central criticism of objective theories of probability in Chapter II was to the effect that, on such theories, judgments of probability were not decidable in finite periods of time, precisely because they allowed the possibility that probability judgments might require revision in the light of subsequent developments — e.g. a fundamental change in science. It now looks — as the reader may have thought all along — that these objective theories are wholly in accord with the beliefs and practices of scientists concerning probability statements — specifically their use of probability 'estimates' — and that my proposed reconstruction of a scientific concept of probability in terms of the l.r.t. cannot be right. It is obvious that the revision of probability judgments, both actual and contemplated, raises fundamental problems for the l.r.t. — in particular my claim about the relationship of the l.r.t. to the concept of probability employed in science — and we must now look explicitly at these problems.

IV
REVISING PROBABILITY JUDGMENTS

I concluded the last chapter by remarking, in a general way, that the provisional character of scientists' judgments of probability — their use of probability 'estimates' — seemed to accord more closely with objective theories of probability than the l.r.t. Not surprisingly, various writers have explicitly formulated arguments against the l.r.t. based on our willingness to revise probability statements in the light of new information, and we would do well to look at these in some detail. During his discussion of the objective aspects of our concept of probability, Blackburn presents a neat and intuitively convincing argument concerning the discovery of additional evidence, which purports to show that no analysis of probability in terms of available evidence will do and that probability (or at least some concept of it) must be explained in terms of objective physical states of the world. Blackburn's argument is illustrated by an example of a gangster and his assistant interested in a proposition Pr: the probability of Eclipse winning the 2.30 is very high. Blackburn remarks:

> We might say: 'The probability of Eclipse winning has gone down drastically' and we all know when this would be agreed upon. The entry of strong competition, the contraction of some ailment, rain when he likes hard going, or in general the determination of some condition affecting the outcome of the race, would lower the probability of his victory. Furthermore it appears that something which affects or might affect the outcome of the race must alter if the probability of Eclipse winning is to alter. If we imagine our gangster ordering his man to decrease the probability of Eclipse winning,

the only way in which he can be obeyed is for his man to tamper in some way with the set-up, by doping Eclipse, entering a stronger horse, etc. (1973, pp. 103-9)

In particular Blackburn points out that

> when we find that Eclipse has 'flu we discover that the probability of his winning is very low, we don't make the probability of his winning very low. It is his catching 'flu which ruins his chances, not our discovery of it. This means of course that one familiar type of analysis is certainly going to be inadequate to propositions like (Pr). If we attempt an analysis which sees (Pr) as asserting a relationship between the prediction that Eclipse will win, and, say, our total available evidence, it will simply misrepresent what would change the probability of Eclipse winning. . . . For consider what would change the truth of: 'The proposition that event e will occur is well supported by the total available evidence.' Clearly the discovery of evidence pointing the other way. But that just corrects our estimates of Eclipse's chances, it does not alter his chances. The gangster's assistant does not obey his command to change the probability of Eclipse winning ('Dish Eclipse's chances') by diligently searching for evidence, even if he changes the truth of 'the proposition that Eclipse will run is well supported by the total available evidence' thereby. Such an analysis then gives a proposition whose truth depends upon entirely different conditions to those upon which the analysandum depends, and is therefore incorrect. (ibid.)

In short, because we regard changes in physical states of the world, e.g. Eclipse's condition, as affecting the truth of probability statements about him, it is such physical states — and not relations to bodies of evidence — that would seem to be the relevant truth conditions.

Blackburn himself despairs of giving a coherent account of a concept of probability with physical states of the world as truth conditions, because he believes such an objective conception of probability leads to the 'desperate' conclusion that 'the actual probability [of events like Eclipse winning the 2.30] is something near 0 or 1, but that normally we don't know which'. The argument here is all too familiar: it is quite natural to think that if every relevant physical factor were known, the outcome of the race could be predicted with certainty — as we saw Reichenbach remark, 'It is only lack of technical ability that prevents us from equalling Laplace's superman.' Whether or not this is true of horse-races, most events ordinarily regarded as probabilistic could be predicted with certainty if all the relevant physical facts were known. However, if we regard probability as determined by the physical state of a system — and not by the knowledge currently available about it — we must hold that the probability of such events is 0 or 1, although we will usually not know which. (Along with Blackburn I regard this as a major difficulty with objectivist conception of chance, which I believe can be avoided on the l.r.t. However, the explanation of this problem in the last chapter is not altogether sufficient to avoid the problem as formulated by Blackburn; only at the end of the chapter will we have the full measure of this problem.)

Another writer, Mellor, has adduced considerations of precisely the same kind employed in Blackburn's intuitive example to demonstrate that *scientific* discourse on probability must be understood in terms of physical states of the world. Mellor's argument is directed against an attempt by Borel to justify as objective those probabilities which are relative to the subjective opinions of scientists fully informed of all current evidence — as will be clear his objection applies as well to the relational account I have already offered. Borel is quoted by Mellor as remarking:

> There are cases in which it is legitimate to speak of the probability of an event; there are cases where one refers to the probability which is common to the judgment of all best informed persons... One could, in order to abridge our language, while at the same time not attaching an absolute sense to this expression, call these probabilities objective probabilities. (1971, pp. 24ff)

But here Mellor replies:

> Now doubtless it is desirable to defer from time to time to the informed opinion of physicists in talking of 'the probability that an atom of radium will explode tomorrow' (Borel's example), but this is hardly what it means to talk so. An objectivist would find it a bizarre conclusion that the properties of radium have respectfully altered down the years to match the changing but ever-infallible consensus of 'the best informed persons' at the Cavendish laboratory and elsewhere (ibid.)

Mellor then elaborates this view in a passage already cited in p. 50, but the force of his argument against the kind of position I advocated in the last chapter should be clear from the above: since estimates of probability made by scientists implementing all current procedures can change as those procedures (or the theories in which they are embedded) change, the probability of that event cannot be relative to the knowledge so gathered, as the probability of the event does not so vary. Because a scientist implementing all current procedures will thereby employ the total available evidence in my objective sense, Mellor's argument would appear to establish that probability is not relative to the total available evidence even in that strong sense.

It is possible (and of some interest) to restate Mellor's argument here with emphasis on the notion of objectivity. Inherent in the idea of an objective judgment (of any kind) is the thought that it is possible to be mistaken about the phenomenon in question. As regards probability judgments, it would appear that only in so far as we regard them as amenable to revision in the light of new information can we be said to be striving to make judgments which are objectively valid. To a *limited extent* the first formulation I gave in the last chapter of the requirement of total evidence captures this notion of objectivity: any individual who makes an ordinary statement of probability on the basis of less specificatory evidence than the local 'objectively' available can be said to be mistaken and his judgment thus will require revision (cf. p. 84). Such an analysis is primarily appropriate to discourse on probabilities in the context of science, but it is of course primarily for such contexts that we require an objective account of probability.

Unfortunately, Mellor's argument cited above points up dramatically the limitations of this attempt to give an 'objective' account of probability within the terms of the l.r.t.: while I can explain the sense in which judgments of probability based on bodies of evidence which are less comprehensive than the total objectively available are mistaken, judgments based on such a totality cannot in the same way be said to be mistaken — they, and they alone, are objectively valid. But, as we have seen, advances in science or technology can provide us with additional information relevant to the phenomenon in question and, certainly on an intuitive level, we regard this new evidence as showing that we were, objectively speaking, mistaken before. But how can this be if earlier judgments based on the total evidence then available are all that can be said to be objectively valid?

In fact, quite independent of any considerations on the objectivity of probability judgments, the revisions or corrections required by new discoveries of evidence appear to be inexplicable on the l.r.t.'s account of probability: on the l.r.t., probability judgments made at different times, each based on different bodies of evidence, will not contradict one another but, rather, will constitute different equally correct judgments about different probability relations.

Actually, this reasoning — which reformulates points made at the end of the last chapter — hinges on a thoroughgoing confusion between full relational probability statements and the elliptical ones we ordinarily make. The revisions to probability judgments which cause the difficulties we have been examining are revisions to earlier elliptical judgments made on the basis of (i.e. relative to) a body of evidence which incorporates the results of new technology; accordingly such revisions are in precise agreement with the l.r.t. as explained throughout the book so far. In fact in the rest of this chapter I hope to show that the revision of ordinary — elliptical — probability judgments over time in the light of the discovery of new evidence can only be properly systematized by the l.r.t. and that the intuitive appeal of the arguments we have just considered in favour of objective theories of probability — and to a large extent those theories themselves — depend on a failure to recognize the true character of this revision. I will first present my argument in a more or less intuitive fashion, then generalize the conclusions in the context of the discussion of previous chapters on realism and effective decidability. Throughout this chapter, I will be almost exclusively concerned with the role played by specificatory evidence in the revision of probability judgments — though I will develop a parallel argument for statistical evidence in the next chapter. Therefore in this chapter, when I speak of evidence — or the available evidence — without further qualification, I will mean specificatory evidence.

Past Tense Probability Statements

It must be obvious that the revision of probability judgments we have been considering occurs over time and we might do well to begin our positive analysis of this crucial phenomenon by examining our ordinary tensed discourse on probabilities. Here we should note that the vocabulary appropriate to the revision of probability judgments over time is embedded in our ordinary use of the term 'probable'. Swinburne, in discussing the l.r.t., says that on it:

many propositions which do not explicitly refer to evidence do so implicitly, and that the evidence refered to implicitly is the total evidence available at the time to which reference is made. This account seems correct. (1973, pp. 23-4)

But he goes on to point out:

If this account is correct it may seem surprising that we do not often use the phrase 'it was probable' saying e.g. 'it was probable two centuries ago that the world began in 4004 B.C.' For if 'it is probable that p' is (often) elliptical for 'it is probable on the total evidence now available that p' we would expect 'it was probable that p' to be used as elliptical for 'it was probable on the total available evidence that p'. We may want to assess the extent to which the evidence we used rendered various hypotheses probable but expressions of the form 'it was probable that p' sound odd. On the other hand we often say 'it seemed probable' that so and so, e.g. 'yesterday it seemed probable that he would come' or '3,000 years ago it seemed probable' that the earth was flat. (ibid.)

Of course we only use the term 'seemed x' as a contrast to 'actually was x' and so our regular employment of the idiom 'seemed probable' when referring to a previous time of greater ignorance is simply a way of indicating that we now regard the probability judgment as mistaken. The correction to a previous judgment implied in this idiom is just another instance of that willingness to revise probability judgments that we have noted as problematic for the relational theorist.

Swinburne himself seems briefly aware of the problems posed for relational theorists by our use of the idiom 'seemed probable' rather than 'was probable' for judgments made on what was previously, but is not now, the total available evidence. However, he is quick to dismiss any qualms: 'I can only conclude that this is a quirk of ordinary language without philosophical significance and I commend the use of the phrase "it was probable" as elliptical for "it was probable on the (total) evidence available".' (1973, p. 25)

Despite underscoring our willingness to revise probability judgments in a manner which apparently conflicts with a relational conception of probability, the usage to which Swinburne has drawn attention can in fact be accommodated within a theory which holds the probability of an event to be relative to available evidence. There is no reason, as far as I can see, that a relational account of probability must give an analysis of past tense statements of probability which makes them relative to the total evidence available at the time in the past with which we are concerned. If 'it is probable that p' is elliptical for 'it is probable on the total evidence now available that p', can we not construe 'it was probable that p' as elliptical for 'it was probable that p on the evidence *now* available'?

This of course is the exact opposite of the proposal commended by Swinburne, but for that reason is able to make sense of the ordinary idioms that Swinburne must dismiss as quirks. On my view we prefer to say that the probability of an event only *seemed* to be so and so when the current expanded information indicates that the probability is otherwise, because our statement about the past probability is relative to our current knowledge. Relative to this knowledge, the probability in the past we speak of is not what we originally thought it to be – thus we say it only 'seemed' to be so and so.

Such an analysis is just a straightforward extention of that offered in previous chapters, where I argued that probability judgments (usually formulated in the present tense) are relative to the total evidence available at the time the judgment is made. Here I simply extend this analysis to probability judgments formulated in the past tense – they too are relative to the total evidence available at the time the judgment is made, a totality which may well differ from that available at the time of the events referred to in the judgment. It is this change in the body of evidence used as the basis for the ordinary judgment of probability which allows the relational theorist to explain the apparent correction of L-true probability statements. The judgment we correct was originally made without reference to evidence; later this judgment is again reported, as it was made (i.e. without reference to any particular body of evidence), and so it is then assessed as any other elliptical judgment would be – relative to the *currently* available evidence. Of course, relative to such evidence, the original elliptical judgment as to the value, or comparative ordering, of the event's probability will be mistaken. Thus the original elliptical judgment is, so to speak, caught betwixt and between – originally formulated quite correctly relative to what was the evidence originally available (although not explicitly mentioning such evidence), it is later assessed relative to the currently available evidence, as that is how we regularly treat judgments of probability not explicitly referring to evidence.

Put another way, the relational theorist can explain both how the ellliptical judgment was correct at the time it was formulated – for it was completely in order relative to what was then the available evidence, and so of course would be correct according to a relational theory of probability — and also how later it would be seen to be mistaken — the eventuality which appeared to count against a relational theory. Here the reader may detect an aura of paradox — for we are concerned all along with a judgment as to what the probability of a given event was at a particular time. Surely, to revert to a schema, no one can make sense of the two contradictory propositions that the probability of an event was correctly p_0 at t_0 — as the original judgment had it — and that it also was *not* p_0 at time t_0, as the current evidence indicates. But a relational theorist can reconcile these apparently conflicting propositions; indeed his account alone can: our ordinary judgment as to what the probability of an event was at a particular time is relational and therefore must tacitly involve some body of evidence. The difficulty is that on the two different occasions the ordinary judgment is understood relative to different bodies of evidence and so can both have been correct and yet later become incorrect. Relative to the evidence e_0 that was available at the time t_0, it is true that the event had probability p_0 at time t_0; relative to the evidence e_1, later available, it is false that the event had probability p_0 at t_0.

To put this analysis precisely it is necessary to make a few brief remarks on criteria of identity for tensed judgments of probability. As I understand it, one and the same complete relational judgment of probability exists in three different forms — a present tense statement involving no explicit reference to the time at which the probability value obtains, e.g. 'relative to e_0, the probability of events x's occurrence is now p_0' (where *now* is t_0), a past tense statement identifying the past time at which the probability value held, e.g. 'relative to e_0, the probability of x's occurrence was p_0 at t_0', or a future tense statement identifying the future time at which the probability value will hold, e.g. 'relative to e_0 the probability of x's occurrence will be p_0 at t_0'. Being different forms of one and the same judgment of probability, these statements will have identical truth conditions, namely the conditions which determine whether or not x's probability relative to e_0 is indeed p_0. A similar criterion of identity can be given for ordinary (i.e. elliptical) probability judgments, and indeed such a criterion has been implicit through the book so far: two sentences ascribing probability values to events will be instances of the same elliptical judgment if, and only if, (a) the sentences refer to the same event and (b) the same probability value is asserted to obtain for the same time. Thus, for example, analogous to the three forms of complete probability judgment just referred to, we would have the following three forms of one and the same elliptical judgment: 'the probability of x's occurrence is now p_0' (where *now* is t_0), 'the probability of x's occurrence was p_0 at t_0' and 'the probability of x's occurrence will be p_0 at t_0'.

Now despite being able to speak of the same — or different — elliptical judgments of probability in virtue of such a criterion of identity, no elliptical judgment can, on the l.r.t., be true or false solely on its own. Only complete two-term probability judgments can be true or false; and so, according to the position I have been defending, only in so far as ordinary elliptical judgments are understood relative to some body of evidence (in fact the total currently available) can they be true or false, correct or incorrect. Perhaps it would be best to say that truth or falsity as applied to ordinary probability judgments are only relative terms, for it is only the full two-term relational statement involving the total evidence available which is, strictly speaking, true or false.

No doubt this is not our ordinary, intuitive way of viewing the matter — we do speak of elliptical probability statements as being true or false in their own right, but as I pointed out in Chapter I, the first goal of a theory on the meaning of probability statements is to make sense in a systematic way of our intuitive procedures for determining the truth of probability statements. The l.r.t. does this by explaining an intuitive judgment that a given ordinary statement is true or false by pointing out that in making such a judgment we always have some body of evidence in mind and so we can be regarded as performing the act of judging whether a specific two-term relational statement is true or false. That we do not immediately perceive we are doing this is hardly surprising: given that we usually omit explicit mention of the evidence we have in mind, we can hardly be expected to note explicitly that we are judging the truth of a two-term relational statement. In any case relatively little significance attaches to the way we ordinarily conceptualize the nature of our judgments on the truth and falsity of a particular kind of statement — it is the philosopher's task to do this and of course I have tried throughout the book so far to present the case for the semantic analysis of probability statements given by the l.r.t.

The overall result of that analysis — at least as regards the problems we are considering at present — is that in so far as it makes any sense to regard an elliptical judgment of probability as true or false, one and the same elliptical judgment can be true at one time and false at another, as its truth or falsity can only be its truth or falsity in relation to the evidence which is available. Conversely, two different elliptical judgments about the probability of the same event (for the same time) need not, despite appearances, conflict in the sense of having as truth conditions states of affairs that cannot both be true. Thus, for example, both the judgment that 'the probability of x's occurrence is now p_0' (where *now* is t_0) and the different judgment, made later at t_1, that 'the probability of x's occurrence was p_1 at t_0' can both be true, in that the two full statements involving different bodies of evidence as the total available at t_0 and t_1 can both be true.

It is just this fact — that one and the same elliptical judgment of probability can be part of two different complete two-term judgments — which, in my opinion, accounts for our repeated revision to probability judgements — and indeed accounts for it in a way which wholly accords with the view that probability judgments are always relative to evidence. What we revise is an *elliptical* judgment omitting mention of evidence: when made initially the judgment that, say, 'the probability of x's occurrence is now p_0' will have been correct in that it was one part of a correct two-term judgment (involving as second term the evidence e_0 available at t_0); later the same elliptical judgment that 'the probability of x's occurrence was p_0 at t_0' will be incorrect and require revision, because with new evidence available the elliptical judgment becomes part of a different (and now mistaken) two-term judgment 'that relative to e_1 the probability of x's occurrence was p_0 at t_0'.

Extending the Argument

Although initially proposed to deal with the problems raised for the relational theorist by the idiom 'it only seemed probable that p', this argument readily provides a resolution to all the problems posed for the relational theorist by our progressive revision of probability judgments in the light of new evidence. One way to put the general form of the problem is this: how can one claim that judgments of unique probability are relative to the total evidence available at the time the judgment is made, if we are always prepared to admit that such judgments were wrong when new evidence becomes available? If such judgments were truly relative to evidence available at the time, would we not regard them as still correct, if perhaps no longer of much interest, when new evidence became available? A simple answer to this is implicit, indeed virtually explicit, in the above discussion: it is only the elliptical judgment, omitting mention of evidence, that we regard as mistaken later, not the full, two-term, relative judgment which we would still regard as correct (e.g. even at t_1 with e_1 available, it will be true that 'relative to e_0, the probability of x's occurrence was p_0 at t_0'). When we admit that a previous judgment was mistaken, as shown by new evidence, we only acknowledge the fact that relative to this new evidence the elliptical judgment we made before is incorrect. Far from contradicting anything the relational theorist claims, such revision actually exhibits the fundamental tenet of his theory of probability: when an elliptical judgment is made it is always to be understood relative to the currently available evidence and its truth or falsity depends solely on the truth value of the full relational statement; then with different evidence available at different times, one and the same elliptical judgments can at first be correct and later require revision.

This I take it explains in a manner wholly congenial to the relational theorist any actual revisions to our ordinary — and elliptical — probability judgments that have been, or will be, carried out on the basis of new evidence. However, it may be thought that a residual problem remains concerning the logical possibility of revision: even if actual revisions, past present and future, to probability judgments can be accounted for in the manner I have suggested, we have not yet explained why at present, possessing nothing more than the evidence currently available, we are prepared to admit that our current judgments may require revision in the light of new evidence. To restate, with an emphasis on logical possibility, a point made earlier: on the l.r.t. theory, it is analytic that a statement of probability relative to a certain body of evidence will be true if, and only if, the probability relation asserted to obtain does indeed obtain. When we are faced with a probability statement lacking explicit reference to a body of evidence, our judgment is to be understood as relative to the total evidence available. Thus, on this account, there should be at present no *possibility* of revision of an elliptical statement of probability, if the appropriate relation obtains between the event or hypothesis in question and what at present is the total evidence available. But the mere suggestion that there might exist relevant evidence, as yet unknown, is in fact sufficient to persuade us we may have to revise our present judgment. Just such a possibility was at issue when Mellor drew attention to the logical possibility of even deeply embedded beliefs about chance being rejected 'in the light of future science' (see p. 50).

For good measure, we should also note that not only can current judgments of probability require revision in the light of new evidence, but also future judgments can require revision if, at a yet later date, further evidence becomes available. Thus we are led to admit the possibility of a never-ending series of judgments of probability, each one being revised later after acquiring new evidence. However, by now it should be obvious that the possibility in question is nothing other than the possibility of new evidence becoming available which would require us to revise our present (or future) *elliptical* judgments in just the manner I have described. Thus our recognition of the possibility that our current judgments of unique probabilities – which are elliptical – may require revision in the light of new evidence only signals the fact that these judgments, as elliptical, may later be assessed relative to such new evidence, rather than relative to the evidence currently available. Similarly, when we admit the possibility that future elliptical judgments may require revision in the light of even later advances in knowledge, our admission simply depends on the fact that these future elliptical judgments may be assessed, and found wanting, relative to a body of evidence which will have replaced the one that had been tacitly assumed when the judgment was originally formed.

Accordingly when, three paragraphs above, it looked as if there was no possibility of revising a judgment made correctly relative to currently available evidence, we simply overlooked the possibility that any elliptical judgment can be assessed relative to bodies of evidence different from the one on which it was originally formulated and so require revision. Because such revision depends only on the presence of a new body of evidence as the total available, there is a genuine possibility, on this account, of an indefinitely long sequence of revised elliptical judgments of probability, each based on ever-expanding bodies of evidence.

We are now, perhaps, in a better position to understand an important aspect of the objectivist's concept of probability which, we saw, was intimately connected with our progressive revision of probability judgments: this was the intuitively natural idea that our progressive revision of probability judgments forms a series, possible infinite, of probability *estimates*, each perhaps a more accurate approximation of a true value, but each liable to correction later on. No doubt as we obtain more and more knowledge about an event, we make a series of judgments on the probability of that event, each omitting reference to evidence and each purporting to be 'unique'; however, the actual probability values ascribed to the event — and asserted to obtain for the same time — differ in each case. Because each judgment in the series ascribes a different probability value, it is a different elliptical judgment, but because they all ascribe probability values for the same time to the same event, each replaces earlier judgments and so is thought of as a revision of earlier judgments. Obviously no one judgment in this series deserves to be singled out as *the* correct one, for even if it has not already been superseded it is perfectly possible that it will be later on. Equally, it would appear, they cannot all be correct, as each apparently conflicts with the other ones. And then it does seem natural to regard this series as a series of ever-fallible *estimates* of probability, each perhaps a better approximation of some true value, as each relies on more evidence.

But the account I have given so far in this chapter provides an alternative explanation of this series and one in which, true to the relationalist's conception of probability, each judgment on the probability value of the event is correct. As elliptical, each judgment is to be understood as relative to the total evidence available at the time it is made; accordingly each judgment in the series will be correct as each is a part of a correct two-term judgment. The appearance of conflict between these elliptical judgments arises because the total evidence available changes over time, and so, different one-term (elliptical) judgments on the probability of the event will be needed to make a series of correct full two-term judgments. Observing only the apparent conflict between different elliptical judgments on the same event, we naturally think each corrects a previous error and, since each is itself liable to be superseded later, we then think each is a still-fallible *estimate* of probability; in reality each is a correct elliptical judgment — correct because it is part of an L-true relational judgment involving the total evidence available at the time it is made — and, as explained before, there is no real conflict between such judgments. In sum, instead of a series of ever-fallible estimates of probability each conflicting with each other on some absolute (or objective) value, we have a series of elliptical judgments each differing as to what the preferential probability of a given event is, but each correct in so far as it is part of a different L-true two-term relational judgment.

REALISM AND THE REVISION OF PROBABILITY JUDGMENTS

To link this analysis of our progressive revision of ordinary probability judgments to our earlier discussion of realism and anti-realism in probability theory, we need only note that the analysis explains the *present* conception of a potentially infinite series of ever-fallible probability estimates in terms of the possibility of our making indefinitely many additions to our knowledge of the physical parameters relevant to the kind of event we are concerned with. Obviously at present the possibility of making indefinite additions to our knowledge of the relevant physical parameters is only a logical possibility, or better, a possibility in principle.

Throughout the book so far I have emphasized that it is finite bodies of evidence (and their logical relations to the hypotheses we are concerned with) which constitute the means by which in principle we can decide the truth of ordinary probability statements. In fact each time we imagine ourselves possessed of such a body of evidence and imagine the revision it requires us to make of an ordinary probability statement made earlier on the basis of a different body of evidence, we envision ourselves affecting just such a decision on the truth of the ordinary statement. Thus, in arriving at the conception of a potentially infinite series of probability estimates in the manner described above, we simply imagine ourselves implementing an indefinite number of times our capacity — which is a capacity in principle — of recognizing the truth of ordinary probability statements by use of finite bodies of evidence (and their logical relations to the hypotheses we are concerned with). From an anti-realist point of view, this capacity is what constitutes our mastery of the meaning of probability statements and any adequate explanation of the meaning of ordinary probability statements must provide a perspicuous characterization of this capacity; in the manner described at length earlier, this is accomplished by the l.r.t.'s treatment of ordinary probability statements as elliptical for two-term L-true statements.

However, the outward form of ordinary probability statements and our method of revising them naturally suggest a different, realist, interpretation, which in any case is probably congenial on an intuitive level. Since the ordinary statement of probability we continually revise refers only to *the* probability of a phenomenon — with no mention of evidence — it is natural to interpret it as about some one single entity. There is of course nothing in this form of speech which precludes this single entity from being a logical relation between the hypothesis we are concerned with and some body of evidence, but the fact that we can imagine circumstances which would make us regard the probability of the hypothesis as different from that determined by the logical relation between it and a particular body of evidence known to us prompts us to believe intuitively that it cannot be. The only other alternative will be some one physical entity that obtains quite independently of the bodies of evidence we know, i.e. obtains 'objectively'.

However, by now it should be clear that the circumstances which prompt us to regard the probability as different from that determined by the logical relation to a particular body of evidence we know are, simply, our possession (actual or envisioned) of a different, more comprehensive or more accurate, body of evidence and *its* logical relation to the hypothesis in question; thus, far from supporting the idea that probabilities are objective physical facts about which we may be mistaken on the basis of limited evidence known to us, this shows that probabilities are *always* relative to such bodies of evidence, as the l.r.t. has it.

Here it might be objected that the difference between the l.r.t. and realist objective theories of probability which I have tried to draw attention to is actually very small, perhaps vanishingly so: the two different approaches simply provide different ways of conceptualizing the same basic phenomenon, i.e. our procedure in revising ordinary probability judgments. On a realist view, our progressive revision depends on the fact that ordinary probability statements are about physical entities in the world, which it is always possible for us to be mistaken about. From the anti-realist point of view, the means by which we carry out revisions to ordinary probability judgments are constitutive of their very meaning, i.e. these statements are construed as elliptical for two-term statements specifying the evidence on the basis of which the revision is carried out. As alternative conceptualizations of the same phenomenon, there might appear to be little to choose between the two approaches: indeed, one might think that realism and anti-realism are just different metaphysical or epistemological conventions, each equally viable in its own right.

Whether this holds for other areas I cannot say, but it does not seem to me so in the case of probability theory and in fact I hoped to establish as much in Chapter II. My main contention there was that objective theories of probability could not explain how we come to know the truth of probability statements without generating a vicious regress, or introducing a second distinct concept of probability or rational credence. Once it is recognized that objective theories of probability require supplementation by some account of how we come to know the truth of probability statements, which, to avoid regress, involves introduction of a separate concept of rational credence, one cannot claim such theories provide an equally valid conceptualization of our progressive revision of probability judgments. The l.r.t. explains this process in terms of a concept of inductive probability — which most agree is necessary in any general reconstruction of knowledge — and that concept alone. The introduction of a concept of objective probability — in addition to that of inductive probability or, more generally, rational credence — to explain this process of revision then constitutes an unnecessary complication. Indeed, if I am correct in claiming that the idea of an objective physical probability derives its intuitive appeal from the way it *superficially* accords with our practice of repeatedly revising one and the same probability judgment — which practice, however, can be explained more simply by the l.r.t. — then the idea of an objective probability should not be viewed as an alternative way of conceptualizing this practice, but as the reification or hypostatization of an additional (and unnecessary) physical entity to correspond to this process.

An additional reason for distinguishing sharply between the conceptualization of our revision of probability judgments provided by the l.r.t. and objective theories of probability — in favour of the former — can also be extracted from the discussion in Chapter III of the methodology of applying the l.r.t. for specific practical purposes. One conclusion of that discussion was that the objective value of probability that scientists were concerned with should be understood as the probability value relative to the total evidence which could be ascertained by all extant technological procedures. In fact, because it is *in practice* only possible to obtain evidence by use of extant technological procedures, such a body of evidence is the maximum it is in practice possible to ascertain at that time; thus a decision on the truth of an ordinary statement of probability made on the basis of this body of evidence would be the best we could in practice make at that time. (This is one of the reasons I called such judgments objective.) The basic problem we have been concerned with in this chapter is that even probability judgments made relative to such bodies of evidence *could* require revision in the light of evidence subsequently obtained by more advanced technology, but it is important to see that at the time we require the probability judgment for the purpose of action, this possibility is, *practically speaking*, totally irrelevant: there is no way we can in practice affect a decision on the truth of a probability statement on the basis of evidence to be obtained by technology not then extant. That is to say, we can imagine all sorts of bodies of evidence that it is in principle possible we will come to possess and, on my view, any such body of evidence can *in principle* be used by us to decide the truth of an ordinary probability statement. However, such a possibility should not blind us to the limitations which exist whenever we wish to decide the truth of a given ordinary statement of probability with a specific practical purpose in mind. The practical need in question exists for a limited time and so only technological procedures extant at that time can be used to decide the truth of the statement that is to guide our action. To put it another way, to determine the truth of a probability statement that is to guide our action for specific practical purposes, we can only use evidence that it is *in practice* possible to ascertain.

This means that the account of the objectivity of relational judgments of probability given in the previous chapter is not seriously undermined by the criticism that even objectively valid judgments of probability may require revision in the light of new advances in technology, as was tentatively suggested at the start of this chapter. In fact the above considerations show that the sense of objectivity elucidated in Chapter III is far more fitting as an analysis of scientists' 'objective' discourse on probabilities than the illusory one provided by so-called objective theories. Since scientific discourse on probability, like ordinary discourse, is concerned with probabilities which answer to practical needs, we must in science content ourselves with making judgments of probability based on the greatest amount of evidence ascertainable by extant technology: we can only guide our actions by probability judgments made in the light of our present knowledge of the world and this is inevitably limited by the technology then extant. In other words, the only way a judgment of probability that is to guide our action in practice can be objectively valid is by utilizing the maximum information it is possible *in practice* to ascertain.

Let me conclude this section by remarking that, while novel in some respects, this treatment of the 'objective' probabilities with which scientists are concerned, is hardly surprising: as we saw Reichenbach remark, only technological limitations prevent scientists from being

Laplace's superman — that is, determining the future with certainty — and so we might expect any account of the role of probability in science to entail that the actual probabilities scientists determine depend on the state of existing technology. This, in effect, is the position I outlined at the start of the previous chapter and have tried to defend in this chapter.

ANALYSIS OF EARLIER ARGUMENTS

My analysis of our practice of revising probability statements in the light of new evidence, its relation to the 'objective' side of our concept of probability — and thus to objective theories of probability — has so far been carried out in an abstract and general way; in fact most of the specific arguments we encountered earlier in the chapter are best understood within the context of this general analysis and it seems appropriate to conclude this chapter by turning our attention to them. The most important argument to analyse is the objection to relational theories of probability put forward explicitly by Blackburn and implicitly by Mellor, namely that we ordinarily regard changes in the physical circumstances surrounding an event, not changes in the information available, as necessary and sufficient conditions for a change in the probability of that event. My own belief is that this claim arises entirely from a failure to appreciate the way in which our revisions of ordinary probability judgments are carried out on the basis of — and thus always remain relative to — bodies of evidence. Put generally, the connection between our intuitive feeling that probability values do not change with the acquisition of new information and our progressive revision of judgments of probability in the light of new evidence is this: when we decide, on the basis of evidence which has become available at t_1, that the probability of a given event was p_1 at t_0, rather than p_0 as thought at t_0, we also of course believe that the probability of this event at t_1 is p_1; thus, at t_1 we in effect believe that the probability of the event has remained unchanged during the period t_0-t_1 in which the new evidence became available. By abstraction, we then reach the general belief that probabilities remain unchanged with the acquisition of new knowledge, though, for reasons I will examine shortly, also believe they change with changing physical states.

It is important here to notice how frequently we actually revise judgments of probability. Both for events that are regularly repeated, e.g. the sun's daily rising, and those that span considerable periods of time, e.g. the earth's being round or flat, it is both feasible and desirable to formulate judgments of probability at different times. Similarly, events that have already occurred, but of which we have imperfect knowledge, e.g. the date of the earth's origin, and those that will occur at a time sufficiently far in the future to permit more than one assessment of probability, also prompt numerous judgments of probability over time. In virtually all these cases our judgments will initially take the form of present tense statements about the probability of the event without reference to any particular body of evidence, that is, what I have called ordinary judgments of a unique or preferential probability. Since later probability judgments are about the same event, or kind of event, it will be natural to compare earlier with later — indeed in certain circumstances this will be highly desirable, e.g. to make sure any earlier mistakes are thoroughly understood and avoided in the future.

But, as we saw above, when we later reconsider a previous judgment of probability not mentioning evidence, we will tacitly employ the currently available evidence as the second term required for a full judgment of probability. We will then be forced to revise the *elliptical* judgment made earlier and the revised judgment will then indicate that the event's probability was the same as it is now — both what we retrospectively judge it to have been as well as what we take it to be now will be relative to the same body of evidence, the total *now* available. To employ Blackburn's example of our learning, at say, 12.00, that Eclipse has the flu, we will not think this has changed the probability from what it was at 11.30 because at 12.00 we will consider his case of the flu as relevant to what his chances were at 11.30 in just the way it is to his chances at 12.00. It should be obvious that in doing this we are simply assessing what his chances were at 11.30 and are at 12.00 relative to the same body of evidence, namely one which includes specification of his illness.

In this light it is not difficult to understand why we are tempted to believe, mistakenly, that unique or preferential probabilities do not change with advances in knowledge. In doing so we in fact confuse two distinct questions concerning the change in probability values over time: the first question is what at any given moment in time t_x we are correct in judging the preferential probability of an event to be or have been at times $t_0 \ldots t_n$, up to and including the present. The second is what at different moments of time $t_x, t_y \ldots$ we are correct in judging the preferential probability of the event to be or have been at times $t_0 \ldots t_n$ up to the present. The answer to the first question, as we saw in the above example, is that at each moment of time t_x (e.g. 12.00) we correctly judge the probability to be the same value p_x for the times $t_0 \ldots t_n$ (11.30 and 12.00) no matter what changes there have been in knowledge during the period $t_0 \ldots t_n$ — all assessments of the probability of this event made at t_x are relative to just one body of evidence. Now if at each stage $t_x, t_y \ldots$ in the advance of knowledge, we are correct in regarding the unique probability to have been the same at the earlier times during which knowledge has previously advanced, what could be more natural than concluding that unique probabilities are not in general changed by advances in knowledge? That is to say, when we consider — either at an intuitive level or in constructing a systematic theory of probability — the question of whether the unique, or preferential, probabilities required for the purpose of action change with the acquisition of knowledge, our most immediate response will be that they do not, for at that moment, and every previous moment, we will have been correct to have judged such probabilities to have been the same for the different times $t_0 \ldots t_n$ during which previous advances in knowledge occurred. Thus, it seems to me, our belief that probabilities do not change with the acquisition of knowledge is essentially a consequence of the first fact cited above, that at each given moment of time t_x the probability of an event is the same for the times $t_0 \ldots t_n$ up to the present during which previous advances in knowledge occurred.

However, we must realize that, in answer to the second question, if we consider different moments t_x, t_y corresponding to the ever-advancing present, we will make different judgments as to what the probability previously was, as new evidence becomes available. Thus while it is correct to judge at t_x that the probability was p_x for the times $t_0 \ldots t_n$, at a later time t_y all judgments of what the probability was during the period $t_0 \ldots t_n$ will be relative to the evidence available at t_y and so a different preferential probability value will obtain for the period $t_0 \ldots t_n$. And it is precisely because at different times t_x, t_y, etc., we quite correctly form different judgments as to what the preferential probability was over earlier periods $t_0 \ldots t_n$ that the unique preferential probability of an event changes over time (e.g. from t_x to t_y) with the advance of knowledge, even though at each of these times t_x, t_y, etc., taken by itself, we are correct to judge the preferential probability to have remained the same over a period

$t_0 \ldots t_n$ during which previous advances to knowledge took place.

Now, as I have argued repeatedly, the proper way to explain the variability over time of our ordinary judgments of probability is to regard such judgments as relational in character. It is therefore most ironic that a process which so manifests the relational character of probability judgments — the revision of ordinary judgments over time — leads us to belief that probabilities do not change with the acquisition of new knowledge, but at least we have uncovered the cause of this above. Not only do we revise ordinary present tense statements on the basis of the information currently available, but we also so revise ordinary past tense statements, giving the impression that there has been no change in the probability of the phenomenon over the time (up to the present) during which our knowledge has advanced.

This analysis also supports my contention that objective probabilities — which do not depend on our state of knowledge — are merely hypostatizations or reifications of (wholly unnecessary) entities to correspond to our progressive revision of ordinary probability judgments. At any given moment of time a statement made then on the probability of a phenomenon — with no body of evidence mentioned — will naturally (and correctly) be interpreted as about a single entity (this, on my view, is a single logical relation to a particular body of evidence); if in addition we believe (again correctly) at each stage of knowledge that the probability of the phenomenon has remained constant from earlier periods to the present during which there have been changes in knowledge — because at *that* stage we judge the probability for earlier times relative to currently available information — we will naturally (but mistakenly) think that the probability is one entity which obtains independently of our state of knowledge, i.e. a so-called objective probability.

Probability and Physical States

With this analysis of the origin — and consequences — of the intuitive belief that probabilities do not change with advances in knowledge to hand, we may turn to consider a closely related aspect of objective accounts of probability, the idea (specifically argued for by Blackburn) that the truth conditions for judgments of probability *must* be empirical conditions of the world, for it is changes in the physical factors associated with an event which are ordinarily thought to affect its probability. Now, no doubt, changes in the physical factors associated with an event do affect its probability, but the relational theorist can give a (reasonably) simple account of this: changes in the physical states associated with an event also change what sets of statements can be used as evidence about it. While this appears at first to be a straightforward enough explanation, there are several complications caused by the argument I have just given which require detailed attention.

Just above I claimed that we do not intuitively regard the probability of an event as changed by increases in knowledge because at every stage in the development of our knowledge we will judge the probability of the event to be, and always to have been, that which is relative to the total evidence currently available. Why, then, do we regard the probability of an event to be changed when the physical factors associated with it are altered? In those cases where we come to learn of the alterations we could, in principle, judge the probability of the event to be, and always to have been, that which is relative to the currently held information including knowledge of the changed circumstances, that is, to be unchanged over the time during which the physical change in question occurs.

The answer is that when a physical factor a associated with an event changes from F to G at time t_n, sets of conjoined statements including specification that factor a is G will only be regarded by us as evidence relevant to what the probability of the event was at times *after* t_n. The rather obvious reason we do not use sets of statements involving the proposition 'a is G' to determine what the probability in question was before t_n is that before t_n, a was F.

This is to say little more than that the evidence we use to determine the bulk of probability statements are sets of statements we believe to be true. Although of course many judgments about unique probabilities have been made relative to sets of statements including false ones, people do not seriously make judgments about the unique probability of an event on the basis of statements they believe are false. (Indeed I think we would regard anyone who did so as quite irrational.) Accordingly, when we make a judgment as to what the unique probability of an event is, we will use only statements which we regard to be true. Similarly, when we judge what the unique probability of an event was at an earlier time, we will use as evidence only statements which we now regard to have been true of the event at that earlier time.

This simple point suffices to explain why we regard changes in the physical factors associated with an event as changing the unique probability of the event. Let us revert to an example of Eclipse's chance of winning the 2.30; if at 12.00 our gangster's assistant dopes Eclipse, we would all regard him as having effectively altered his chances, just as, on an intuitive level, we would wish to deny that he had done so by discovering some new relevant information, e.g. about his having the flu. The crucial difference between his uncovering new information at 12.00 and his doping Eclipse at 12.00 is that the information he uncovers pertains to Eclipse's physical condition prior to 12.00, as well as after. Accordingly such information can be used at any time as part of the evidence relevant to what Eclipse's chances were both before and after 12.00. In the case of the doping, it is not true that he was doped before 12.00, and so information of his drugged condition can only be used in assessing what his chances were after 12.00.

Thus when at, say, 2.15 we reflect on what Eclipse's chances were before and after 12.00, we will regard the two cases quite differently. Using all the information currently available about the event as it was prior to 12.00 we will, in the case of our having discovered that he had the flu, regard his chances as having been as low prior to 12.00 as they are after 12.00 — at both times his chances are low relative to this information. In the case of doping, however, we will at 2.15 judge his chances to have been good prior to 12.00 but poor afterwards. Relative to all the information we have at 2.15 about the event as it was prior to 12.00, his chances are, and were, good; relative to all the information we now have about the event as it was after 12.00, his chances are quite poor.

Put generally, the probability judgments made relative to evidence including specification of a relevant physical factor as it was after a change at time t_n will of course be different from those made relative to evidence not including this information. (This is just what we mean by calling the change 'relevant'.) Since evidence including specification of this factor will not ever be used by us to assess what the probability was prior to t_n, but will, if known, be used to assess what it was after t_n, we will quite rightly regard the event's probability as changed by this change in the physical circumstances. But it is then quite mistaken to use this fact to criticize a relational account of probability: the real reason that we regard the probability of an event as changing when physical factors associated with it change is that different bodies of evidence can be used to access what the probability was before and after the change, and this is wholly compatible with the relational theorist's account.

As the reader will have appreciated, this account of why changes in the physical conditions associated with an event determine changes in the probability of the event — without thereby constituting the truth conditions of statements of probability — depends on a distinction between sets of statements (as evidence) which apply to the event before the time the change occurs and those which do not. Although at an intuitive level this distinction should be perfectly clear, it does raise at least one longstanding problem bearing directly on the probability of future events — the question of the truth value of statements pertaining to the future, as in Aristotle's problem of 'The Sea Battle Tomorrow'. To take an example of the change from F to G at time t_n (where the event will transpire or fail to transpire at a time t_r later than t_n), we see that if a was F at t_m prior to t_n, it is (arguably) the case that at t_m it was true that at t_n a would become G. If the presence of G makes the event far more likely at the appropriate t_r, then (again, equally arguably) at any time t_n or later when we assess what the probability was at t_m, we should use as relevant evidence the fact that at t_m it was the case that at t_n a would become G. In terms of our example of Eclipse being doped at 12.00 for the 2.30, we should, by this line of argument, hold at 2.15 that at 11.30 his chances were quite poor because at 11.30 it was the case that at 12.00 he would be doped for the 2.30.

Of course such a line of argument is highly unwelcome for it becomes difficult, if not impossible, to see why we regard the probability of an event to be changed by changes in the physical circumstances surrounding the event. The origin of this difficulty is fairly clear: if propositions about the future are true or false at earlier times (an assumption many have regarded as being brought into question by Aristotle's discussion of the Sea Battle), then a physical change at time t_n in a factor associated with an event will always entail some true proposition about the event as it was prior to t_n specifying the change to occur later. If such a statement is permitted as evidence relevant to assessing what the probability of the event was *prior* to t_n, there is no reason to think that the change at t_n of the physical factor affects the event's probability. This argument, in effect, erases the distinction between evidence which applies to an event before a change occurs and evidence which applies after, and it was by reference to just such a distinction that I hoped to explain how changes in the physical circumstances surrounding an event changed the probability of the event.

Although I believe such a distinction is both viable and important, it may, at the moment. appear that the theories of objective chance I have criticized have a clear advantage in this regard; by identifying the truth conditions of probability judgments with physical conditions, rather than relations to sets of sentences or propositions (bodies of evidence), such theories apparently can give a simple account of why changes in the physical condition associated with an event change the probability of that event: the physical conditions simply are the truth condition for the probability judgments. But the argument cited in the previous paragraphs cuts both ways: if it is correct, the objectivist is in just as much difficulty as anyone in accounting for our ordinary belief that changes in the physical condition associated with an event give rise to changes in the probability of the event. The difficulty the objectivist faces can be put this way: for any change in the physical conditions associated with an event at time t_n (e.g. our change from F to G), there will obtain a corresponding physical condition associated with the event *prior* to time t_n, namely the condition that the event is of such a kind that from time t_n onwards a will be G.

Once we have admitted as a physical condition obtaining prior to t_n the circumstance that from t_n onwards a particular factor obtains, there is no easy way for the objectivist to explain how the probability value of an event is changed by changes in the physical conditions surrounding an event. Although, to employ our example, a changed from F (at t_m) to G at time t_n (thus constituting one change in the physical conditions surrounding the event), another material condition remained unchanged from time t_m to t_n, the condition that from t_n onwards a would be G. Why should we not consider the condition obtaining at t_m, that from t_n onwards a is G, in assessing the probability of the event at t_m, and so conclude that the probability remains the same from t_m to t_n despite the change of a from F to G? Put another way, if at t_m it is the case that a will be G from t_n onwards, then would not the objective probability at time t_m be determined by this 'fact'?

Once again, now on an objective theory of chance, we are faced with the difficulty of accounting for the ordinary belief that the change of a from F to G at t_n changes the probability of the event in question. Here one may be tempted to deny that there are such 'physical conditions' as 'a being G from t_n onwards' which can obtain prior to t_n. In one sense I am in sympathy with such a proposal — it seems to me very similar to maintaining that there is a useful distinction between evidence which applies to an event before a change takes place and evidence which applies afterwards — but it is important to see what is involved in such a move. One cannot simply stipulate that all genuine physical conditions must be definable without use of temporal predicates involving a future time, for, although it is such reference to a future time that causes the difficulty here, many genuine scientific properties — constituting physical conditions associated with events in the laboratory -- necessarily involve such temporal predicates. What is required to resolve the difficulty posed above for objective theories of probability is a general method for distinguishing physical conditions, such as the properties F and G, changes among which genuinely affect the probability of an event, and so-called physical conditions involving changes in those properties at future times (e.g. it being the case from t_n onwards that a is G); the latter so-called conditions remain the same during the time in which the former changes occur and thus cannot be regarded as material to the probability of the event in question, if this is to change over time. I do not doubt that there is such a distinction — though it seems to me rather difficult to make precise. However, the important thing to note is that such a distinction allows the relational theorist, as well as the objectivist, to account for the intuition that probability values change with changes in the physical conditions associated with an event.

That is to say, once we have available the distinction between genuine physical conditions, such as 'a being F' or 'a being G', and those involving reference to future changes in these conditions, we may simply (and naturally) stipulate that the only sets of sentences specifying genuine physical conditions can be used as evidence in assessing the probability of an event. Thus, for example, while 'a is F', 'a is G', etc., could be used as evidence in assessing what the probability of an event was at time t_m — with 'a is G' ruled out as it does not apply at t_m — 'a is G from t_n' onwards cannot be used as evidence in assessing the probability at t_m — although, arguably, it applies — as it involves the kind of illegitimate physical condition including reference to the future which no theory of probability, relational or objective, can permit to be used in the assessment of probabilities.

Admittedly I have not provided here a satisfactory characterization of this distinction between genuine and illegitimate physical conditions, but I hope it is clear by now that any objective theory of probability, which might appear to provide an alternative to the relational approach I advocate, must rely on just such a distinction to explain the way changes in the physical conditions associated with an event change the probability of it. And, to conclude, this means that the relational account of probability provided by the l.r.t. is no more or less capable than objective theories of explaining why probabilities change with changing physical conditions.

Probabilities of 1 and 0

Of the specific arguments we examined earlier concerning objective features of our concept of probability, it only remains for us to consider Blackburn's contention that any account of probability that did justice to these features leads to the unhappy conclusion that probability values are usually 1 or 0, but that we ordinarily do not know which. Actually it is quite easy to avoid this conclusion on a relational account of probability (cf. Hacking, 1965, p. 24), but the reasoning which apparently leads to this conclusion is so closely bound up with our practice of revising probability judgments in the light of new evidence — and thus to the entire question of the objectivity of probability judgments — that we cannot avoid examining it in detail.

We may begin by recalling from the previous chapter that we could be led to the conclusion that probabilities are usually 1 or 0 (but that we do not ordinarily know which) by applying criteria for available evidence inappropriate to the context in question: if we employed the objective criterion to a gambling situation with explicit or implicit rules forbidding certain procedures of measurement, we would reach the unwelcome conclusion that games of 'chance' were not genuinely probabilistic. But it was admitted at the time that this was only a partial solution to such difficulties, and that a more serious form of the problem was not resolved by the proposals in Chapter III.

The most serious form of this problem — and the one which is most closely connected with objective theories of probability — is this: if probabilities are absolute values not changed by the acquisition of new knowledge, the very real possibility of our eventually predicting an event with certainty means that, all along, the probability for that event will have been 0 or 1. Our current judgments of other probability values must therefore be regarded as mistaken estimates based on insufficient evidence. As we have seen, proponents of objective theories of chance do believe that probability values remain constant despite changes in knowledge, so they are of course liable to be driven to such a conclusion, as Blackburn noted. Mellor only avoids such a conclusion by denying determinism; this blocks the argument in question by denying that we will eventually be able to predict the outcome of all events with certainty. Such a move, familiar though it is, is unhappy in its own right: whatever we think of determinism, it seems undesirable to formulate a theory of probability which depends on its denial. As Hacking, who is regarded by Mellor as advocating views similar to his own, has argued, 'far be it from a theory of chance to preclude that august philosophical ogre [determinism].' (1965, p. 24.) This contrasts markedly with Mellor, who begins his chapter on the relationship between propensities and determinism by remarking: 'If propensities are ever displayed, determinism is false.' (1971, p. 151.)

In fact, I believe the account of probability I have given so far does justice to objective features of our discourse on probability without denying determinism, and the considerations I have adduced in favour of it show what has gone wrong in the reasoning by which we are apparently faced with the choice of denying determinism or concluding that probability values are ordinarily 1 or 0. Blackburn himself provides a very clear example of this reasoning (1973, pp. 103-6) and we can usefully consider it in some detail: after considering the example of a gangster and his assistant attempting to change the probability of Eclipse winning the 2.30, Blackburn formulates his 'Supervenience Condition' (SC):

> (SC) A change in the probability of an event entails a change in some of the conditions which affect or may be going to affect the occurrence of the event.

Blackburn then asks us to imagine someone extremely knowledgeable about the world, both in regard to particular facts and general laws:

> Call this man the Present Tense Knowledgeable Being: PKB for short. Now I say that the probability of Eclipse winning the 2.30 is very high. Let us suppose that he disagrees. Inevitably he wins the argument ... I start off making my probability assertion, and for each piece of evidence I produce, the PKB can produce more, qualify my evidence, show its lack of significance, show that other events are in train which mean it is irrelevant, or in some way demonstrate that he has a better basis for prediction than me. And at each stage of the argument I will express my defeat by admitting that the probability is not as high as I thought.

So far, of course, there is no problem, but Blackburn continues:

> Now suppose that the PKB's knowledge falls short of actually entailing that Eclipse will or will not win. Suppose that all that he can do is assert that the probability is that Eclipse will not win. Then it is logically possible that there should exist a superior PKB — one with a shade more knowledge — who could in turn use his acquaintance with what is the case to make the original PKB admit

that the probability of Eclipse is higher, or lower, than he took it to be. And we can imagine an endless hierarchy of possible revision, until eventually someone's knowledge enables him to deduce the outcome of the race. We can express this as a Revision Condition: (RC) For any aggregate of knowledge K about what is the case and what laws exist, if on the basis of K we think that the probability of an event has some value other than 0 or 1, it is always logically possible that someone by adding to K, should make us admit that the probability of the event has some higher or lower value than we took it to have.

Blackburn then points out that (SC), which 'forbids us to suppose that the mere existence of a PKB alters the probability of the event', taken with (RC) apparently

> lead hopelessly to the conclusion that probabilities are really all 0 or 1, or near to 0 or 1, but that in the absence of a PKB we do not know which. For if a PKB does not alter the probability of an event and if he can always make us revise our estimate unless that reaches something near 0 or 1, it follows that the actual probability is something near 0 or 1, but that we do not normally know which.

Besides its status as a formal argument, Blackburn here has admirably put his finger on many of the considerations which prompt the ordinary layman to reflect that, perhaps after all, unbeknown to us, probabilities are generally 1 or 0, save for events which are intrinsically indeterministic. Put at its most intuitive level, the argument is that the possibility of certain knowledge about the outcome of future events (perhaps now possessed by God alone) entails the possibility that such events are already somehow certain, despite our current ignorance. Then, just as we saw with Mellor, one is naturally lead to deep ruminations on determinism: if many of the events we ordinarily regard as probabilistic are truly so, then it can only be due to an indeterminacy in the causal structure of the world. Current scientific theory in quantum mechanics may be called on to bolster such a position, followed perhaps by reflections on the freedom of will in human action.

But such ruminations, whether on an intuitive level by the layman or a systematic one by the philosopher of science, are beside the point: both Blackburn's detailed argument and the parallel intuitive line of reasoning are mistaken. Blackburn's argument depends on the assumption, formulated in (SC), that probability values do not change with the acquisition of new knowledge, and I have of course tried to explain how such an assumption is wrong. But condition (SC), mistaken though it is, would not in itself lead to the conclusion that probabilities are generally 1 or 0, despite our ignorance of the actual value. What leads to this conclusion is the combination of condition (SC) with the condition (RC), which in my opinion, simply states a possibility that shows probability values do change with additions to knowledge — the possibility being that of progressive revision to probability judgments in the light of new evidence.

It is obvious that Blackburn's condition (RC) depends on precisely the kind of revision we considered at length in this chapter. 'Each stage of the argument' in which we are made to admit 'defeat' in the face of information brought to our attention by a PKB, and each stage where a less informed PKB admits defeat to a logically possible superior PKB, constitutes a stage in which previous elliptical judgments of probability are assessed as incorrect relative to an increased body of evidence made available by the pronouncements of a PKB. As pointed out earlier, the sequence of successively revised judgments of unique probability which condition (RC) thus relies on is just the kind of sequence which, according to the relational theorist, exhibits a change in the preferential or unique probability of an event with additions to our knowledge (see for example p. 136). Given that condition (RC) was coupled by Blackburn with a condition (SC), denying such a change, it is hardly surprising that the two together lead to unwelcome, but incorrect, conclusions.

Perhaps as important as seeing where Blackburn's argument went wrong is seeing why it might appear convincing at all — indeed if we understand this, we will also see why many people are intuitively attracted by arguments resembling Blackburn's. In fact these arguments contain a germ, or rather two germs, of truth. As to the first, assuming we eventually reach the stage of knowledge at which we can predict with certainty the outcome of an event, then it is true that *even now* the probability of that event is 1 or 0. Here the reader may be forgiven for thinking I have unwittingly accepted the nub of Blackburn's and thus cannot avoid his conclusions but this is not so — as a relational theorist, I believe probability statements only make sense when understood relative to some body of evidence, and this, as before, is crucial. Relative to the knowledge with which we can predict its outcome with certainty, the probability of a given event is now, has been, and will always be, 1 or 0. Of course, relative to different bodies of evidence, the probability of the event will be different. Blackburn's error from this point of view is twofold.

First of all he is quite mistaken in emphasizing, as he does, that knowledge sufficient to predict the outcome with certainty will, if it becomes available, show that the probability now is *really* 0 or 1. All that is the case is that relative to such knowledge the probability is now 0 or 1: but it is equally true that relative to, say, current knowledge, the probability is now different. The probability of the event is not *really* either 1 or 0 or a different value. *The* probability is not really anything in itself; it is always a relation that can only be spoken of when some particular body of evidence is understood.

Blackburn, however, persistently speaks of *the* probability of the event without reference to any body of evidence — indeed he argues that relational accounts indicating the need for such references are mistaken. But on the relational account — which I tried to show meets all of Blackburn's objections — such talk of 'the probability' must be understood as relative to the total evidence available at the time the statement is made. And this is the other part of Blackburn's error: if anything deserves at the moment to be spoken of as the *real* probability, it could only be that probability which is relative to currently available evidence — this alone is what we can mean when we speak now in elliptical fashion of 'the' probability. Thus it is quite misguided to conclude from the fact the probability of the event is now 1 or 0, relative to some knowledge, that the real probability is now this *simpliciter*. If it is now really anything, when no mention of evidence is made, it is the value relative to the evidence currently available.

However, even this error contains a second germ of truth: in discussions of this kind it is all too easy to think of probability values relative to evidence other than the total amount currently available, for in doing so we simply employ (or rather misemploy) the precept of using the total evidence available. In Blackburn's argument we are specifically asked to imagine a situation in which more and more evidence becomes available, until there is sufficient knowledge to predict the outcome with certainty — in the parallel intuitive argument we imagine a body of knowledge (perhaps now known to God) which, again, is sufficient to predict the outcome with certainty. Having imagined, or hypothesized, the existence of such extensive evidence we implicitly rely on it, rather than the currently available evidence, when we consider what the probability of the event is; and, of course, relative to it the probability now is 1 or 0. The reason we rely on this evidence rather than the actual evidence available seems to me to be the familiar practical maxim to employ the total evidence available rather than a lesser body. In the argument in question we specifically are asked to envision a PKB who makes such additional information available and we then rely on this greater body of knowledge to assess the probability of the event; since it is quite correct that relative to such body of evidence the probability is now 1 or 0, we conclude that this is the most preferable, or real, probability now *simpliciter* — omitting as usual any reference to the body of evidence we have in mind. The problem, of course, is that by hypothesizing a body of evidence as available — via a PKB — we do not actually make it so, and thus cannot actually use it to determine what 'the probability' of the event is. If we do not explicitly mention evidence, this can only be the probability relative to the total evidence actually — not hypothetically — available.

In fact Blackburn's error in confounding the total evidence actually available with a totality hypothetically available seems to me symptomatic of a deeper confusion, one which, I think, can only be clarified on the basis of our earlier discussion of possibilities in principle and possibilities in practice. Since Blackburn's error here not only parallels an intuitive mode of reasoning, but also exhibits features similar to (fallacious) reasoning on statistical probabilities, I will conclude this chapter, and prepare the way for next, by explicitly stating the connection of his argument to that earlier discussion.

The bodies of knowledge possessed by each of Blackburn's PKB's are simply finite bodies of evidence, any of which, in my view, can *in principle* be used by us to determine the truth of an ordinary probability statement. Indeed our present capacity to recognize the relevance of the hypothesized pronouncements of Blackburn's succession of PKB's to determinations of probability for the event in question simply reflects the fact that such bodies of evidence are the means by which we can recognize the truth of ordinary probability statements; thus this capacity is simply part of our mastery of the meaning of probability statements. The reason we regard the pronouncement of each successive PKB as *superseding* that of earlier ones is, however, a precept governing the practical application of relational probability judgments to guide our actions: the requirement of total evidence.

Now on a number of occasions I have pointed out the importance of distinguishing the means by which we can actually (or in practice) decide the truth of an ordinary probability statement with a specific practical purpose in mind and the means by which it is in principle possible to do so and this is just what has become confused in Blackburn's argument: to guide our action on a given occasion with an ordinary probability statement we must actually — or in practice — decide the truth of that statement. To do so we must use some body of evidence (and an appropriate logical relation), and the best we can do is follow the requirement of total evidence and use the total evidence which can in practice be ascertained, i.e. the total amount actually available. This will be limited by the technology then extant and, in particular, will not include bodies of evidence of a kind known only to God or Blackburn's hypothetical PKB. Although such bodies of evidence can in principle be used to determine the truth of our ordinary statement, they cannot be so used in practice at the time in question.

Thus it would be quite misguided to think of the bodies of evidence known to a hypothetical PKB as serving via the requirement of total evidence as the basis for determining at a given time the truth of an ordinary statement: the requirement of total evidence is a practical precept intended to guide our (actual) actions, and for this purpose a possibility in principle only is quite useless. However, in effect, this is just what Blackburn has done by regarding the hypothesized knowledge of each superior PKB as 'superseding' that of any lesser being: probability judgments made relative to the total evidence available do supersede (or are preferable to) those made on lesser bodies of evidence, when we wish to make a practical decision on a course of action; however, since we cannot in practice use the hypothetical knowledge of a PKB to guide our action, probability judgments relative to such knowledge do not in any way supersede those made relative to the total evidence actually available at the time we wish to act. Thus, as I remarked on p. 147 at the end of a more intuitive discussion of Blackburn's error, when we speak elliptically of the probability of an event — by which we mean the probability most desirable for the purpose of action — this can only be the probability relative to the total evidence actually available.

V
STATISTICAL PROBABILITIES

Although I have not yet specifically discussed statistical evidence, the argument of the last chapter carries over from the case of specificatory evidence to that of statistical evidence and, I believe, provides the key to understanding what has often been called 'statistical probability': my view is that most of the intuitions which seem to favour a distinct concept of statistical probability can be explained as intuitions about probability values relative to statistical evidence; in a similar way, all the main formal techniques developed by statisticians and employed by scientists for inferring probabilities from statistical data can be understood as techniques for using statistical evidence to determine the relational probabilities of the l.r.t. Obviously this is a considerable claim that will require a lengthy justification − the more so, because it is the notion of 'statistical probability' (variously explicated) which has most often been put forward by objectivists as a rival to the l.r.t.'s conception of inductive probability.

In any event, we would have to spend a good deal of time examining the notion of 'statistical evidence', for, on my view, it is such evidence, and such evidence alone, that allows us to determine numerical probabilities. That is to say, I have argued that the measure function we should employ to determine logical probabilities is what Carnap called $\lambda = 0$. Such a measure function only determines probabilities relative to statistical evidence of observed frequency and so such evidence plays a central role in my account of probability.

As a preliminary to analysing the notion of statistical evidence in detail, it may be useful to make explicit certain assumptions implicit in the last two chapters concerning the relationship between statistical and specificatory evidence. When I speak of the statistical evidence relevant to the probability of a specific outcome, I mean a body of evidence concerning results in a series of trials similar to the one under consideration. Of course 'similarity' is a notably flexible concept, relative to the properties we have in mind — event A may be similar to event B in respect of some properties and different in respect of others — but this is precisely where specificatory evidence comes in. For any body of specificatory evidence about a particular trial — say, that the trial is one in which a die of such and such a weight and balance is tossed — there will exist a similarity class of sets of trials which are also tosses of die weighted and balanced in just this way. Statements about results in any such set constitute what I understand as statistical evidence relevant to the outcome of tosses of die weighted and balanced in this way. A question closely related to one discussed at length by frequency theorists is just how to define the similarity class that is to be taken in determining *the* probability of a particular individual event, e.g. this toss of this die. The answer is implicit in the last chapter — the similarity class we use for this purpose is that corresponding to the total available specificatory evidence relevant to the outcome in question. Thus if we know nothing else relevant about this toss of this die, save that it is a toss of a die with such and such a weight and balance imparted with a particular velocity, the statistical evidence which would be relevant to the outcome would be reports of the results of trials consisting of tosses of dice with this construction, given the same initial velocity.

In general, on my view, when we determine a preferential, or unique, probability to guide our action over a particular event, we consider all the relevant specificatory evidence, then consider a body of statistical evidence concerning the frequencies in trials of the kind specified in that body of specificatory evidence; finally we assign a numerical probability to the outcome on the basis of a particular measure function on that body of statistical evidence, and, for the reasons given earlier, I myself favour $\lambda = 0$ as a measure function[†]. This of course still

---

[†] In this sketch of the way statistical evidence combines with specificatory evidence to determine the unique or preferential numerical probability desired for the purpose of action, I have deliberately skirted over a number of problems centring on the question of how we use statistical evidence to determine what physical attributes are 'relevant' to particular outcomes. I believe there are no insurmountable difficulties for the l.r. theorist in this area; however, as indicated in the introduc-

Statistical Probabilities

leaves open the question of just how much statistical evidence we should use — just which of a number of different possible sets of alternatives containing different numbers of trials — in determining the unique or preferential probability for a given individual event. This is one of the questions I will deal with later in this chapter.

This much said as a preliminary, we may now turn to our main concern in this chapter, the question of how statistical evidence relates to objectivists' conception of statistical probability. As I see it, many probability theorists (Carnap included) have accepted the existence of a concept of statistical probability not reducible to that of inductive, or epistemic, probability solely because we are willing to revise probability judgments when new statistical evidence is uncovered; it is for this reason that I have delayed discussion of the entire topic of statistical probability until this point. As explained in the last chapter, our willingness to revise probability judgments seems at first glance to conflict with the conception of probability judgments as logically true; on closer analysis, we see this impression is deeply mistaken, for the central tenet of the l.r.t. is that elliptical judgments (which are what people usually have in mind when discussing these issues) are relative to evidence, and so require revision when one body of evidence supersedes another as the basis for the elliptical judgment. It is particularly important to keep this in mind when we are concerned with statistical evidence and I will begin my analysis of the idea of statistical probability by examining the way various writers have tried to exploit our willingness to revise, or reject, probability statements in the light of changing statistical evidence to formulate theories of objective statistical probability.

REJECTION RULES AND EMPIRICAL PROBABILITY

Logical relation theorists have previously noted that one important belief of scientists on the connection of probability and frequency can

---

tion, a careful examination of the way scientists determine relevance and independence would involve, *inter alia*, examination of the χ^2 method of testing and random selection procedures. I think it is possible — indeed illuminating — to analyse these matters in terms of the l.r.t., but the issues involved are highly complex and require separate treatment.

easily be accommodated on the l.r.t.: the belief that an event with probability p can be 'expected' to occur with frequency p 'in the long run'. Lewis (1946, p. 291) pointed out that any numerical judgment of probability can be construed as an estimate of a numerically equal frequency in the long run, and this idea was subsequently formulated quite precisely by Carnap. All probability$_1$ values in Carnap's system are also probability$_1$ mean estimates of frequency (a balance of possible frequencies weighted by the probability$_1$ each frequency has of occurring); the reason scientists expect a phenomenon with probability p to exhibit p as a figure in a large finite series of trials (or for that matter an infinite series) can then be explained by the fact that p is the most rational, i.e. probability$_1$ mean, estimate of frequency in any class, finite or otherwise.

But this analysis does not explain another perhaps more important feature of scientists' beliefs (and practices) concerning probability and frequency — the belief that subsequent observation of a frequency in a finite sample outside the interval $p \pm \lambda\sigma$ provides grounds for rejecting an earlier hypothesis that the probability of the phenomenon in question is p. The possibility of such a rejection is precisely why the initial value of p — based on our initial observations — is regarded as an *estimate* of probability, and this feature of scientists' beliefs on probability has never been satisfactorily explained by l.r. theorists. In the end, I believe that the practice of rejecting hypotheses about numerical probabilities in the light of observation of frequencies outside such intervals can be explained in terms of the l.r.t., but on first analysis such a practice does appear to favour an empirical conception of probability: on an empirical conception of probability the rejection of an earlier probability hypothesis in the light of subsequent observations on frequency can be viewed as the outcome of an empirical test of the probability hypothesis.

Empirical tests are of course fundamental to science, and if a particular hypothesis is to be accepted or rejected on the basis of certain empirical data, it is wholly natural to interpret that data as constituting an empirical test of the hypothesis. But in the case of probability hypotheses, this is tantamount to accepting the concept of empirical or statistical probability, which Carnap called probability$_2$: granted that a concept's meaning is given by its truth conditions (or at least its assertion conditions), there seems no alternative but to admit that the concept of probability employed by scientists is one of long-run frequency, for our 'tests' for hypotheses on the probability of specific

Statistical Probabilities

phenomena are tests involving observation of the frequency occurring in various samples.

In this context it is significant that various philosophers who favour a theory of 'objective chance', or 'empirical probability', have explicitly appealed to procedures for rejecting probability statements to support their theory of probability. When Popper accepted the frequency theory of probability, he characterized it as a 'physical definition of probability' and emphasized that the 'value [of probability] is empirically determined through a long series of experiments to any degree of approximation' (1968, p. 198). Popper believed that the procedures for rejecting probability statements on the basis of observations of frequency were the *experimental* procedures which determined the value of this physical probability: the rejection procedures can readily be interpreted as procedures for falsifying probability statements, and Popper of course held that genuine attempts to falsify statements or hypotheses were, *par excellence*, empirical tests of those statements.

Braithwaite offered a similar, but far more elaborate, argument in favour of construing the rejection procedures found in statistics as empirical tests of probability hypotheses. (I should point out that what Braithwaite (and others) mean by the term 'probability hypothesis' is what I called in previous chapters an 'elliptical' probability statement or judgment, namely one indicating a numerical value of probability, but omitting mention of evidence. I have already used the term in this sense in this chapter, and will continue to do so.) Braithwaite was unwilling to accept the standard frequency theory's identification of empirical probability with limit of frequency in an infinite series of trials, but did believe observed frequencies were crucial to the meaning of probability statements: he claimed that rules for rejecting probability statements fixed, in and of themselves, an empirical meaning for probability statements, much in the way that rules of truth, or specification of truth conditions, are usually thought to fix the meaning of a particular concept. Like Popper, Braithwaite also claimed that the data on which a hypothesis might be rejected provided an empirical test of the hypothesis (1953, p. 191). Pressed to explain how empirical tests of probability hypotheses could also constitute rules for fixing the meaning of those hypotheses, Braithwaite appealed to the traditional positivist account of theoretical concepts in science: the meaning of theoretical terms is often said to depend on the observational consequences derived from theoretical hypotheses, and if the derived observational consequences are not observed, scientists reject the theoretical hypotheses. For Braithwaite, probability hypotheses were similar: their meaning was to be explained in terms of a class of derived observational results, which would have to occur if we were not to reject the probability hypothesis in question.

This theory seems to me particularly interesting because of its apparently anti-realist character, and it has heavily influenced the anti-realist account of statistical reasoning I will present in later sections of this chapter; as such, it will be useful to consider it in some detail, and, it turns out, its shortcomings indicate the limitations inherent on objective theories of statistical probabilities.

Braithwaite's Theory

Braithwaite's suggestion that standard scientific procedures for rejecting probability hypotheses fix an empirical meaning for those hypotheses appears, on the surface, to accord admirably with an anti-realist conception of probability. The information on frequency which serves as the grounds for rejecting probability hypotheses may naturally be thought of as the evidence, or means, by which we recognize the truth and falsity of such hypotheses. Indeed Braithwaite's theory appears to be just the kind of anti-realist, yet objective, theory of probability that was canvassed as a possibility in Chapter I. The suggestion there, eventually rejected, was that an objective, yet anti-realist, theory of probability could be given by stating finitely ascertainable conditions which justified the assertion (or conversely the rejection) of statements on empirical probability; crucially, the justification for the assertion or rejection of a probability statement was, on this proposal, to be probabilistic; that is, the conditions which justified assertion or rejection of the probability statement were conditions which made that statement *probably* true or *probably* false. This is precisely the proposal made by Braithwaite:

> Consider now the sentence 'The probability of a birth being the birth of a male is 51/100' or, as it is synonymously expressed, '51 per cent of births are male births' — a case of the general form of proposition expressed by 'the probability of a member of β being a member of a is p', where p denotes a proper fraction, i.e. a rational number between 0 and 1. This form of sentence is given a meaning by the following rule of rejection (to be called a k-rule-of-rejection): choose any small positive number k (e.g. 1/20). On the basis of a set of n observations of members of β, reject the hypo-

thesis that the probability is p that a member of β is a member of a if the a ratio is this set of n observations (i.e. the number of members of a in this set divided by n) is less than $p - \sqrt{\frac{pq}{nk}}$ or is greater than $p + \sqrt{\frac{pq}{nk}}$. (1953, pp. 153-4)

As Braithwaite makes clear, the mathematical basis for his proposal is the Chebyshev inequality for the binomial distribution. Roughly speaking, this states that for binomial trials with probability p (i.e. those with a constant and independent probability of p), there is a probability of less than $k^{\frac{1}{2}}$ that the frequency in a series of n trials will be outside the interval $p \pm k\sqrt{\frac{pq}{n}}$. Equivalently, there is a probability less than k that the frequency will be outside the interval $p \pm \sqrt{\frac{pq}{nk}}$. The interest of this theorem is that it holds for any binomial probability p whatsoever, and this is what permits Braithwaite (following standard statistical practice) to use it for inferring the probability less than k of rejecting a true probability hypothesis, even when we do not know what probability hypothesis is true. By the Chebyshev inequality, no matter what probability p obtains, there is a probability less than k of rejecting it by the rule: reject if the observed frequency is outside the interval $p \pm \sqrt{\frac{pq}{nk}}$.

As we have noted repeatedly, all 'objective' theories of probability involve the possibility that probability judgments may be revised indefinitely, and Braithwaite's theory is no exception: 'Since we can never know at any one stage whether or not further observations, which we have not made, would reject the hypothesis at a later stage, we can never know that a hypothesis is to be definitely rejected.' (1953, p. 160.) Braithwaite considers the objection that *provisional* rules for rejecting probability statements do not provide an adequate meaning for them, but tries to refute this suggestion:

> Does this provisional character of the k-rule-of-rejection imply that it will not serve to give an empirical meaning to statements of statistical hypotheses i.e. to probability statements? I think not . . . It seems to me that we perfectly well can take as the criterion for empirical meaningfulness that there should be empirical conditions under which the statement in question would be accepted or empirical conditions under which it would be rejected — irrespective of whether such acceptance or rejection is definitive or is provisional and capable of revision on the basis of further experience. With this extended 'verification' criterion, the k-rule-of-rejection gives empirical meaning to probability statements. (ibid.)

This also accords with the suggestion in Chapter I concerning how an objectivist might formulate an anti-realist theory of probability — following remarks made by Dummett, we noted that such a theory would make probability judgments indefinitely subject to revision. Moreover, the statistical information on which a probability hypothesis is rejected or a previous rejection cancelled is, for Braithwaite, always finite, and of course this is required of an anti-realist theory.

But if the main body of argument of Chapter I is correct, there can be no viable anti-realist theory of objective or empirical probability along the lines Braithwaite envisions. Specifically, I argued that an objective or empirical theory of probability (which did not rely on a second epistemic concept of probability or confirmation) could not explain without circularity how we come to know the truth of probability statements from finite amounts of evidence. In effect, Braithwaite tries to resolve this problem by an appeal to mathematical techniques of statistical inference, and there is no doubt that the techniques that he refers to are customarily interpreted so as to allow us to infer the probability of a phenomenon from the evidence of small samples. Significantly, we only 'know' the probability of the original phenomenon to a second-order degree of probability — for example, we infer that there is a 95 per cent chance that we have not rejected a value within a certain interval of the true value — but our knowledge of this second order of probability is wholly certain, as it has been obtained by mathematical reasoning alone. This blocks the regress described in Chapter I, which arose through making the truth of probability statements an empirical matter itself only knowable probabilistically. The second-order judgment of probability in question then was in turn only knowable probabilistically, and so on *ad infinitum.* However, if our second-order judgment of probability is known with certainty, no such regress arises, and this is the effect of Braithwaite's proposal.

Unfortunately, though the circularity uncovered in Chapter I is blocked in this fashion, Braithwaite's theory generates a new and different circularity, and does so necessarily: mathematical techniques alone can never resolve the question of how a finite body of evidence justifies knowledge of a probability — our basic question — because the mathematical techniques only allow us to infer new probabilities from others of the same kind. If we cannot see how a certain 'objective' definition of probability justifies us in inferring the probability of a specific phenomenon on the basis of a finite amount of evidence, we cannot be reassured by being given other probabilities of the same

Statistical Probabilities

kind for more complex events, as our original doubts recur as queries about these second probabilities.

Such an objection applies with particular force to Braithwaite's theory: the mathematical reasoning — which of its nature cannot lay to rest any worries about the validity of a particular definition of probability — are invoked as meaning rules which fix the very meaning of probability statements. Braithwaite was acutely aware of the possibility that his proposal involved a vicious circularity of this kind, and went to some lengths to disabuse his readers of their natural inclination to regard his proposal as viciously circular:

> I do not wish to deny that there is a type of circularity involved in giving as the justification for the mode of definition of a probability statement another probability statement but it is not a vicious circularity; it does not vitiate the definition. What has happened is that we first give a rule according to which meaning is given to probability statements by virtue of there being such statements as are rejectable according to the rule on the basis of empirical knowledge; this provides a definition of probability statements as a particular sort of empirical statements. There is no circularity of any kind in using this method of definition. If then we ask why this method of definition should be used rather than any other, we are then asking for the reasons why probabilities defined in this way do what we want them to do; and the reason for this is another probability statement. Herein lies the circularity. But it vitiates nothing that has been said. (1953, p. 166)

Braithwaite was, I suppose, correct in maintaining that there was no vicious circularity in his definition of probability taken on its own — one can stipulate anything one chooses as the conditions for asserting or rejecting a particular kind of statement and this, for the anti-realist, fixes a particular meaning for that kind of statement. But then, as Braithwaite appreciated, there is the substantive question of showing this definition serves some purpose. In this case what is required is some demonstration that 'probabilities defined in this way [i.e. by the k-rejection rules] do what we want them to do', and it is just here that a vicious circularity arises. Specifically, in answer to our question as to the point of defining probability by use of the k-rejection rules, Braithwaite tells us that such a procedure ensures a low probability (less than k) of rejecting a true probability hypothesis. But what, on Braithwaite's theory, is a *probability less than k* of rejecting a true hypothesis? It is certainly not a limit of frequency less than k in an infinite series of trials, nor is it a proportion less than k in any *one* specific finite set of trials (see Braithwaite, 1953, pp. 122-6 for his statements on these points). On Braithwaite's theory, *meaning* is given to the statement that there is a probability less than k of a certain kind of occurrence by the k-rejection rule whose justification we are seeking. In effect, to justify the procedure of rejecting our first probability statement on the basis of a certain rule, we are only offered a statement whose meaning is a set of conditions *determined by the very same rule*. If we are in doubt as to the justification of rejecting the original probability statements in accordance with this rule, we are hardly going to be satisfied by being given a statement whose meaning is a set of conditions determined by the same rule.

Another way to put the objection is this: obviously no one wishes to reject true hypotheses of any kind and so, at first glance, it appears that we should adopt a policy with a low probability of rejecting true probability hypotheses. But the advantage of adopting such a policy depends on an antecedently understood — or independently accepted — definition of probability, one by which (to take two pertinent examples) a low probability of rejecting true hypotheses corresponds to a low limit of frequency of rejecting them in an infinite series of trials, or a low degree of rational credence in the statement that we will reject the true hypothesis. Since Braithwaite does not accept either the standard frequency definition or the l.r.t., he cannot appeal to either of these notions of probability to justify use of the k-rejection rules; appeal to his own definition of probability here is circular, as it is the justification of this definition which is in question.

Braithwaite obviously intended his theory to give a satisfactory explication of the idea that probability was 'frequency in the long run' with the concept of frequency in the long run defined by the k-rejection rules; accordingly a low probability of rejecting a true hypothesis is meant to be equivalent to 'a low frequency in the long run' of rejecting such hypotheses, and it certainly appears desirable to adopt the policies which lead to low frequencies in the long run of rejecting true hypotheses. But, again, this is to trade on some ordinary notion of frequency in the long run, and the difficulty is that Braithwaite does not accept such a notion of 'long-run frequency', but rather proposes to fix the meaning of this idea via his k-rejection rule. Since it has no independent meaning, he cannot, then, appeal to the 'long-run' success of the k-rejection rule in justifying its adoption.

Statistical Probabilities

Though there is obviously an appearance of circularity to Braithwaite's theory, the reader may be at something of a loss to decide the respective merits of our claims: Braithwaite believed there was a circularity in the justification of his definition of probability, but that was non-vicious, while I have just claimed the opposite. Though it might not be possible to settle this question at the highly theoretical level of what constitutes a vicious circularity in the justification of a definition of probability, it is notable that Braithwaite's one specific attempt to refute the charge that his definition involves a wholly arbitrary stipulation of rejection conditions fails, and fails for precisely the reason I have tried to bring out above. Braithwaite poses the question 'What is the reason for using this criterion [the k-rule of rejection] rather than any other' for fixing the meaning of probability statements? He goes on to consider a radical criticism of the k-rejection rule along these lines, namely

> that the criterion in no way connects the rejection of the hypothesis with its falsity rather than its truth, and that it is the distinction between the truth and falsity of a hypothesis with which an empirical criterion of meaningfulness must be concerned, and not the circumstances under which I, or indeed the 'cultural circle' of mathematical statisticians, agree to reject it. Unless some connection can be shown between rejection and falsity, the criterion is worse than useless, since to use it would delude us into thinking that there was some such connection.

He believes, mistakenly, that there is a reply to this criticism:

> Fortunately a quite satisfactory answer can be given by considering the extreme cases when the probability hypothesis states either that the probability of every member of β being a member of a is zero or that this probability is 1. For if this probability is zero, the hypothesis will be refuted if any observed member of β is found to be a member of a, since such an observation is logically incompatible with no member of β being a member of a, *which is what is asserted by the probability statement*. Consequently finding one member of the class $(a\,\beta)$ will prove the probability hypothesis to be false. But applying the k rule of rejection will reject the hypothesis if the a ratio in a set of n observation falls outside the interval $(0 - \sqrt{\frac{0(1-0)}{nk}}, 0 + \sqrt{\frac{0(1-0)}{nk}}$ i.e. if the a ratio differs from 0. Since this degenerate interval, which consists only of the point 0, does not

Statistical Probabilities

depend on the values of n and of k (provided that neither is 0), a k-rule-of-rejection will reject the hypothesis if, in any number n of observations, at least one member of a is found, whatever positive number k may be. Thus, for any positive n and for any positive k, the rule of rejection will reject those hypotheses ascribing a probability of 0 *which are false*. (1953, pp. 164-5, my italic)

After giving a parallel argument for the case of probability is equal to 1, Braithwaite concludes:

So in the cases in which the probability is either 0 or 1, to use the k-rule of rejection comes to the same thing as using the rule of rejecting statements known to be false. This establishes a connection between rejection and falsity in the two extreme cases, and thus seems to me to establish the required connection in the other cases also.

Whether establishing a connection between rejection and falsity in the two extreme cases would suffice to justify the definition of probability based on the k-rejection rule is not altogether clear, but if Braithwaite cannot establish even this connection, his definition simply involves an arbitrary stipulation of rejection conditions for probability statements. The passage I have italicized in the text indicates precisely where Braithwaite's argument goes wrong; as I understand it, what is asserted by a probability statement depends on what the statement *means*. But according to Braithwaite the meaning of probability statements (apart from their syntactic content) is fixed by the k-rejection rule and, thus, *any appeal by Braithwaite to the meaning of probability statement in justifying the k-rejection rule is viciously circular*. However, as the italicized passage clearly indicates, his argument crucially involves an appeal to what probability statements *assert* in the extreme case of the probability values of 1 and 0. Of course it is natural to think that a statement that there is a 0 probability of β being *a means* or *asserts* no c's are *a*'s, but this is to trade on some antecedently accepted definition of probability, here a vague and intuitive one. (It should be noted that there exist definitions of probability, such as the standard frequency definition of probability in terms of limits of frequency, in which this does not hold.) Such an antecedently accepted meaning for probability statements cannot be appealed to if we are trying to justify a quite different, and rather technical, definition of probability, and this is just what Braithwaite wishes to do.

Thus, to tie this argument together, Braithwaite's definition of probability involves an essentially arbitrary stipulation of rejection conditions to fix the meaning of probability statements, and this is inevitable because no justification can be given for his k-rejection rule without circularity — the point made earlier. What plausibility his proposal has stems from the plausibility of other definitions of probability — what I called antecedently accepted definitions of probability. Since Braithwaite proposes to fix the meaning of probability statements by the k-rejection rule, he cannot appeal to such independent definitions of probability and so his justification for the k-rejection rule must lapse into vicious circularity.

It seems to me highly significant that Braithwaite's theory eventually breaks down: it incorporates existing statistical techniques in a perspicuous manner and appears, on the face of it, to be an objective, but antirealist, account of a notion of statistical probability. Moreover, it is a formulation of an intuitively attractive idea — found also in Popper's writing — that observations of finite frequencies provide empirical tests for probability hypotheses. Braithwaite simply took this idea one step further: he stipulated that the meaning of probability statements was fixed by their test conditions. If such a promising proposal founders on circularity, there seems to me little hope of finding an alternative theory along similar lines, and so the prospects for an anti-realist theory of objective statistical probability must look exceedingly dim.

CONFIDENCE INTERVALS AND OPERATIONAL DEFINITIONS OF PROBABILITY

Before proceeding to give what I think is the correct account of the notion of the statistical probability, as it occurs in science, I will consider another possible account of statistical probability, closely related to Braithwaite's. Braithwaite relied on the Chebyshev inequality, and though this is a powerful and useful theorem, there exist even more powerful techniques for estimating probabilities, most notably the Neyman-Pearson theory of confidence intervals. While Braithwaite was only able to derive necessary conditions for the acceptance of probability estimates from the Chebyshev inequality (which were expressed as rejection conditions), the Neyman-Pearson theory yields necessary and sufficient conditions for the acceptance of probability estimates. The mathematical basis for the Neyman-Pearson theory is similar to that used in establishing the Chebyshev inequality (cf. Braithwaite, 1953, p. 248ff), but the theory allows us to infer from a finite sample a high degree of probability (usually 95 per cent or 99 per cent) that the 'true probability value' for a phenomenon is within a certain interval. The interval within which the true probability is estimated to be is the so-called confidence interval; the degree of probability with which we expect it to occur within this interval is the confidence coefficient.

Since the Neyman-Pearson theory appears to provide necessary and sufficient conditions for knowing (to a high degree of probability) what the probability of a phenomenon is (to a specified degree of accuracy), it might be thought to constitute an *operational definition* of the notion of probability itself. I do not know of any philosopher who has argued explicitly for this position, but I suspect it is the way many scientists think of probability. Certainly, the Neyman-Pearson school of statistics is the one most widely accepted by scientists, and scientists are usually quite ready to treat any accepted technique for measuring a phenomenon as an operational definition of that phenomenon.†

† A populization of quantum mechanics I recently came across illustrates well the currency such an operationalist view of probability has among scientists. The author — a mathematical physicist — points out (without approving) that 'mathematicians have never succeeded in giving a precise definition of randomness or the associated task of defining probability. If you go to a maths library you will find lots of books on probability. How is it possible to have written so much about a topic that has not been precisely defined? ... how do the mathematicians write all those books without defining randomness or probability? They get away with it by becoming operationalists — they give an operational definition of randomness as that which obeys the theorems they derive about it. The mathematical theory of probability begins after probabilities have been assigned to elementary events. How probability is assigned to elementary events is not discussed, because that requires an intrinsic definition of the randomness of events — which is not known. This operationalist approach if applied to geometry would be like proving all sorts of theorems about triangles without actually precisely defining what is a triangle. An operational definition of "triangle" is simply the logical object that obeys all these theorems. When asked only for consistency, not for definition, you can really go very far with this approach, and this is what is in all those probability books.' (Pagels, 1982, pp. 105-8.) Of course both the Neyman-Pearson theory of confidence interval testing and the Chebyshev inequality are established by mathematical reasoning of the kind the author refers to, and since these techniques provide a way of measuring probabilities numerically, they could be expected to play a pivotal role in any operational definition of probability.

Statistical Probabilities

Attractive though such a proposal might appear, it suffers from two decisive drawbacks. First of all, any attempt to justify such a definition of probability by reference to the high probability it ensures for correct estimates of probability suffers from the same circularity we found with Braithwaite's theory: since the rules for estimating probabilities are thought to be constitutive of the notion of probability itself, any attempt to justify this definition by reference to the high probability of successful estimation presupposes that probability defined in this way serves some useful purpose, cognitive or practical. This is just what is in doubt when we ask for a justification of the definition and, as far as I can see, no answer can be given to this question. This is identical to the problem we noted in connection with Braithwaite's theory.

But perhaps it would be thought that *operational definitions* of scientific concepts do not require justification, or at least justification in this fashion. A common view is that operational definitions are justified by reference to their success in predictions; what precisely that would come to in this case is far from clear, and I suspect any attempt to work such a view out in detail would founder on circularity. However, these are matters we need not go into here, for there is a second reason why we cannot use the theory of confidence interval testing to provide an operational definition of probability: the confidence interval method of testing only allows us to determine probabilities within certain intervals, or margins of error. Though this presents no practical problem — the purposes to which we put probability judgments do not require precise real numbered values — a grave theoretical problem arises if we try to use this method as the basis for an operational definition of probability: on such a definition, probabilities become *intrinsically* imprecise. By this I mean that probabilities, so defined, are, by their very nature, magnitudes which only have interval values.

Although, as I said, I have not been able to locate in print any argument in favour of the view that probabilities are to be operationally defined by the confidence interval method of testing, the view that probability is an inherently imprecise magnitude seems fairly widespread. Mellor gives a particularly forceful statement of this view:

Precise values of chances, and hence of propensities, are notoriously not ascribable even in principle. On any recognised theory of testing statistical hypotheses (e.g. Neyman, 1952, Chapter 1) all that can ever be shown is that a chance lies in an interval of values . . . This all stems not from errors of measurement but from the very nature of chance. (Mellor, 1971, p. 101)

What seems to me interesting about this view is the claim that there is an imprecision inherent in the concept of probability. There is no doubt such a claim follows immediately if probabilities are regarded as operationally defined by the confidence interval method of testing (which is the one Mellor refers to), for this method can only yield probability values within certain intervals.

The one great problem with the claim that probabilities are inherently imprecise is that the axioms of the probability calculus are formulated for quantities which are single real numbers. Indeed in almost all systems, a basic axiom of probability is that probabilities are single precise real numbers; in more mathematical treatments probabilities are treated as single value real number functors. If this is so, how can we specify as an interpretation of the axiomatic concept of probability some magnitude which by its very nature is imprecise, taking only interval values?

My objection here is not to the not implausible view that as a matter of working practice we adopt procedures which yield only interval values of probability. Nor does it necessarily apply to the view that it is in principle impossible to *measure* probabilities with precision, so long as we are prepared to admit a different between what we can in principle measure and what actually obtains (and realists, I suppose, are prepared to accept such a difference). The objection only applies to the radical view that probabilities *themselves* are imprecise, for if that is the case, we cannot make inferences about probabilities with the mathematical calculus of probabilities (or should I say so-called mathematical calculus of probabilities because of course on the view we are considering, quantities which take on precise real numbered values could not be probabilities).

But it is this radical view which Mellor states quite explicitly, and, what is of more interest, it is this radical view that follows from the proposal to define probabilities operationally by the confidence interval method of testing. Indeed such a proposed operational definition must now look quite absurd, since the Neyman-Pearson method of confidence interval testing is based on the pure mathematical calculus of probability. If we accept that probability is to be operationally defined by this method, we would be in the absurd position of holding that the concept of probability had, by definition, a character (namely of imprecision) which prevented one from using the theorems necessary to define it.

This seems to me an insurmountable objection to construing the Neyman-Pearson technique of confidence interval testing as providing an operational definition of probability — and one which also would apply to any proposal to define probability operationally on the basis of other statistical techniques (say, Fisher's method involving the fiduciary argument) which yield interval probability values.

One final point should be made concerning statistical techniques for inferring probabilities, and it applies both to relatively uncomplicated procedures, such as rejection rules based on the Chebyshev inequality, and more sophisticated techniques, such as the Neyman-Pearson method of confidence intervals. While the above arguments show that such statistical techniques cannot be used to *define* a viable notion of statistical probability, these techniques may be thought to provide an answer to a crucial objection I have raised to objectivist theories of probability — that such theories cannot provide a plausible account of how we come to know probabilities on the basis of finite observations. The statistical techniques we have just considered allow us to make certain inferences concerning probabilities on the basis of finite observations — for example, that we may have a 95 per cent degree of confidence that the probability value of a given phenomenon is within a certain interval of the frequency observed in a small sample — and thus such techniques appear to provide us with justified knowledge of objective, empirical, probabilities (whether these are taken to be limiting frequencies, or some form of propensity). But such techniques give us the justified knowledge that a particular objective probability value obtains *only on the assumption that there exists a single, although as yet unknown, objective probability*. Characteristically they embody reasoning of the form 'no matter what *the* probability is, there is a probability not less than ... that of this sample will be within ...'. However, if there is no single, stable objective probability, these methods cannot be used and, as I have pointed out in several places already, an unnerving consequence of objective definitions of probability is that, for all we know (now or at any time in the future) no such prob-

Statistical Probabilities

ability may, in reality, exist.† The sequence of observations we are concerned with may not have a limit — despite apparent convergence — or — if we adopt a propensity theory — the chance set-up we are dealing with may not have a propensity of the requisite kind. Thus unless we are also given an explanation of how we are justified in believing on the basis of our observations of a sample that a single objective probability actually obtains — and this is never provided — the statistical techniques we have been considering are of no avail in answering the crucial question of how we can have justified knowledge of probabilities, that is, the question how we can know the truth of probability statements on the basis of finite amounts of observations.

STATISTICAL EVIDENCE AND THE REVISION OF PROBABILITY JUDGMENTS

As the reader may have anticipated, I believe that the correct explanation of how we can know the truth of ordinary probability statements

---

†In this context, it is interesting to note that the statistical techniques we have been considering (as well as such similar techniques as Fischer's 'Fiduciary' method) rely on reasoning of a non-constructive nature; specifically, they involve the assumption that a single probability value exists, although there is no effective method for calculating it. Mathematicians and statisticians have not been concerned by the non-constructive character of statistical reasoning because, of course, they regard probability values as magnitudes given by, or in, experience. However, if we accept Dummett's claim that a realist viewpoint — both in mathematics *and* other areas — manifests itself in the use of classical, rather than intuitionist, methods of inference, the non-constructive character of statistical inference is significant. Unless there exists an independent (and effective) method for determining probability values on the basis of observational evidence, the assumption that a single value of probability exists (and the statistical inferences drawn from that assumption) will not be intuitionistically valid. As we have seen — and will continue to see — the main difficulty with the conception of an objective, statistical, probability is that the statistical techniques we have been considering constitute the *only* method for determining the value of statistical probability, on the basis of observational evidence; that is, no independent method for determining such magnitudes exists and so the reasoning involved in the statistical techniques will not be intuitionistically valid. This provides yet another reason for regarding theories of objective, statistical, probability as irremediably realistic in nature.

Statistical Probabilities

on the basis of finite amounts of statistical evidence is the one offered by the l.r.t.: probability is a logical relation between evidence (including statistical data) and hypotheses concerning various outcomes; ordinary probability statements are elliptical for two-term L-true statements, whose truth then is known by (a) our awareness of evidence (statistical and specificatory) and (b) our immediate apprehension of logical relations. Moreover, I believe such an analysis can be extended to the statements scientists make on probability, which of course are to be construed as elliptical as they do not explicitly mention evidence. (Indeed for the sake of continuity I will often refer to scientists' statements on probability as ordinary probability statements, particularly when I am concerned with their elliptical character.)

I also believe that scientists' practices in inferring probabilities by the use of standard statistical techniques can be satisfactorily explained in terms of inductive probability, and that the belief — explicitly argued for by philosophers of science and implicitly accepted by many scientists — that a distinct 'objective' concept of statistical probability is necessary to systematize scientific discourse on probability arises from a failure to see how the l.r.t. can explain the way scientists determine probabilities.

The demonstration of this hinges on a careful analysis of various notions of possibility and their relation to the practical application given to probability judgments. Much of the demonstration will parallel arguments in Chapters III and IV concerning specificatory evidence and the requirement of total evidence. The parallels are in no way arbitrary for, as we saw in the last chapter, a crucial part of objectivist accounts of probability is their commitment to the possibility of indefinite revisions of probability judgments in the light of increased scientific knowledge of physical parameters. Precisely the same can be said of objectivist attempts to explain a notion of statistical probability: from the discussion of earlier sections of this chapter it should be obvious that a central feature of the statistical methods used in science to determine probabilities is their 'provisional' character. For the scientist, probabilities are inferred on the basis of finite observations of repeated trials (i.e. finite bodies of statistical evidence), but scientists regard the probabilities so determined as fallible 'estimates' of probability. The role played by statistical evidence in the progressive revision of apparently always fallible probability estimates is as simple as it is crucial, and no one puts the matter better than Braithwaite.

If the probability statement were interpreted according to a mode of interpretation which depended upon the class of reference being a finite class, a finite set of observations — namely, observations of the members of this finite class — would suffice conclusively to establish the truth of the probability statement. But this is just what cannot happen with scientific hypotheses; however many observations we have made a further observation may serve to refute the hypothesis. Thus the class of reference in a scientific hypothesis must be a class which is not limited in advance by the way in which the expression of the hypothesis is interpreted. (1953, pp. 123-4)

This simple argument would appear to preclude any analysis of a scientific concept of probability along the lines of the l.r.t., for statements of logical probability can be conclusively settled on the basis of observations of members of finite classes. The observations constitute the evidence required as second term for a relational judgment of probability, and the truth of such a relational judgment is settled with certainty by our capacity to grasp relations of partial entailment which constitute probability. Thus the provisional character of scientific probability judgments based on observations of repeated trials — provisional because the observations can later be superseded by observations of more trials — appears to be incompatible with the basic conception of probability advanced by me and other l.r. theorists.

But all of this has a familiar ring to it by now. The possibility that later observations of additional trials may force us to revise a probability judgment made on the basis of earlier observations is really no different from the possibility we considered at the end of Chapter III and throughout Chapter IV, save that we were there concerned with the revision of probability judgments on the basis of additions to our knowledge of the physical attributes relevant to the outcome of an event, and we are now concerned with additions to our knowledge of the frequency of a particular phenomenon observed in repeated trials. In Chapter IV it emerged that there was only the *appearance* of conflict between the l.r.t.'s claims on the certainty of probability judgments and scientists' practice of revising probability judgments in the light of newly discovered specificatory evidence: what was revised was an elliptical judgment of probability, not explicitly mentioning evidence, and the revision only betokened the fact that we had, tacitly, changed the second term required for a complete L-true probability judgment. The same applies to statistical

Statistical Probabilities

evidence; indeed it must, for the second term of a complete probability judgment is a combination of specificatory and statistical evidence, which I have only separated out for the purpose of analysing the different philosophical issues surrounding each part. Specifically, the second term in the full probability statement indicates that the kind of outcome we are concerned with has occurred with a certain frequency (the statistical part) in some finite class of trials sharing a specific set of characteristics (the specificatory part). Thus, just as one and the same elliptical judgment of probability may have to be revised if we change the specificatory part of the second term of the full statement, one and the same elliptical judgment of probability may have to be revised if we change the statistical part of the evidence, to encompass a larger class of trials sharing a fixed set of characteristics. This — and this alone — explains how and why we revise or refute probability hypotheses on the basis of statistical data as described by Braithwaite in the above quotation: having initially formulated an L-true probability statement on the basis of one body of statistical evidence, we find ourselves forced to revise the part of the statement stating the probability value in light of observation of more statistical evidence, for, following the precept of using all the evidence we know, we adopt a new and larger body of statistical evidence as the second term for another, still L-true, judgment of probability. In a similar way, we can explain why an earlier rejection of a probability hypothesis may later have to be cancelled: it is always possible that after rejecting a probability hypothesis on the basis of observing one body of evidence greater than that known when the hypothesis was formulated, we will observe yet more evidence. If the original elliptical probability hypothesis is correct relative to this body of evidence, we will cancel our rejection and, again, accept the original hypothesis.

As explained at length in Chapter IV in regard to specificatory evidence, this practice of revising the elliptical part of probability judgments cannot be construed as supporting, or requiring, a concept of probability distinct from that of epistemic probability investigated by the l.r.t.; rather, such revision can only be understood properly on the basis of the l.r.t. This is particularly so in regard to statistical evidence, for to my mind virtually everything that has been written concerning the need for a separate concept of statistical probability in explaining scientific discourse on probability stems from a failure to appreciate the way in which the revision of ordinary elliptical probability judgments is carried out on the basis of the changing amounts of statistical evidence. To substantiate this, I will now examine in detail a number of specific doctrines philosophers have put forward in regard to the notion of statistical probability, and try to show how these doctrines relate to the analysis just sketched.

Limit Statements

The oldest, and to this day, still the most influential account of statistical probability is the definition of probability as limit of frequency in an indefinitely repeated series of trials. Now in Chapter IV I claimed that in coming to believe in the existence of an objective or physical probability, we simply reified an entity in a misguided attempt to make sense of our practice of revising probability judgments in the light of new specificatory evidence: if any judgment of probability based on a finite body of specificatory evidence could conceivably require revision, the truth condition of judgments of probability would appear to consist in some objective or physical state not necessarily knowable to us, and most definitely not knowable with certitude. A similar, though more precise, argument shows that the frequency theory of probability stems from a misguided attempt to make sense of our practice of revising probability judgments in the light of statistical evidence.

To begin with we may remind ourselves that the *rejection* of an earlier probability statement is itself provisional in character, like the original statement. That is to say, if on the basis of one set of observations of, say, 5,000 out of 10,000 A's being B, we ascribe a probability of 50 per cent to an A being a B, then later observe, say, 600,000 out of 1 million A's being B and so 'correct' our earlier estimate of probability, we might yet conclude (on the basis of observing 5 million in 10 million A's to be B) that the first probability value was 'correct' and that the first revision of this value was 'mistaken'.

Of course the most intriguing aspect of such provisional rejection procedures is that *any* step — the original assertion of a probability statement, its rejection, the cancellation of the rejection, etc. — can always be overruled in the light of further observation, for the sequence of our observations is indefinitely extendible. It then is natural to wonder what, if anything, constitutes the truth conditions of probability statements, for there is nothing that we can observe which definitively settles the truth of a probability statement. Put another way, how can any statement of probability be said genuinely to be true or false if that statement, its rejection, the cancellation of its

Statistical Probabilities

rejection, etc., can all require emendation? The question is pressing because, of course, without there being something which makes the probability statements true or false, the very process of revision we are considering seems to make no sense — we revise in order to have a better approximation to the truth of the probability statement we are concerned with.

Given the possibility of indefinitely many revisions to our judgments of probability, on the intuitive level it must appear that a particular probability statement would only be *genuinely* true (or false) if there existed a certain stability or convergence among the successive rejections, cancellations, etc., made on the basis of ever-increasing numbers of observations. That is to say, intuitively it is natural to think that a probability statement is genuinely true if, and only if, there exists some point in the indefinitely extendible series of our observations at which the statement is not rejected, and *thereafter is never again rejected*. Conversely, if, and only if, there is some point in the series at which the statement is rejected and thereafter *always* remains rejected would we intuitively regard it as genuinely false, as opposed to only apparently so, given some limited number of observations. Such an intuition remains faithful to the essence of the practice of revising probability hypotheses — that a judgment based on a greater amount of evidence supersedes one made on a lesser amount — as it equates true probability statements or correct rejections, with ones which are sustained by *all* subsequent observations of greater amounts of evidence.

If this is an accurate account of our intuitions on contemplating the possibility of an indefinitely extendible sequence of cancellations and revisions based on increasing observational evidence, it is not difficult to see why the definition of probability as a limit of frequency has had considerable intuitive appeal: if we adopt any of a very large class of rejection procedures and append it to the intuitive conception of truth and falsity just sketched, only a limit of frequency in an indefinitely repeated series of trials can constitute a 'true' value of probability.

To see this, we should first note that there is always a limitation on the degree of accuracy required by probability judgments that are to serve a given practical purpose; we may call this margin of error ϵ. Now, for the sake of argument, let us assume we adopt the simplest and most natural procedure for rejecting probability hypotheses, the one based on the so-called straight rule of induction. Since, for a given practical purpose, it does not matter if we adopt a value of probability ϵ more, or less, than the 'true' value, the rejection procedure based on the straight rule would take the following form: given observations of a frequency $\frac{m}{n}$ in n trials, reject any hypotheses on the probability outside the interval $\frac{m}{n} \pm \epsilon$. It is readily demonstrable that if a limit of frequency p exists in our indefinitely extendible series of trials, a probability hypothesis asserting the value of p will be true by the above intuitive criteria: given a fixed margin of error ϵ, there must be some point in the series after which such a probability hypothesis is never rejected.

The same of course can be said for all probability hypotheses stating values within the interval $p \pm \epsilon$, for a given margin of error ϵ; thus the argument so far does not explain why we might take the true value of probability to be the limit p, rather than any other value 'sufficiently' close (i.e. $\pm \epsilon$) to p. But of course ϵ is only a fixed value for a given practical purpose, and different practical needs concerning the same phenomena can — and will — require different standards of accuracy. Indeed there would appear to be no general method of limiting the standard of accuracy appropriate to probability statements. No matter how small a margin of error ϵ is appropriate for one practical purpose, it is always possible to imagine practical exigencies requiring a greater degree of accuracy.

This makes all the difference to what we will intuitively regard as the true probability of a phenomenon: any probability value insufficiently close to the true value for some practical purpose is *a fortiori* not the true value of probability. Since we can always imagine circumstances requiring a smaller margin of error than a given one ϵ, the true value of probability must be such that there is some point in our indefinitely extendible series of observations after which it is never rejected, *no matter how small a margin of error ϵ we have chosen*. It is obvious from the definition of limit of frequency that the value of the limit alone is such that for any ϵ (no matter how small) there is some point in the indefinitely extendible series of our observations after which it is never rejected by the rule 'after observing a frequency of $\frac{m}{n}$, reject all probability values outside the interval $\frac{m}{n} \pm \epsilon$'.

Of course from the point of view of the l.r.t., the reasoning which thus leads to the identification of probability with limit of frequency is deeply confused — what I have just been describing is a natural, though misguided, attempt to make sense of the process of revision of ordinary (elliptical) probability judgments on the basis of increasing amounts of statistical evidence. The successive observations of cumulative frequency which prompt the rejections, cancellations of

Statistical Probabilities

rejections, etc., are actually just different bodies of knowledge (or evidence), which form the second term of different L-true relational statements of probability, with the measure function $\lambda = 0$ providing the numerical values of the successive relational judgments. However, the important thing to note is that the process of revision in question only applies to the elliptical part of these statements (the part stating the numerical value, but not the evidence used), and it is for this reason that the process of forming successive different L-true relational statements using $\lambda = 0$ for different bodies of evidence may appear to be a process of revising one and the same genuine probability judgment. But what needs 'revision' is only one and the same elliptical judgment mentioning numerical probabilities, because it is taken in relation to different bodies of statistical evidence. Our faith in the idea that the conclusions drawn on the basis of larger and more inclusive bodies of statistical evidence should be preferred — which means that the 'revision' can go on indefinitely — stems from the fact (long acknowledged by l.r. theorists) that elliptical judgments of probability are always made relative to the total evidence known, which here increases with each subsequent observation. The rejection rule described above depends on the fact that the $\lambda = 0$ measure function is used to determine the successive relational probabilities which replace earlier ones, with the proviso that different numerical values within the margin of error corresponding to our practical need may be regarded as interchangeable. Save where the different relational values are sufficiently close for a given practical purpose, the successive different relational judgments appear to require reversion of one and the same probability statement, for relative to different bodies of evidence one and the same elliptical judgment will require revision. But rather than an indefinite series of revisions to one and the same full *genuine* probability statement — which is how frequentists view this process — we actually have a series of different, genuine, L-true relational statements. In effect the $\lambda = 0$ measure function which determines the numerical value of these relational probabilities becomes misconstrued as part of a rejection rule, and the succession of different relational probabilities becomes misconstrued as revisions of statements about one and the same nonrelational, or objective, probability.

Faced with the possibility of unending revisions and counter-revisions to one and the same elliptical judgment of probability — carried out just because such a judgment must always be relative to evidence — we have little choice on the *intuitive level* but to identify the truth and falsity of such judgments with the existence of the kind of stability described above; this in turn yields the belief that limits of frequency alone can be the true probability. In reality any stability in the sequence of observations — in the sense of convergence to a limit — is purely fortuitous, and as such has nothing to do with the truth or falsity of probability statements.

Misconceived though it is, the reasoning I have endeavoured to uncover is natural enough — indeed it includes a number of intuitions quite sound in their own right — and this, I believe, accounts for much of the appeal of the frequency theory. If this is so, the intuitive appeal of the earliest, and most influential, account of statistical probability can be traced to a failure to appreciate the true way in which logical probabilities, determined by the $\lambda = 0$ measure function, are determined relative to different successive bodies of statistical evidence; moreover, the postulation of an unobservable limit of frequency (whose existence is at best purely fortuitous), and the identification of this with probability, can be seen as a hypothesization or reification of a (most dubious) entity to provide something sufficiently stable for statements of probability to be genuinely true or false, given the apparent possibility of endless revision to probability judgments. However, once the process of revising what are, in reality, elliptical probability judgments is correctly understood in terms of the l.r.t., the need, and the appeal, of postulating such a dubious entity should, I hope, vanish.

The Pragmatic Justification of Induction

This analysis of the intuitive origin of the frequency theory can be thought of as an inversion of a familiar argument often used to support that theory, namely Reichenbach's (and Peirce's) pragmatic justification of induction. This argument is succinctly expressed by Salmon in regard to an infinite sequence of observations of cumulative frequency:

> Suppose first that the sequence $F^n(A,B)(n = 1, 2, 3 \ldots)$ has no limit. In this case any attempt to infer the value of that (non-existent) limit is bound to fail, whether it be by induction by enumeration [the straight rule] or by any other method. In this case, all methods are on a par: they are useless. Suppose, now, that the sequence does have a limit. Let us apply the rule of induction by enumeration and infer that the observed frequency matches the limit of the relative frequency to whatever degree of approxi-

mation we desire. We persist in the use of this rule for larger and larger observed initial parts of our sequence as we observe larger numbers of members. It follows directly from the limit concept that, for any desired degree of accuracy whatever, there is some point in the sequence beyond which the inferred values will always match the actual limit within that degree of approximation. To be sure, we cannot say beforehand just how large our samples must be to realize this condition, nor can we be sure when we have reached such a point, but we can be sure that such exists. There is a sense, consequently, in which we have everything to gain and nothing to lose by following this inductive procedure for ascertaining probabilities — i.e., for inferring limits of relative frequencies. If the probability whose value we are trying to ascertain actually exists, our inductive procedure will ascertain it. (1967, p. 86)

Of course this highly realist† argument fails to persuade the l.r. theorist, who believes probabilities exist even if limits of frequency do not. Here, however, the anti-realist will be reminded of Wittgenstein's view that the real meaning of a concept may be found in the explanations philosophers give of how to apply that concept: the net import of this purported pragmatic justification of induction is that finite bodies of statistical evidence, of increasing size, are the conditions which justify the assertion of probability statements. According to the anti-realist, such conditions — rather than some allegedly real entity (which may or may not exist) — constitute the meaning of probability statements. My position throughout the book has been that the l.r.t. — which construes ordinary probability statements of the kind in question as relative to such evidence — provides an anti-realist definition of just this kind. (The interested reader may wish to compare this with Reichenbach, 1949, p. 460. There he states that the deductive conception of probability (the l.r.t.) confuses the 'probability relation' with the grounds for assertion of the probability relation. For the anti-realist, of course, the matter is the other way round: the meaning of probability statements is fixed by their assertion conditions, and it is the realist who hypothesizes an objective entity to correspond to these conditions that is confused.)

†Given Dummett's characterization of anti-realism as a generalization of the intuitionist position, it is interesting to note the above argument is not intuitionistically valid, for it relies on the assumption that a limit either does or does not exist.

Statistical Probabilities

As Reichenbach and Salmon pointed out, their pragmatic justification of induction would vindicate not only the straight rule for inferring probabilities, but also any 'convergent' rule, i.e. any rule which yielded values which converged to those determined by the straight rule, as the number of observations $n \to \infty$. This result also has its anti-realist 'inverse': it means that the above analysis of the intuitive origin of the frequency theory does not depend on the assumption that the $\lambda = 0$ measure function is at the base of our intuitive concept of (logical) probability. If any of the wide class of measure functions convergent to $\lambda = 0$ is chosen as the basis for determining logical probabilities† in the light of indefinitely increasing bodies of observational data, a probability hypothesis stating the limit of frequency will have the same special status described above: it, and it alone, is such that no matter what margin of error ϵ we adopt in carrying out the progressive reversion of one and the same (elliptical) probability hypothesis, there will exist a point after which it never need be revised.

At this stage it may be objected that, although my analysis of the intuitive origin of the frequency theory does not depend on any special assumption concerning choice of the $\lambda = 0$ measure function, it does involve a very simplistic view of the use of margins of error in determining probabilities. My argument assumes that a scientist (or statistician) trying to determine probabilities for a specific practical purpose will adopt a given margin of error ϵ, and then carry out repeated revisions to elliptical probability hypotheses on the basis of numerical values determined by $\lambda = 0$ (or convergent measure function) in the light of increasing observational evidence. Actually — as our earlier consideration of Braithwaite's theory shows — the use of margins of error in formulating rejection criteria for probability hypotheses is far more complex and involves sophisticated probabilistic reasoning of a kind we have yet to examine in relationship to the l.r.t.; in the above I was only concerned to explain the *intuitive* or pre-theoretic basis of the frequency theory, rather than the sophisticated mathematical reasoning often used to support, or supplement, statistical conceptions of probability. The explanation the l.r. theorist can give to the sophisticated statistical techniques for establishing binomial hypotheses — involving margins of error and second-order probability

---

†It is noteworthy that at one stage Carnap — following a suggestion by Putnam — considered adopting an axiom which would limit choice of measure functions to this class (cf. Jeffrey, 1980, pp. 120ff).

Statistical Probabilities

statements — is quite a different, and far more complicated, matter, and it is that question I wish to turn to now.

Statistical Methods for Inferring Binomial Probabilities

We have in fact already encountered two of the most common statistical methods for inferring probabilities on the basis of observations of statistical samples, the Neyman-Pearson confidence interval method and the use of rejection rules based on the Chebyshev inequality. The mathematical reasoning employed in each method is not directly in dispute, as it only involves theorems of the pure probability calculus; what is in dispute is the semantic interpretation assumed for the concept of probability with which the pure mathematical inferences are made or, what is more alarming, the way these methods of statistical inference are used to provide *semantics* for a concept of statistical probability otherwise lacking. That was Braithwaite's explicit intention, and there seems to me little doubt that many practising statisticians and scientists see these rules as fixing conditions for justified assertions of probability statements — perhaps by constituting an operational definition of probability, as discussed earlier. I have already indicated why I think such semantic accounts of statistical probability are mistaken, and I now wish to explain what I think is the intuitive origin of most of the mistakes that have grown up surrounding these methods of statistical inference. For this purpose, I will consider in detail the Chebyshev inequality and its use to justify rejection rules. My analysis can easily be extended to cover other techniques which rely on theorems for the binomial distribution (or the normal distribution as an approximation thereof), e.g. the Neyman-Pearson method of confidence interval testing, but in view of our detailed consideration of Braithwaite's theory, the prominence I have given to the idea of successive rejections of probability hypotheses in explaining the intuitive appeal of the frequency theory, and the somewhat controversial character of the Neyman-Pearson school of statistics, it will be more convenient and straightforward to concentrate our attention on the Chebyshev inequality.

To proceed with an analysis of the rejection procedures based on the Chebyshev inequality, let us take a simple numerical example: suppose a scientist wishes to measure precisely the probability of heads with a particular coin; on the basis of a very small number of observations e_0, say 100, he very tentatively concludes that the probability of heads with this coin is p_0, 60 per cent, having observed 60

Statistical Probabilities

heads. Being scientific, he knows he can, and should, perform considerably more trials and use accepted statistical practices for inferring probabilities. He then performs 1,000 trials, observes 500 heads (formulated in an evidence statement e_1) and, by use of the Chebyshev inequality, rejects the probability value of 60 per cent with a 95 per cent degree of certainty that this rejection is not mistaken. (With k as 1/20 he would reject all figures outside the intervals 50 per cent $\pm$ 7 per cent for n = 1,000.) On the analysis of revisions to probability judgments I have given, it is easy enough to understand rejection of the value p_0, when e_1 has been observed: p_0 is the correct value relative to e_0 (using $\lambda = 0$), but (still using $\lambda = 0$) p_0 is incorrect relative to e_1; once our scientist has observed e_1, he will use it, rather than the smaller e_0, when making ordinary elliptical statements of probability (which, I maintain, is what he is doing whenever he makes statements of probability without explicitly mentioning evidence).

All this is familar — the question which concerns us now is why the scientist should use the Chebyshev inequality to qualify his rejection of values outside a specific interval by a second order of probability statement asserting a 95 per cent chance of the rejection not being mistaken. The rejection of p_0 on the basis of e_1 is definitive and certain for the l.r. theorist; i.e. relative to e_1 it is L-false that the probability of the coin is p_0. In effect, my basic claim is that in rejecting p_0 after first observing e_0, then observing e_1, we simply make two first-order relational judgments of logical probability involving one and the same elliptical statement (i.e. that the probability is p_0). The first L-true relational judgment is that the probability relative to e_0 is p_0, the second is that it is false that the probability relative to e_1 *is* p_0; since the latter judgment, like the former, is purely logical in character, there would appear to be no possibility of *it* being an error, contrary to the assertion that there could be as much as a 5 per cent chance the rejection is mistaken.

But this misses the whole point of my analysis so far: in thinking that the rejection of p_0 when e_1 is observed can be mistaken, the scientist only has in mind the possibility that some more extensive number of observations, say, of 1 million trials, could be made, and these might reveal that the original figure of p_0 was correct and the rejection therefore mistaken — this would be the case if we observed, say, 600,000 heads. That is, relative to such a body of evidence, e_2, the original elliptical judgment would be correct (again assuming $\lambda = 0$). In a manner I have indicated several times already, this wholly explains why the scientist thinks the rejection of p_0 when e_1 is observed

Statistical Probabilities

may be mistaken — the possibility of cancelling a rejection, like the possibility of rejecting the initial judgment of probability, only depends on the possibility of observing a different and more inclusive body of evidence, and assessing one and the same elliptical statement of probability relative to that different body of evidence.

But the basic question concerning our statistical practice still remains: even if we explain the possibility of error in rejecting probability statements in this way, why do scientists use the Chebyshev inequality to probabilify and quantify the possibility of the error of a rejection (as well as using it to set the bounds of what constitutes permissible error)? The answer, as might be expected, involves the interpretation given by the l.r.t. to the standard theorems of the probability calculus used in determining the Chebyshev inequality. The theorems are, of course, the binomial law and Bernoulli's Law of Large Numbers, and I will follow Carnap's interpretation of them in terms of the l.r.t. Carnap's formulation of the binomial law applies to what he called direct (or downward) inductive inferences, that is, inferences from knowledge (or evidence) of the frequency in a population to a conclusion on the inductive probability of samples drawn from that population exhibiting certain frequencies. Put in Carnap's symbolism, the theorem provides a means for determining the degree of confirmation $c(h,e)$ given to hypotheses concerning the frequency of a property M in samples, relative to evidence e of the frequency r_1 of M in the entire population. As Carnap himself remarks, this formulation is not the traditional one found in probability theory, for it

> refers to an evidence stating the *rf* r_1 of a property M in a population to which the sample belongs. The traditional formulation does not refer to this *rf*; it speaks of r_1 rather as the probability of an individual's being M; a restricting condition is usually added to the effect that r_1 must be the probability of M for each individual in the sample or each trial in the series of experiments, 'independently' of the other individuals. This independence is meant in the sense that, even after some of the individuals have been observed, the probability for any other one is still r_1. (1962, p. 499)

Carnap, citing Keynes, adds that this condition is very seldom fulfilled, but 'is fulfilled with good approximation as long as the sample is small in relation to the population'.

The important point is that when the sample *is* small in relation to the entire population, the binomial law determines inductive probabilities for hypotheses concerning samples, *relative to information about the frequency r_1 in the overall population*, in just the same way that the traditional application of it determines probabilities for hypotheses about samples on the assumption that r_1 is the probability of the phenomenon in question. For example — though Carnap does not do this specifically — we can establish the Chebyshev inequality for the binomial distribution under this interpretation, which will then state that no matter what frequency p obtains in a population (of sufficient size) there is, relative to knowledge or evidence of that frequency, a degree of probability less than k that a sample of size n drawn from the population will be outside the interval $p \pm \sqrt{\frac{pq}{nk}}$.

Though the numerical values here are, of course, identical to those found in any use of the Chebyshev inequality, the reader may wonder what bearing this interpretation of the inequality has on the formulation of rejection rules. We had reached the point of enquiring why a scientist would quantify probabilistically the possibility of his rejection of a value p_0, based on observations of a sample e_1, being mistaken by use of the Chebyshev inequality; in keeping with the general analysis of revisions to ordinary probability judgments I have given, I argued that the source of the scientist's belief that this rejection might be mistaken was his awareness that observations of a larger body of evidence e_2, say, of a million trials, might require him to cancel any rejection based on e_1. But now the relevance of the Chebyshev inequality's interpretation within the l.r.t. to the use of rejection rules should be obvious: given that it is the possibility of making an observation such as e_2 which prompts the scientist to regard rejections based on e_1 as possibly in error, it would be wholly natural for him to regard the *probability of the sample e_1 of 1,000 failing to approximate (within an agreed margin of error) the result in the series of a million trials* as a measure of the possibility of the results of the sample leading him to make a mistaken rejection.

Moreover, as I have stressed earlier, if the rejection of p_0 based on e_1 were to be cancelled on the basis of observations e_2, this would only be because the original elliptical probability statement was considered in relation to e_2, relative to which it was correct. Thus it is obvious that such a cancellation would be based on, or made relative to, the evidence e_2. Accordingly the probability underlined just above — the probability which is to measure the possibility of the rejection based on the sample e_1 being in error — should be the probability relative to the evidence e_2, in virtue of which the rejection would be cancelled. The direct, or

Statistical Probabilities

downward, inductive inference described by Carnap permits one to assess this probability by use of the mathematical techniques involved in the Chebyshev inequality, because of course the initial sample of 1,000 is part of the very much larger population of a million described in the evidence statement e_2. What we obtain on this interpretation of the Chebyshev inequality is the knowledge that, relative to the information on the results of a million trials, there is a logical probability of not less than 95 per cent that the results of the sample will approximate to within 7 per cent the outcome in the series of a million trials.

It is natural here to persist in wondering what such a purely mathematical conclusion on logical probabilities has to do with scientists' practices in estimating probability. By the l.r.t.'s interpretation of the Chebyshev inequality, we can only conclude that relative to the information on the results of a million trials there is at least a 95 per cent probability that the sample of 1,000 approximates these results to the desired degree, but what use is this, since, for the case we have in mind, we do not have results of the million trials? Admittedly, if we knew this information e_2, it would provide a better basis for determining the probability value in question than e_1, and so *would* be used by our hypothetical scientist as the basis for his ordinary statements on probability, but we simply do not have this information.

However, this is no deterrent whatsoever to employing the Chebyshev inequality here; the whole point of using the Chebyshev inequality in rejecting probability statements is that it provides a means of determining the probability of frequencies in samples matching those frequencies in overall populations which are thought to determine the probability in question, *without knowledge of the latter frequencies.* (Indeed the same is true for all related statistical techniques for estimating probabilities, e.g. the confidence interval method of testing.) Thus there is no objection to appealing to knowledge, or evidence, not yet obtained in explaining how the Chebyshev inequality functions in determining rejection procedures — it is accepted by all that the main interest of this theorem (in regard to evaluating binomial hypotheses) is to allow us to fix criteria of rejection in absence of the statistical data which would validate that rejection.

But perhaps it will be further objected that I have now been driven to a most strange position for someone advocating a notion of epistemic probability, in that I am committed to speaking of probabilities relative to an *unknown* body of evidence (in the above example, the results of a million trials). To some extent this seems to me a trivial point: one can easily recast the above argument in terms of probabilities conditional upon the description of the frequency in the million trials, and appeal to the Chebyshev inequality as a means for establishing that no matter what the correct description of this frequency is, conditional upon (or relative to) this description, there is a logical probability of 95 per cent of small samples approximating the frequency so described.

The reason such a logical probability is of interest to us is that it is only because our hypothetical scientist envisions the possibility of carrying out a million trials (and recording the frequency observed) that he regards his rejection based on the sample of a thousand as susceptible to later cancellation. Since it is just such a possibility of carrying out a more extensive body of observations that leads the scientist to regard the rejection based on the sample as possibly in error, nothing could provide a better measure of the probability of this error than the probability relative to, or conditional upon, a correct description of the outcome in the more extensive series of trials.

A far more interesting objection to this line of argument is that it involves a vital oversimplification: it ascribes to the scientist the belief that the results of the million trials constitute the correct basis for determining the probability of the phenomenon in question; on this assumption alone is it plausible to characterize the probability of error of the rejection based on the sample of a thousand as the probability relative to, or conditional upon, a true description of the outcome in a million trials. But no scientist would regard a statement of the results in the million trials (which I will revert to calling e_2) as *the correct* basis for a judgment of probability: it is clearly preferable to e_1 being more comprehensive, but any probability judgment based on e_2 is also amenable to revision in the light of evidence of a yet more comprehensive body of trials e_3, say, of 10 million trials. Indeed the crucial aspect of the probability judgments in science, as we have seen, is that they are *indefinitely* revisable.

However, and this seems to me the main interest of the discussion above concerning the Chebyshev inequality's interpretation within the l.r.t., the binomial law and Bernoulli's theorem, which serve to establish the inequality and related theorems, hold on the l.r.t.'s interpretation for *arbitrarily* large finite populations. Indeed for finite populations in general, the results given above are only good approximations, with the approximation increasing as the size of the population increases relative to the sample. Thus we could easily have substituted 100 million as the

Statistical Probabilities

number of trials described in the evidence statement e_2 used in the example above, or any other figure for that matter. Perhaps more to the point, we may draw conclusions of the kind reached above for *each and every* successive finite population corresponding to successive initial segments of the indefinitely extendible series of trials we can observe. Thus not only is there at least a 95 per cent probability, relative to information on the results of a million trials, that the frequency in the sample of a thousand will approximate to within 7 per cent of those results, there is also a probability of at least 95 per cent, relative to the information of the results in 10 million trials, that the frequency in the sample will approximate to within 7 per cent of those yet more extensive results, and so on *ad infinitum*.

The significance of the fact that the second-order probability of a sample approximating the frequency in a very large population holds for arbitrarily large populations is this: the arbitrarily large populations are successive initial segments of a potentially infinite sequence of repetitions of the kind of event we are concerned with. As regards epistemic probabilities, the frequencies which obtain in these populations constitute the information we would obtain if we kept on indefinitely carrying out this kind of experiment − the successive and cumulative bodies of statistical evidence, relative to which we can determine the probability of the phenomena in question. In effect, I have already explained how the belief that no one finite body of evidence can constitute the correct, irrefutable, basis for determining the (first-order) probability of a given phenomenon arises from reflecting on the succession of different cumulative bodies of evidence obtained in this way: statements about such a probability value are actually elliptical utterances, tacitly involving evidence of the total number of observations that have been made up to a given point in time, and as we envision ourselves subsequently extending − indefinitely − the number of repeated observations of the same phenomenon, the total body of evidence we think of as determining the first order probability changes, and so this first-order value of probability will seem to us to change if the frequency specified in the different bodies of evidence is different. But, as we have just seen, relative to each and every successive large body of evidence we would obtain if we continued to repeat the experiment in question, there is a virtually constant second order of probability that the evidence of a given small sample will yield values which are close approximations to the true descriptions of the frequency in the successively larger populations specified by the bodies of evidence in question. This means that the scientist who regards the statements about the first order of probability of the phenomenon as estimates (indefinitely) amenable to revision will regard statements on the second order of probability of the accuracy of an estimate procedure involving a small sample as indubitably correct, i.e. not amenable to revision: it is the successive cumulative statistical evidence obtained by indefinitely extending our observations which constitutes the grounds for revising judgments of probability – treating a judgment of probability as in error – and relative to each of these successive bodies of evidence there is a virtually constant second order of probability of an error being made through the use of a given estimate procedure and a given sample.

Let me put this point – which I regard as crucial to understanding a great deal of what has been written on the notion of 'statistical probability' – in a more general way that makes its connection to my earlier claims (particularly those of Chapter IV) clearer. On the elaboration I have given of the l.r.t.'s analysis of probability statements not explicitly mentioning evidence, revisions to such statements of probability only reflect changes in the body of evidence we tacitly adopt as the second term required for a genuine L-true statement of probability. Specifically, such revisions are carried out as more evidence becomes known – or are envisioned as possible when we contemplate the possibility of such increases in our knowledge – and when we do not explicitly mention evidence we rely on the total amount known. The crucial point to emerge from the above discussion of scientists' techniques for estimating probabilities is that the succession of finite totalities of statistical evidence obtained by indefinitely extending our observations of a given kind of phenomenon not only gives rise to the idea of an error in regard to a first order judgment of probability, but also thereby serves as a basis for the second-order probability judgments on the amount and probability of such error. The idea of an error in a first-order probability judgment is explained by reference to this succession of bodies of evidence, for whenever we think a particular first-order probability judgment is in error we envision some larger class of observations which makes us revise an earlier judgment of probability made on the basis of a smaller body of evidence. As explained on page 180, the second-order probability of such an error being made on the basis of the observation of a small sample should then be regarded as the probability of this sample failing to approximate the results in such a larger class of observations; since we regard this larger body of evidence as superseding that of the sample as the basis for probability judgments on the phenomenon in question, this second-order probability should be relative to the evidence of this larger class (as also explained on page 180).

Now, the bodies of observational data which so give rise to the notion of an error in a judgment of probability form an indefinite succession of ever-larger totalities corresponding to an indefinite extension of our observations and so we might anticipate that a scientist reflecting on this succession of evidence would intuitively come to think that second-order judgments of the probability of error were, like first-order probability judgments, indefinitely amenable to revision. But the considerations adduced above indicate why this is not so: the scientist only regards the first-order judgment of probability based on the evidence e_1 of a small sample as subject to error because he envisions the possibility of some larger class of observations being made which indicate a different value of probability; since there will obtain second-order probability relations between the evidence e_2 describing such results and the small sample he has already observed, he can quantify the second-order probability of an error of a specified size. For him to regard this second-order judgment as subject to error he must envision a different and yet larger class of observations which, following the precept of adopting the total evidence, is then also regarded as the correct basis for judgments of probability for the phenomenon; moreover, the second-order probability of the sample being in error relative to the evidence e_3 of the results of this larger set of observations would have to be a different numerical value from what he originally regarded the second-order probability of error to be, i.e. the value relative to e_2. He easily can envision such a larger class; indeed he can (and does) envision an indefinite succession of ever larger classes of observations serving, successively, as the basis for judgments of probability, but for each of these classes there is a virtually constant second-order probability — relative to evidence of its results — of the original sample approximating the results of that class of observations. Because there is in this way a virtually constant second-order probability of the sample approximating the results in the successively larger classes which alone could lead the scientist to revise a first-order judgment of probability based on the evidence of the sample, he naturally regards the second-order value as not amenable to revision.

In general the scientist comes to believe that the statistical techniques we have been examining provide an indubitable method for

Statistical Probabilities

determining the second-order probability of a small sample being in error, for whatever he envisions as correctly determining the probability, both first and second order, of a given phenomenon — and this is just the frequency in each of an indefinite succession of ever larger bodies of observations, taken successively — is such that it can be estimated by these techniques; indeed, as the above analysis shows, there is a virtually constant second-order probability determined by these techniques for a given small sample approximating what our scientist envisions as determining the probability of the phenomenon, namely, the frequency in each of the succession of ever-larger bodies of observation.†

The effect of this analysis is to explain in terms of the l.r.t. three quite different intuitive beliefs which at first sight appear to favour objective theories of probability. First of all, scientists, statisticians, and the ordinary layman all believe that there is usually a single, uniquely correct, probability for a given phenomenon, indeed one that remains constant over time unless there are changes in the physical circumstances surrounding the kind of event in question. Secondly, however, although they believe that observations of frequency in repeated trials of this event are relevant to determining this unique value of probability, they do not believe that observations of the frequency in any one finite class can serve to determine this value with certainty. Thirdly, scientists and statisticians believe — and the ordinary layman is prone to defer to such expert knowledge — that statistical techniques involving probabilistic reasoning of the kind we have seen exemplified with the Chebyshev inequality provide a means for knowing how probable it is that estimates based on the observations of a given finite class (usually quite small) are accurate. Although objective theories of probability purport to provide a systematization of beliefs one and two, they encounter grave difficulties from an epistemological point of view (or so I argued in Chapters I and II); moreover, as I argued

---

†As so far explained, this argument assumes that the probability value relative to a given body of statistical evidence is determined by the $\lambda = 0$ measure function (cf. p. 178). However, I believe this could be generalized to cover all measure functions yielding values convergent on those determined by $\lambda = 0$, though the details of such a generalization would be rather complicated. In any case, I hope the above analysis of a standard technique of statistics — carried out, as it is, in terms of $\lambda = 0$ — is sufficiently plausible to persuade the reader that scientists and statisticians do implicitly rely on this measure function, rather than any other.

Statistical Probabilities

earlier in this chapter, such theories cannot provide a justification for the third belief and, in fact, this is symptomatic of the difficulties such theories have in explaining how we have justified knowledge of probabilities.

As to the first belief, it is indeed possible in most cases to determine a single, unique, probability for a given phenomenon at a given time, for the total evidence available at a given time usually is such that there exists a single probability relation between it and hypotheses on the phenomenon in question (though, as explained in Chapter I, this is not invariably the case). The single value of probability determined in this way will change over time with the acquisition of new knowledge; however, since such a change usually takes the form of adopting a different (and larger) body of evidence as the basis for our (elliptical) judgments of probability, we are naturally led to believe that there exists a unique value of probability which does not change over time with the acquisition of new knowledge: at every stage in the development of our knowledge there is a single, unique probability value which — at that stage — we judge to have been the correct value for all times up to the then present, and this naturally leads us to believe that this value of probability does not change over time, as I explained at length in Chapter IV.

The basic argument of Chapter IV concerning the revision of elliptical judgments of probability is easily extended to explain the second belief mentioned above — that the unique probability of a phenomenon cannot be established with certainty on the basis of observations of the frequency in any one finite class as I explained at pp. 167ff. The above discussion of the Chebyshev inequality's interpretation within the l.r.t. provides the explanation of the third belief, that such techniques provide an unassailable basis for estimating probabilities from observations of given samples. A probability value determined on the basis of observations of a given sample is regarded as an estimate of probability only because there exist larger bodies of evidence concerning repeated observations of the same phenomenon which, if known, would require us to revise judgments on the probability of the phenomenon made relative to the smaller body of evidence constituting the sample. In fact the class of potential observations of most of the phenomena we are concerned with in probability theory will be unlimited in size and so gives rise to an indefinitely increasing succession of bodies of observational evidence of the kind which requires (an indefinite succession of) revisions to a given elliptical judgment on the (understood

Statistical Probabilities

unique) probability of a given phenomenon. However, the frequency in each of the successive classes of observations which would so determine (a succession of) unique probabilities for a given phenomenon can be estimated from observations of a small sample, and in fact there is a virtually constant second-order probability for such estimates being 'correct', i.e. approximating the results in each of the successive classes. Since each of these classes is thought of as (successively) determining the correct, unique probability of the phenomenon, it is natural to regard techniques for estimating the results in each of these classes as an unassailable method for determining the unique probability of the phenomenon: just as a belief in a single value of probability which did not change over time with the acquisition of new knowledge arose from the fact that at each stage of our knowledge there exists a single probability value constant over time up to then (relative to the total evidence available then), the fact that for each stage of our progressively increasing knowledge of the frequency in repeated trials of the same phenomenon there is a virtually constant second-order probability of a given small sample approximating the knowledge of frequency at that stage — relative to that knowledge — leads to the belief that there is a single second-order probability for accurately estimating first-order probabilities, which is determined with 'certainty' by mathematical techniques of statistical inference.

The common thread which runs through objectivist attempts to systematize the beliefs I have been describing is a failure to appreciate the relational character of probability statements, which in fact alone makes these beliefs intelligible; indeed, in failing to appreciate the relational character of probability statements, scientists, statisticians and ordinary laymen are virtually driven to a belief in objective, or empirical, probabilities, despite the myriad other difficulties with such a conception. Failure to recognize the relational character of probability statements leads them to misconstrue the revisions required of one and the same elliptical statement of first-order probability, relative to ever-increasing bodies of statistical evidence, as ever-fallible estimates of some one probability value, which then is naturally conceived of as an objective and empirical fact holding independently of the knowledge we gain through repeated observations of the phenomenon in question; in a similar way the genuine, but relational, second-order probabilities of a small sample approximating the results in each of the successively larger populations of events, which constitute our ever-increasing observational knowledge of the phenomenon,

Statistical Probabilities

are misconstrued as a single, infallible, second-order probability of an estimate based on the sample being a good approximation to the first-order objective, or empirical, probability.

DECIDABILITY IN PRINCIPLE AND IN PRACTICE, AGAIN

Since these mistaken beliefs on objective probability have wide currency among scientists and statisticians, it may be useful to explain the nature of the error involved in them quite generally in terms of our earlier discussions on the meaning and methodology of application for probability statements. To do this properly, we need to recall an important distinction made earlier between evidence which can be known in principle and evidence which can be known in practice. This distinction was, in the first instance, derived from a commonplace distinction made in the discussion of recursive decidability. Recursive procedures are those which terminate (positively or negatively) after *some* finite number of steps, although, crucially, there is no fixed or (as I will also say) limited finite number of steps within which such a procedure must terminate. Thus, as is generally recognized, the number of steps in which a recursive procedure terminates may be so great that no one person, or indeed the whole human race taken together, can decide them within a fixed time-span. Any proposition decidable by a recursive function is said to be decidable in principle, though the necessity of carrying out a vast number of steps may prevent such a proposition from being decidable in practice by the human race as currently constituted.

Following Dummett's suggestion to use the intuitionist's explanation of the meaning of mathematical concepts as a paradigm of an anti-realist theory of meaning, we noted that the l.r.t.'s claim that ordinary probability statements were short in meaning for statements on evidentiary relations could be seen as an anti-realist explanation of the meaning of such statements, as evidence, and the relation of partial entailment such evidence bears to hypotheses, constitutes the way in which we decided the truth of ordinary probability statements. But paralleling the distinction between those mathematical statements which are in principle decidable by recursive procedures, i.e. those terminating after *some finite* number of steps, and those which are in practice decidable by procedures terminating within the *limited finite number* of steps which some individual, or at least the human

Statistical Probabilities

race as a whole, can actually effect, we should distinguish between the capacity in principle to decide the truth of some ordinary statement by examining some body of evidence and the capacity in practice to decide its truth by examining evidence. This distinction was explained in Chapters III and IV for the case of specificatory evidence; as regards statistical evidence, this distinction hinges on sheer numbers (as, to some extent, it does in the case of recursive functions, namely in respect of the number of steps required in carrying out a particular calculation). While we can in principle decide the truth of some ordinary statement of probability by coming to know the results in 10^{100} trials (i.e. using information on this number of trials as evidence), we cannot do this in practice, for the very simple reason that we cannot in practice observe such a vast number of trials. That is to say, to use a set of statements as evidence to decide the truth of some ordinary statement of probability, we must be appraised of the content of these evidence statements and so any decision on the truth of an ordinary probability statement we actually make can only rely on evidence we can actually ascertain.

Now — as I have indicated several times since the outset of the book — for the anti-realist, the meaning of a concept is given by reference to the conditions by which *in principle* we can decide the truth of statements in which the concept occurs. Ironically, it is only by reflecting on such conditions for the case of probability statements that scientists and statisticians are led to the beliefs on the relationship of probability and statistics we have been discussing. In effect, I argued that these beliefs arose by reflecting on the *possibility* of obtaining more and more statistical evidence, which would require repeated revisions to one and the same elliptical judgment of probability. Since the amount of statistical evidence we can in practice ascertain at present is strictly limited, it should be obvious that the process of reflection by which we arrive at these beliefs merely involves taking note of the conditions by which we can *in principle* recognize the truth of ordinary probability statements. These conditions crucially involve finite, but unlimited, amounts of statistical evidence; the finite, but unlimited, amounts of statistical evidence we can in principle use in deciding the truth of an ordinary probability statement form a succession of finite totalities, ever-increasing in size — this is what I characterized in the previous section as the indefinitely extendible, or potentially infinite, series of observations of cumulative frequency. Contemplating such a succession of finite totalities, we mentally carry out an indefinite series of revisions to one and

Statistical Probabilities

the same ordinary, i.e. elliptical, statement of probability, corresponding to increases in the amount of evidence we envision ourselves observing. Since these successive finite bodies of evidence constitute the means by which we can in principle decide the truth of a given ordinary probability statement — rather than those by which we can in practice decide its truth on any given occasion — we have, in arriving at our beliefs on statistical probability, simply manifested our mastery of the meaning of ordinary probability statements — our capacity to recognize the truth of these statements on the basis of finite bodies of statistical evidence.

The Requirement of Total Evidence

Of course I do not think scientists, statisticians (or philosophers of science) realize that this is the process by which they arrive at the beliefs in question, and this accounts for much of the confusion and controversy surrounding the notion of statistical probability. Indeed if the analysis I have given of the origin of beliefs on statistical probability is correct, these beliefs involve a thorough misunderstanding of the relationship between probability and statistical evidence. To have full measure of the error involved in these beliefs, it is important to note the role played by the practical precept of using the total evidence known in the above reconstruction of the beliefs of scientists and statisticians on statistics and probability.† A brief glance at earlier sections will serve to remind the reader that adherence to just this precept was — and indeed had to be — attributed to scientists and statisticians in this reconstruction. In the first instance, the scientist was led to the belief that any probability statement made on the basis of observations of the frequency in some fixed finite class could not be definitively correct, as further observations might require revision of this judgment. The correct explanation of this crucial process of revision was seen to be that scientists made their probability statements relative to bodies of statistical evidence, but, in accepting the precept

---

†Since I have not yet elucidated any notion of the 'available' statistical evidence I have so far in this chapter only attributed to scientists and statisticians a belief in the weakest form of the requirement of total evidence, namely to use all the evidence known in determining the truth of an ordinary probability statement. Unlike the more complicated formulation of the requirement of total evidence I will give at the end of the chapter, there seems to me little doubt that in this weak form the requirement of total evidence is adopted by everyone.

Statistical Probabilities

that one should use the total evidence known, came to believe that when greater numbers of observations were made, probability statements made relative to the increased body of evidence would be preferable to ones made earlier, relative to lesser bodies of evidence. The possibility that such revisions might go on indefinitely was seen to lead to two other beliefs on statistical probability, namely that limits of frequency in infinite series of trials alone could constitute true probabilities and that mathematical methods of statistics (such as the Chebyshev inequality) provided a firm basis for measuring statistical probabilities.

Taken in combination with the remarks of the above paragraphs, these considerations yield the following general picture of the beliefs on statistics and probability we have been examining: our mastery of the meaning of ordinary probability statements consists in our capacity to recognize the truth of these statements by reference to the frequencies observed in finite numbers of trials; moreover, this capacity, as befits a mastery of meaning, is not limited by specific practical restrictions – in particular, this means that the finite bodies of evidence by which we can in principle recognize the truth of ordinary probability statements are not limited in any way in size. When scientists and statisticians reflect on the successively larger numbers of trials which we can in principle observe and use to recognize the truth of a given ordinary probability statement, they implicitly adopt the precept for applying probability statements for practical purposes which enjoins us to use the total evidence known, and this leads to the erroneous, but natural, beliefs on statistical probability described earlier.

At first glance it might seem quite implausible to diagnose any belief of scientists and statisticians as, in effect, a consequence of implicitly adhering to a form of the requirement of total evidence when they contemplate the sequence of ever-increasing bodies of statistical evidence it is in principle possible to ascertain, for such reasoning inevitably involves a serious confusion between what is in principle possible and what is in practice possible, as I will explain in detail shortly. However, the confusion is a subtle one and it is masked by complex issues concerning the time at which judgments of probability need to be made. Here it is important to note that the distinction between the statistical evidence we can in practice ascertain and the statistical evidence which can in principle be ascertained is one that breaks down if we assume unlimited amounts of time are

Statistical Probabilities

available for gathering statistical evidence. The number of repeated experiments we — meaning the human race as a whole — can in practice perform in the near future, or in any other limited finite span, is a strictly limited finite amount; the number that it is in principle possible for finite beings to perform is not so limited. However, if the human race were to continue to exist indefinitely in time, the number of experiments which could — in practice — be performed by the human race as a whole during that time would grow indefinitely; indeed it seems natural to regard the indefinitely extendible sequence of experiments which could in practice be carried out by the human race over indefinitely long periods of time to be of exactly the same character as that of the potentially infinite sequence of experiments which represents all the trials which can in principle be carried out by finite beings. (Indeed, from the point of view of probability theory, there is no reason to distinguish between the unlimited, or potentially infinite, number of experiments which represent the events which can in principle be performed by finite beings and the indefinitely extendible — or potentially infinite — sequence of events that can in practice be performed by humans over indefinitely long periods of time and I will continue to treat them as equivalent characterizations of the same sequence in what follows.†)

This of course means that it is not in the least 'implausible' to diagnose scientists' beliefs on statistical probability arising from implicit adherence to a precept for applying probability statements in practice — the precept of using the total known evidence — when they contemplate the indefinitely large bodies of statistical evidence which can in principle be ascertained: all that scientists need be doing when they

---

†The reasons for regarding these 'two' sequences as essentially the same seem to me to go fairly deep and indeed are themselves worthy of extended study: the capacity of the human mind to conceive a single item or event repeated or occurring again and again over indefinite periods of time is at the heart of the intuitionists' conception of the natural numbers and this forms the background of the discussion given above of statistical evidence. Moreover I believe general considerations about the relationship of meaning to practical application supports the idea that the means by which we can in principle recognize the truth of a certain class of statements are such that we can in practice recognize their truth, given ample resources, particularly ample amounts of time. However, such general questions on the nature of meaning, as well as general questions on the nature of infinity as construed by the intuitionists, go beyond the scope of our present inquiry.

contemplate bodies of evidence indefinitely increasing in size — while adhering to a precept for the practical application of probability judgments — is conceiving of each of the larger bodies of evidence as one which could be used in practice to decide the truth of an ordinary probability judgment if enough time were available for performing repetitions of one basic experiment. This in fact seems to be very close to what scientists *do* when they think of statistical trials — they imagine indefinitely long periods of time in which some ideally indefatigable experimenter performs repetitions of the same trial, yielding ever-increasing amounts of statistical evidence. (Indeed the reason I first presented my account of scientists' beliefs on statistical probability in terms of the effect of coming to know at successive times larger and larger bodies of statistical evidence was that this way of putting them remains close to the scientists' intuitive way of thinking.)

Once the reasoning of scientists and statisticians on statistical probability is diagnosed as arising from the possibility that, over time, a succession of ever-growing bodies of statistical evidence can — in practice — be gathered, and so can lead to the indefinite revision of one and the same elliptical probability statement, a deep error in this line of reasoning becomes apparent. The error parallels one explained in the previous chapter in regard to specificatory evidence, but it will be useful to state the matter explicitly for the case of statistical evidence. We noted that while the number of experiments relevant to the probability of a particular outcome which can in practice be performed by the human race as a whole will grow indefinitely if the time available increases indefinitely, the number which can be performed in a finite time-span is strictly limited. Now it seems to me indisputable that any actual practical concern — whether it be of an individual or the human race as a whole — is such that it obtains for a limited duration of time. The needs or desires of a gambler to win money occur at a particular point in time and pass away with time, certainly with the end of his life, but, arguably, in the far shorter time-spans of a night or a week. Inveterate gamblers can be thought of as ones with a succession of numerically different, though qualitatively similar, practical needs to win certain amounts of money within some relatively short period of time. In a similar way, the practical needs of the human race as a whole should be thought of as the sum of the needs of individuals which come into existence in time, passing away, or changing radically, over time. Much of the same is true of the practical needs of the scientist or statistician. As we noted before (and will have occasion to note

Statistical Probabilities

again), this is obviously true in such practical areas of science as medicine — the doctor who waits too long for statistical data to decide what drug to use may well have a dead patient — but is also true of the theoretical sciences: to use the half-life of a particular substance to test a theory or hypothesis requires one to obtain statistical data on the half-life within the time-span appropriate for the test. Although in special cases this might be a longish period, say a decade or so, it is not an indefinitely long period of time, and indeed could not be as long as, say, 10^4 years.

This means that there is a serious incoherence in the way scientists imagine successively larger amounts of statistical evidence being used as the basis of probability judgments concerning a particular phenomenon: the indefinitely large amounts of statistical evidence which we can in principle gather, and so can in principle use to recognize the truth of ordinary probability statements, can *in practice* only be gathered if indefinite amounts of time are available, while any probability judgment corresponding to a practical need must be completed within a strictly limited time-span. Since all probability statements answer to specific practical purposes — even in the theoretical sciences — the possibility of gathering indefinitely large amounts of statistical evidence to use as the basis of a judgment of probability is wholly idle, as it cannot *in practice* be done in the time available. For probability judgments that are to be applied to fulfil some practical purpose, the best one can hope to do is gather an amount of statistical evidence that it is in practice possible for the human race as a whole to gather within the time dictated by the particular practical purpose in question. This means that any precept which is to guide us in the practical application of probability judgments — such as the requirement of total evidence — can only be formulated so far to require us to consider evidence which can in practice be ascertained in the time-period in which we must make our decisions. (In the last section of this chapter I will present what I believe to be the appropriate formulation of the requirement of total evidence, together with an account of what constitutes the statistical evidence available to scientists.)

In this light, the process of reasoning by which scientists and statisticians arrive at their beliefs on statistical probability is thoroughly misguided: evidence which can in principle be ascertained, and so can *in principle* be used to decide the truth of an ordinary probability statement designed to serve a particular practical purpose at a given time, is envisioned as known; adhering to the requirement of total evidence the scientist then thinks this body of evidence, rather than a lesser one, is to be used to decide the truth of the ordinary statement. However, since the evidence in question cannot *in practice* be ascertained within the time-span in which the practical decision is required, it is totally inappropriate to use this evidence to guide an action and so decide the truth of the ordinary statement on its basis.

A FINITE FREQUENCY THEORY

Before I give my positive account of the statistical evidence available for probability judgments, which, I believe, avoids the confusions we have just examined, I should like to consider in some detail an interesting — though in the end unsatisfactory — attempt by one prominent frequency theorist to grapple with just the issues at stake in the above. This is Reichenbach's attempt to formulate a 'finite' frequency theory based on the idea of 'practical' limits observable by humans. I believe a careful examination of this theory will show the general picture given above of the interplay between conditions by which we can in principle recognize the truth of ordinary probability statements — which include bodies of statistical evidence of no fixed or limited size — and the methodological precept of using the total known evidence for giving practical application to probability judgments is correct, and that the problems that Reichenbach's theory inevitably face can only be resolved along the lines suggested there.

Reichenbach begins by noting an all too familiar objection to the frequency theory:

> We saw the logical difficulties in the fact that the statement about the limit appears meaningless for extensionally given sequences of an infinite length. A limit at a given value p is compatible with every finite beginning of the probability sequence; since we can count the frequency only in a finite initial section all limit statements must be called non-verifiable and consequently meaningless. (1949, p. 347)

In an attempt to resolve this objection (in fact unresolved to this day), Reichenbach claims that:

> In fact we are interested only in finite sequences because they will exhaust all the possible observations of a human lifetime or the life-

Statistical Probabilities

time of the human race. We wish to find sequences that behave, in a finite length of these dimensions, in a way comparable to a mathematical limit, that is, converging sufficiently well within that limit and remaining within the interval of convergence. If a sequence of roulette results or mortality statistics were to show a noticeable convergence only after billions of elements, we could not use it for the application of probability concepts, since its domain of convergence would be inaccessible to human experience. However, should one of the sequences converge 'reasonably' within the domain accessible to human observation and diverge for all its infinite rest, such divergence would not disturb us; we should find that such a semi-convergence sequence satisfies sufficiently all the rules of probability. I will introduce the term practical limit for sequences that, in dimensions accessible to human observation, converge sufficiently and remain within the interval of convergence ... It is with the sequences having a practical limit that all actual statistics are concerned. (ibid., pp. 347-8)

This proposal obviously turns on Reichenbach's claim that finite sequences 'exhaust all the possible observations of a human lifetime or the lifetime of the human race', and it is clear that Reichenbach has in mind here what I have called limited finite sequences; his claim is that experiments exceeding in number some fixed amount would be 'inaccessible to human experience'. Indeed he cites the figure of billions of elements as being beyond the domain 'accessible to human observation'. However, the main thing which limits the domain accessible to human observation is time, and Reichenbach's argument would only succeed if there were a fixed finite limit to the lifetime of the whole human race, which Reichenbach appears to believe. What Reichenbach has in mind when he distinguishes between the domain within and beyond human experience is, in fact, the distinction I have discussed above between statistical evidence which can in principle be gathered by finite beings and statistical evidence which can in practice be gathered by a single individual, or the entire human race; as we noted, the latter formed a limited finite whole if, but only if, the time available to the individual, or the race as a whole, for gathering evidence is a limited finite amount. By citing the limited duration of a single individual, and hypothesizing the same for the entire human race, Reichenbach succeeds in fixing a strict finite limit on the number of possible human observations, for indeed the number of observations which can *in*

Statistical Probabilities

practice be made by an individual, or the entire human race, in a limited finite period will be a limited finite amount.

Further confirmation that Reichenbach has in mind — though it is somewhat differently expressed — the distinction I discussed in the previous section comes later when he discusses 'finite attainability'. In discussing his pragmatic justification of an induction, he notes that a particular procedure of positing the limit in an infinite sequence is justified by

> the principle of finite attainability. If the sequence has a limit, the anticipative posit is justified because, in repeated applications, it leads to any desired approximation of the value of the limit in a finite number of steps (ibid., p. 347)

It is obvious that here Reichenbach means by finite attainability what I have called decidability in principle: we know the procedure of the anticipatory posit terminates successfully after some finite number of steps, but there is no limitation on how many steps this may be and the actual termination may not occur for billions and billions of millennia. Such a time-period is obviously a bit long for most practical purposes, and so Reichenbach extends this argument to the large, but limited finite, sequences he claims exhaust all possible human experience:

> These results must now be extended to the concept of practical limit, which was introduced in section 66. The concept refers to a sequence which reaches sufficient convergence after a fairly large number of elements, but which may diverge in later parts that lie beyond the reach of human experience. It is obvious that the rule of induction is justified, too, when the condition of the limit is replaced by that of a practical limit. The justification, in fact, will be improved, since finite attainability then means an attainability for human capacities. A sequence that converges so late that human observers cannot experience the convergence has, for all practical purposes, the character of a sequence without limit. In the following discussions we should therefore regard the limit condition as referring to a practical limit. (ibid., pp. 447-8)

The conception introduced here of 'attainability for human capacities' — in contrast to 'finite attainability' — can, I think, only mean attainability in practice in some fixed time-span; in fact Reichenbach chooses the lifespan of a single individual and the (hypothesized) limited duration of the human race as a whole as the relevant time-spans. But why does Reichenbach regard these particular time-spans as specially significant? These periods obviously have something to do with the practical needs to which probability judgments are put (and this is why Reichenbach uses the term 'practical' limit throughout this discussion), but Reichenbach makes no explicit defence for choosing these periods. Here one might be tempted to suggest that the duration of a single human life, or that of the human race as a whole, has an obvious practical significance which justifies Reichenbach's proposal: events after these times cannot practically affect the individual or species. But no such justification is available to Reichenbach here; throughout most of his lifetime, an individual cannot in practice know the frequency of events in the total class of events made up of all the relevant observations he can make, or could have made. He can only know this on his death-bed, when probability judgments will be singularly lacking in interest for him. Similarly for the entire human race: collectively we can in practice only know the cumulative frequency among all observations which can — actually or in practice — have been made up to the present moment. Thus there is no way we can — actually or in practice — bring the frequency among the totality of 'possible human observations' to bear on a matter of individual or collective practical interest. For this reason, Reichenbach's proposal seems to me to be devoid of practical justification along the lines just suggested.

In fact, in making this proposal, Reichenbach has relied on a process of reasoning discussed repeatedly in this chapter, but heretofore under the assumption that the group we are concerned with is the entire human race as a whole and that this group's existence was unlimited in time. In this chapter I have argued that the correct way to understand the most common beliefs on statistical probability was to see them as natural, though misguided, attempts to systematize the practice of revising one and the same elliptical judgments of probability, with each revision made relative to each of a succession of ever-increasing bodies of statistical evidence. Such bodies of statistical evidence represented the ever-increasing amounts of statistical evidence it is in principle possible to ascertain, or the ever-increasing amounts of statistical evidence that could in practice be ascertained by the entire human race as a whole over ever-increasing time-periods. Adherence to the practical precept that probability judgments relative to the total evidence known are preferable to those made relative to lesser bodies of evidence led to the conception of a never-ending series of revisions to apparently ever-fallible judgments of probability; this in turn led to a number of ideas on the nature of 'statistical' probability, including the identification of limits of frequency in potentially infinite series with probability.

However, if we assume that the time in which observations of statistical data can in practice be made by the human race as a whole is strictly limited, the same reasoning leads to a related, but subtly different, conclusion: with the total amount of statistical evidence which can in practice be ascertained by the human race limited, the practical precept that probability judgments should be made on the basis of the total evidence known would not lead one to conceive of a never-ending series of revisions of ordinary probability judgments; rather, one would be led to believe that the judgment relative to the total amount of evidence which could in practice be ascertained by the human race as a whole, would constitute an 'absolute', or objectively correct, judgment of probability, immune from revision.

Since any revision to what is actually one and the same elliptical judgment of probability is only required by virtue of observations of a greater body of statistical evidence on the basis of a precept designed for the *practical* application of probability judgments, a judgment relative to the total amount of evidence which could *in practice* be gathered would naturally appear to be one which did not require revision. By hypothesizing a limit on the amount of evidence the human race as a whole can – in practice – gather, we in effect limit the amount of evidence we envision as capable of being used to decide the truth of a given ordinary probability judgment which is to answer some specific practical purpose or purposes. That is to say, adopting the practical precept of using the total evidence known to guide our actions, but also envisioning the possibility of subsequent increases to our knowledge of statistical data – which I maintain is at the heart of the idea of statistical probability – we would naturally regard a limit on the amount of evidence which the entire human race could in practice ascertain as fixing a limit on the evidence to be used for revising an ordinary probability statement designed to guide our actions. Thus a limitation on the amount of evidence which can in practice be gathered appears to constitute a limitation, or boundary, beyond which the practice of revising one and the same statement would cease, and the probability value relative to the maximum amount of statistical evidence which can in

Statistical Probabilities

practice be gathered appears as an 'absolute', or correct, value immune from revision. This, then, seems to me to be the *essence* of Reichenbach's proposal that the frequency in the class of experiments constituting the total number of observations which could be made by the human race as a whole in its limited duration is to constitute, by definition, the true probability for a given phenomenon.†

Since the reasoning which motivates Reichenbach's finite frequency theory is so similar to that examined earlier in the chapter under the assumption that the time available to the entire human race as a whole is unlimited, it is easy to reformulate our earlier general findings concerning the meaning and practical application of probability judgments to explain precisely the nature of Reichenbach's error. In fact there are two errors Reichenbach's proposal suffers from, the first (paralleling the discussion at pp. 192-5) concerns the practical application of probability judgments, the second (paralleling the discussion at pp. 188-9) concerned the meaning of probability statements. The objection to Reichenbach's proposal from a practical

---

† Actually, Reichenbach's proposal is slightly more complicated than I have made out above and this is why I only claimed to have captured *the essence* of the motivation behind it. He does not, as I suggest in the above paragraphs, propose to use the cumulative frequency in the class of all possible observations as a whole to fix the probability of a given phenomenon — rather he proposes that a practical limit in this class fix the probability. This is a figure within which fall the cumulative frequencies in the successive sub-classes of observations occurring after a 'reasonable convergence' begins. Obviously the cumulative frequency in the entire class must be within this domain of convergence, and so there is little, if any, difference between proposing that such a practical limit constitutes the probability in question and proposing that the cumulative frequency in the entire class constitutes this probability.

As far as I can see, Reichenbach only uses the practical limit in this class (as opposed to the frequency in it as a whole), in order to parallel the usual frequency definition of probability in terms of limits in potentially infinite classes. Because his finite frequency account in terms of practical limits follows the usual frequency account so closely, it would be possible to refine a version of the argument concerning the rationale for identifying limits of frequency, in potentially infinite sequences, with probability (given earlier in this chapter) to explain Reichenbach's proposal to define probability by reference to practical limits in limited finite sequences. This would be substantially more complicated than the argument given first above, and would not affect the substance of the matter, as far as I can see.

point of view has in fact already been hinted at — the probability value for a phenomenon relative to the total evidence which can in practice be ascertained by the entire human race as a whole is not a value which can be known by humans, either individually or collectively, at the time when it is necessary to make the probability judgments in question. The medical researcher who wishes to know the probability of a certain drug affecting the course of a disease cannot know, in the time in which he must make his decision, the frequency of its success among all humans who at some point take it — he certainly cannot wait until the termination of the existence of the entire human race to observe this, as he must act within relatively short time-periods. Similarly for the physicist who wishes now to test a theory by reference to the value of a particular substance — he requires a figure now, and cannot await information on the results of its cumulative frequency millions of years hence.

Thus, just as it was wholly idle to think that we could use, as the basis for any probability judgment which is to serve our actual practical needs, the vast and ever-increasing number of observations which could in practice be made if the time available to the human race as a whole was unlimited, it is also wholly misguided to think that the limited, but possibly quite vast, number of observations which could in practice be made by the end of the (hypothesized) limited time-span of the human race as a whole can be used as the basis for a probability judgment designed to serve such practical needs.

However, there is a yet more serious error involved in Reichenbach's proposal and this pertains to what is, after all, our central philosophical interest, the meaning of probability statements. Even if we accept for the sake of argument — and I do not see why we should do more than this — that there is some finite limit in time to the duration of the entire human race, we are entitled to ask just what time-period this is. This is, in effect, to ask the precise number of observations which are possible — in practice — from the human point of view. There is obviously no way this can at present be answered, but far from being a small matter of detail, which is how Reichenbach seems to regard it, this is a crucial question: it is the frequency in just this class which is, on the proposal in question, to fix *the meaning* of statements of probability. That is to say, Reichenbach's suggestion is to substitute the frequency in a limited finite class for the idealized notion of limit of frequency in an infinite class as the meaning of probability statements. Then, as far as I can see, in order to give a genuine definition of the

Statistical Probabilities

meaning of the probability statements about a certain kind of phenomenon, one must state precisely what class this is — specifically, how many instances of the phenomenon in question this class has — and this is just what cannot be done. Conversely, if it is assumed that at present we have a grasp of the meaning of probability statements on a certain kind of phenomenon — which to my mind is hardly an unreasonable assumption — we should know on the basis of this mastery the limits beyond which human experience is not possible. But how can this be if there can be no way of knowing at present what the limit of all human experience is, if indeed there is one?†

A more perspicuous way to put this crucial point is this: it is clearly a contingent matter of fact that the human race as a whole has a finite existence in time (if indeed it is a fact), and such a contingent matter cannot be essential to a semantic definition of probability, as Reichenbach's proposal has it. One reason Reichenbach's proposal has a veneer of plausibility is that it comes close to accommodating, but actually misses the entire point of, quite legitimate strictures on the way considerations of finitude figure in a definition of probability, or any other concept: any adequate theory of probability must explain how probability judgments are justified on the basis of finite numbers of observations, as we humans who make probability judgments can of course only observe finite numbers of trials. The verificationist objection which Reichenbach addresses is, to a large extent, just a variant formulation of a similar point, stated in terms of meaning and the possibility of verification. However, despite the fact that only finite numbers of observations can be used as the basis for making or verifying probability judgments, there is no specific limit to the number of observations which can be used in making, or verifying, a statement of probability. The condition of finitude which both anti-realists and verificationists insist upon is a logical condition, as one would expect since it is concerned with matters of meaning: one does not require that

---

†Objections of a similar kind can be made against any attempt to define probability in terms of the frequency in some *one* finite class. If, in order to resolve the specific objection I have made above, one proposes to stipulate the probability of a given phenomenon is the frequency in a large finite class with a specific number of members, this stipulation can be nothing but wholly arbitrary. Thus, for example, Kyburg, who actually recommends use of a googleplex for just this purpose, is forced to admit that this is a wholly 'arbitrary' limitation (see Kyburg, 1961, p. 230).

probability statements must be made, or verified, on the basis of finite numbers of observations because, as a matter of contingent fact, there is a limited finite number of observations the human race as a whole will actually be able to perform, but, rather, because finite observations (whether small in number, or stupendously large, *it matters not*), are the only means by which we can know the truth of such statements. For the anti-realist and verificationist this is what is crucial to the meaning of probability statements.

It is just this which is missed out by Reichenbach, and for just this reason his proposal to fix the frequency in some large finite class as the meaning of a certain kind of probability statement is wholly unsatisfactory: the meaning of probability statements — or any other kind — is fixed by the conditions by which we can in principle recognize the truth of those statements, not those by which we can in practice recognize their truth within a specific time limit. As I have repeatedly said, finite bodies of statistical evidence — with no limit on size — are a crucial part of such conditions for ordinary probability statements, and so the proposal to fix the meaning of such statements in terms of a class delimited by reference to specific practical limitations confuses issues on meaning and application that it is essential to keep straight. In effect, in Reichenbach's proposal what may be genuine restrictions on the conditions by which we can actually ascertain the truth of an ordinary probability statement of some kind are mistakenly used to fix limits on the conditions which constitute the *meaning* of the statement.

Of course the time-periods Reichenbach has chosen are not actually appropriate as the periods within which probability judgments must be made (as explained above), but are, rather, the maximum periods in question, though this does not bear directly on issues concerning the meaning of the probability statements. What matters from that point of view is that the limitations Reichenbach is concerned with are still only practical limitations; the domains beyond human experience he speaks of are domains which humans cannot *in practice* experience, and there is no reason why such limitations in practice should affect the meaning of probability statements.

I have dwelt at length on Reichenbach's finite frequency theory because the errors he has committed are not trivial ones: rather, they go to the very heart of probability theory and its relation to statistics, involving, as they do, issues concerning the statistical evidence which can in principle be observed, the amount which can in practice be

Statistical Probabilities

observed during fixed time intervals, and the question of just what time intervals are appropriate for probability judgments. These are issues which I believe have the profoundest impact on probability theory and, as I am sure the reader will have anticipated, are issues which I believe can alone be satisfactorily treated within the context of the l.r.t. The general framework within which such a resolution can be given has already been outlined in this chapter; however, to give a precise resolution to the issues on the meaning and application of probability judgments we have just been considering, it remains for me to provide a satisfactory account of the methodology of handling statistical evidence in order to apply the l.r.t.

THE AVAILABLE STATISTICAL EVIDENCE

Despite our lengthy examination of the role statistical evidence plays in scientific discourse on probability, we have yet to resolve one central problem concerning the use of statistical data to determine inductive probabilities suitable for scientific discourse. The problem is a familiar one, discussed at length in Chapter III concerning specificatory evidence, where indeed I deliberately postponed the parallel question concerning statistical evidence. It is of course the question as to which of many different relational probability judgments (involving different amounts of statistical evidence) we are to use to determine a unique probability on a given occasion, for a particular practical purpose (whether that purpose be the pressing needs of medical science or the more theoretical needs of other sciences). Throughout earlier chapters I stressed that the probability statement relative to the total available evidence was the one singled out as most desirable from the point of view of action. In regard to specificatory evidence, various explications of 'availability' were offered in Chapter III, corresponding to subjective, inter-subjective and objective statements of probability. But no explication was given to the notion of availability as regards statistical evidence, and various considerations already adduced suggest that this is no easy matter. The total available specificatory evidence — understood objectively — was the total specificatory evidence ascertainable by known procedures for discovering relevant empirical parameters, but what would be analogous to this for statistical evidence?

In fact there are two related difficulties for the parallel proposal, i.e. that the statistical evidence available for a particular decision be taken to be the evidence on repeated trials which could be obtained if some extant experimental procedure were implemented. First of all, the procedures known for obtaining statistical evidence on the results in repeated trials are extremely simple, and it is unclear if this proposed explication would be in any way illuminating: to obtain statistical evidence of the results in n trials of a certain kind, we simply perform the relevant experiment n times. In what sense, then, have we fixed the notion of the statistical evidence which is available, if we identify this with the statistical evidence which would be ascertained if the relevant procedure were implemented? The basic procedure in question is a single performance of an experiment, and the crucial question of how many times is this one procedure to be implemented receives no answer on this proposal.

This brings us to the second, and particularly acute, problem with such an explication for the idea of available statistical evidence: if the available statistical evidence is the evidence which would be ascertained by implementing known procedures, and the only relevant known procedure is performing a particular test n times, there appears to be no limit to the total statistical evidence available. If one has gathered statistical evidence about the results in n trials, it would appear, on the proposed explication, that more statistical evidence would still be available – all one needs to do to obtain more statistical evidence is repeat the same experiment one more time and this would yield the results in $n + 1$ trials. Crucially the performance of one more experiment involves no new procedure; we simply repeat one more time the experiment we have already repeated n times.

Happily there is a relatively simple solution to these two problems, and it provides the basis for giving an explication to the idea of the statistical evidence available to a scientist quite similar in spirit to that given in Chapter III for specificatory evidence (though slightly different in details). The solution depends on the distinction between the evidence which can in practice be ascertained and the evidence which can in principle be ascertained, a distinction explained in Chapter IV for specificatory evidence, and discussed extensively in the previous sections of this chapter for statistical evidence. Since, in explicating the notion of the statistical evidence available to a scientist, we are really concerned with the question of how much statistical evidence should be used as the basis for a probability judgment which is to answer to a specific practical purpose, the possibility referred to above of *indefinite* repetitions of a single kind of experiment is wholly idle.

Statistical Probabilities

Any serious sense of 'availability' that is to capture the amount of statistical evidence a scientist can bring to bear on a particular question involving judgments of probability, must be such that the scientist, alone or with others, can actually — that is in practice — ascertain it within the time-span dictated by the practical purposes to which the probability judgment is to be put. As we noted earlier, for any given finite group of finite beings the amount of statistical evidence which can in practice be gathered within a limited finite time-span is a strictly limited finite amount, although the amount of statistical evidence which finite beings can in principle ascertain is unlimited. Thus, while in principle it is always possible to add to extant statistical knowledge by performing additional experiments — which is the possibility referred to in the paragraph above — this is not always possible *in practice*; since we are concerned with elucidating a notion of the evidence available to a scientist when he wishes to apply probability judgments to a specific practical purpose, this is of crucial importance, and serves to limit the amount of evidence 'available'.

Accordingly we may say that the statistical evidence available to a scientist is the evidence which he, alone or with others, can in practice ascertain *within the time-span* dictated by his practical needs. In effect, because probability judgments in science, as elsewhere, answer to specific practical needs, and such needs obtain for specific limited time-periods, the limitation on the amount of statistical evidence which can be gathered by a finite group of finite beings in a finite time serves to fix a limit on the amount of statistical evidence 'available' to scientists wishing to make judgments of probability.

The same point can be made in terms of the notion of technical possibility, which, in Chapter III, I treated as equivalent to that of possibility in practice. Following some remarks of Reichenbach's, we noted that the specificatory evidence we could bring to bear on a particular matter involving judgments of probability was limited by the existing technological resources. Now the amount of time required to perform an experiment and the number of people living who can perform that experiment fix the number of times an experiment can be performed within a certain period, and so limit the statistical evidence that can be brought to bear on a particular problem, just as the specificatory evidence that can be brought to bear on a problem is limited by the state of existing technology. Thus it seems appropriate to speak of the technological limitations on the amount of statistical evidence which can be gathered in a certain period; the point of the above two paragraphs can be restated to the effect that a scientist who wishes to use statistical evidence in making a judgment of probability can only rely on information on the results of trials which can be performed within the given time-period with existing technological resources.

It is now an easy matter to give an exact — and objective — formulation to the requirement of total evidence, in respect of statistical evidence. As we saw in regard to specificatory evidence, the requirement that an individual use the total evidence *known* to him in deciding what relational probability is most desirable for the purpose of action is very weak, leading to a variety of subjectivism: the unique, or preferential, probabilities determined in this way depend on the subjective matter of what information that individual happens to know. Similarly with statistical evidence — if we merely require that an individual use the statistical evidence he happens to know to determine the numerical probability of a phenomenon most desirable for the purpose of action, the actual values determined will depend on the subjective matter of what statistical information he happens to know. (This in effect was Carnap's proposal, and this is just why his theory has been objected to as subjectivist in character.) Conversely — and this parallels the strategy of Chapter III for specificatory evidence — if an individual uses all the statistical evidence he *can possibly* ascertain in determining such a unique, or preferential, numerical probability, his judgment will be as objective as it can be expected to be.

The crucial point to emerge above is that the relevant sense of possibility (in the phrase in italics above) is possibility in practice. The amount of statistical evidence which an individual can in principle ascertain is unlimited, while the amount he, alone, or with a finite group of other finite individuals, can in practice ascertain within a finite amount of time is a strictly limited finite totality. It is just such a strictly limited finite totality of statistical evidence which alone can be relevant to his determination of the probability value most desirable from the point of view of action: for him to be able to use a certain amount of evidence as second term of a probability judgment for a decision is actually to take, he must be able actually — or in practice — to ascertain this information.

Using these considerations to give the requirement of total evidence an objective formulation, we may say that the total statistical evidence available to a scientist who wishes to make a probability judgment within a certain time is the total amount it is possible in

Statistical Probabilities

practice for the entire human race as a whole to ascertain within that time-span. The reason this formulation refers to the capacities of the human race as a whole — rather than those of an individual in isolation — should be obvious: no one regards scientific research as an activity carried out by an individual in total isolation from others; indeed no scientist can wilfully ignore information which others have obtained, and so the amount of statistical evidence which can be used for making a probability judgment in science cannot be fixed by reference to the capacities of an individual in isolation.

I should stress that a central feature of my proposal is that the statistical evidence available for a judgment of probability in science is the amount of statistical evidence that *can* in practice be ascertained rather than the amount which has actually been ascertained in practice — it is this which allows judgments of probability relative to such a body of statistical evidence to be objective. It should be obvious that the limited finite number of experiments relevant to any kind of outcome which *can* in practice be carried out is usually so large that no scientist or group of scientists *would* actually — or in practice — carry them all out. To take our familiar example of coin-tossing, within a year or so (an appropriate time for a scientific study of this phenomenon to be concluded), one person could perform the relevant experiment some 500,000 or more times, save for the strain on his sanity. A team of a dozen or so researchers would be able to perform this experiment many millions of times in the same period. (I calculate one person tossing a coin at the rate of one toss per ten seconds would toss a coin in excess of 700,000 times in 52 weeks, working a 40-hour week.) If we consider the amount of experiments of this kind which could be carried out in a year by the entire human race as a whole, the number is immense.

Even in genuine scientific research the number of repetitions of a single experiment that can in practice be carried out in a relatively short period of time is enormous — there is nothing, other than good sense, to prevent every trained nuclear physicist (and competent student) from abandoning all other work to carry out repeated tests for the half-life of a particular substance. Of course it would be ridiculous if scientists actually did this, just as it would be ridiculous for the entire human race to spend one year repeatedly tossing coins; however, I am not proposing that scientists actually do this, but rather only wish to point out that the number of experiments relevant to any phenomenon that could actually be done is an immense, though limited, finite amount.

Estimating Inductive Probabilities

But if neither the scientist, nor the ordinary layman, *is* actually going to carry out such a vast number of experiments, what is the point of proposing — as I did — that the probability value relative to such a body of statistical evidence constitutes a unique, objective value of probability? In particular, how are we to come to know this unique or preferential objective probability, since I am certainly not suggesting such vast numbers of experiments actually be performed and the results used to determine relational probabilities? This is exactly where statistical methods for estimating probabilities are called for and where, on my view, such methods find their proper explanation in terms of probability.

Granted that the probability value relative to the total statistical evidence objectively available would constitute a unique, preferential, value for the purpose of action, but that such a body of evidence is so large that no one would seriously attempt to gather it, we might reasonably settle for some method of choosing small statistical samples which would lead to probability values quite similar to those we would obtain if we were to go to the (very great) trouble of ascertaining such statistical evidence. It should be clear that no method of choosing statistical samples is *certain* to yield probability values based on the frequency observed in the samples which are close approximations to the values of probability which would obtain if we used this vast body of statistical evidence, for we do not know what the latter values are. The best we can hope to do is find some method of choosing small samples which *probably* display frequencies that are close approximations to the frequency we would obtain if we carried out all the experiments which can in practice be performed. If we then use the $\lambda = 0$ measure function on the evidence of such a small sample (which is the one I have recommended as most appropriate for a reconstruction of scientific discourse on probability), we obtain a numerical probability value which *probably* approximates closely the value we would obtain if we actually used the evidence of the result in this vast series of trials to determine the probability in question (again via $\lambda = 0$).

But how is the l.r. theorist to find such a method of selecting samples? For him any probability must be a probability relative to some evidence, but what evidence is appropriate to use in the present context? That is, relative to what body of evidence are we to determine the probability that the frequency in a small sample is a good approximation to the frequency we would find if we actually performed the vast number of trials we *could* perform given existing technology?

Obviously we desire what I have called a preferential, or unique, relational probability value here, because we are, in effect, faced with a practical decision requiring a single action, namely choosing one small sample in the hopes of obtaining a good approximation of the results we would obtain if we performed the very great number of trials we can perform given existing technology. Our guide for identifying such a preferential probability value is the requirement of total evidence, and if the proposal of this section for explicating this requirement in the case of statistical evidence is to be taken seriously, we should base our action on information of the results in the total number of repetitions of the same basic phenomenon we are concerned with which can be performed at present, given existing technology, namely what I have called the total available statistical evidence. But now we appear to be in some trouble, edging towards a hopeless regress: we are at present trying to find a general method for approximating probability values relative to such a vast amount of evidence, and we now see that to find such a method we require knowledge of a probability value relative to just this vast amount of evidence.

But actually there is no regress here, for we have at our disposal the means to resolve this difficulty. The resolution of it hinges on the fact that any small sample we actually observe is a subset of — i.e. is drawn from — the vast population comprising the total number of experiments that can be performed given existing technology, and that the standard statistical methods for estimating probabilities from small samples, as interpreted within the l.r.t., provide a means for determining the probability of a sample approximating the results in an entire population, *relative to information on the results in that entire population*. If we regard the total number of experiments which can be performed given existing technology — the results of which I have called the total statistical evidence available — as a parent population from which any small sample we actually observe is drawn, these methods provide just what we need at present: a means for determining *the second-order probability* of probability values relative to the evidence of a small sample being a good approximation of the values relative to the total available statistical evidence, where this second order of probability is itself relative to the total available statistical evidence.

It may be useful to illustrate my suggestion here by reference to

Statistical Probabilities

the Chebyshev inequality, as already studied. As we have seen, the standard statistical procedure based on the Chebyshev inequality is to take a small sample of size n, observe a frequency p in it, and then reject all values of probability outside the interval $p \pm \sqrt{\frac{pq}{nk}}$; the rational being that the procedure of rejecting values outside this interval has a probability less than k of rejecting a true value of probability. On my view the only thing which could be called a true value of probability is the unique, or preferential, probability value relative to the total available statistical evidence. The difficulty we have been examining is that the population of events which make up the total available statistical evidence is so large that no one would be prepared to examine it in its entirety. I have proposed to use the standard methods of statistics for estimating probabilities — as interpreted within the l.r.t. in terms of the downward inference from a population to a sample — as a way of overcoming this difficulty. Thus in the case of the Chebyshev inequality we are to choose a sample of size n from the vast populations of experiments which can be performed given existing technology, observe a frequency p and then reject all probability values outside the interval $p \pm \sqrt{\frac{pq}{nk}}$. By the Chebyshev inequality as interpreted within the l.r.t., we know there is a probability less than k relative to information on the results in this vast series of trials that we will have rejected a figure which approximates closely to the frequency in this vast population. Since information on the frequency in this vast population is what I have called the total statistical evidence available, we may reformulate this by saying that we know our procedure of rejection has a second order of probability less than k — *relative to the total available evidence* — of rejecting a first-order probability for the phenomenon close to that which obtains relative to the total available statistical evidence.

This is highly, indeed doubly, significant, given that we believe that the probability relative to the total available statistical evidence is the preferential relational probability to adopt for practical decisions involving the phenomenon in question. First, and most obviously, this conclusion is significant because it assures us that rejections based on observation of the value p in the small sample are unlikely to be rejections of a value close to that which holds relative to the total available statistical evidence, which is the most desirable, but as yet unknown, value for us to use for the purpose of action. Secondly, the probability less than k of our sample leading to a rejection of this most desirable value is itself relative to the total available statistical evidence. It is crucial that this second-order probability less than k is relative to the total available statistical evidence as, for the l.r. theorist, this is the most desirable basis for any action concerning the phenomenon in question, and so our decision to reject probability values on the basis of the evidence of the small sample is guided by a probability judgment which is the most desirable for the purpose of this or any other action.

The only objection to using second-order probability values relative to the total available statistical evidence to justify rejections based on observations of a small sample is that we are obviously not in possession of the total available statistical evidence; indeed it is the probability value relative to this unknown body of information that we wish to avoid rejecting. But this is where the Chebyshev inequality becomes so important: by it, we know that no matter what probability values obtain relative to the total available statistical evidence, there is a second-order probability of less than k, relative to this information, that our sample will lead us to reject a value close to this preferential value. I should add that this is precisely the kind of role usually reserved for the Chebyshev inequality in statistical inferences of probabilities: lacking information on what a certain frequency is (which is believed to fix correctly the probability for the phenomenon we are concerned with), we use observations of a small sample to reject probability values outside a certain interval, with the degree of second-order probability that our sample has led us to reject the correct value determined by the Chebyshev inequality.

Of course, as we have noted before, the Chebyshev inequality is just one statistical method based on the binomial distribution used in estimating probabilities, and other more powerful techniques – such as the Neyman-Pearson confidence interval techniques – are frequently employed in the practice of science. However, the account I have given of the role of the Chebyshev inequality in terms of the l.r.t. can be extended in a straightforward way to justify the use of these other techniques. In fact, as we have just seen in detail with the Chebyshev inequality, the only difference between the interpretation I have given to the methods of statistics and the usual one concerns the idea of a 'correct' or 'true' probability hypothesis or statement; for me, this is not a physical or empirical probability, but rather the probability relative to the total available statistical evidence, a vast, but limited, finite totality. Since most of the influential techniques of statistical estimation of probabilities are formulated to apply to inferences to the frequency in *either* very large finite populations or potentially infinite populations (indeed Neyman, for one, seems to prefer formulations of the former kind), such methods can be interpreted as methods for inferring probabilities relative to the total available statistical evidence, as I have explained that concept.

In general, any technique for inferring probabilities from samples, where the true probability is thought to be fixed by the frequency in some large finite class, can be employed in the same manner: since as we have noted, the binomial law and Bernoulli's Law of Large Numbers can be used in conjunction with large finite populations, virtually all techniques for estimating binomial, or probability, hypotheses can be interpreted as methods for estimating probabilities relative to the total available statistical evidence, construed as evidence on the outcomes in a very large finite class.

One interesting consequence of my interpretation of scientists' procedures for estimating probabilities is that on it these procedures emerge as mere practical *conveniences*, devoid of any greater significance — that is, on my view, they are theoretically dispensable, though practically convenient. In essence, my view is that in science, as in ordinary life, the 'correct' probability value of a given phenomenon can be known with full certainty at a given time, both in principle and in practice: it is the probability value relative to the total evidence objectively available, both specificatory and statistical. However, the total available statistical evidence is so vast that, while it is possible in practice to ascertain it (indeed this is just how I have defined it), it is not in the least practically *convenient* to do so, and so we never actually do so. Here is where the methods of statistics become useful: they provide an extremely convenient, though theoretically dispensable, method for approximating the ideal values relative to the total available statistical evidence.

This view of statistical methods for inferring probabilities as practically efficacious devices, allowing us to use conveniently small samples to approximate some ideal value — which it is far from convenient to ascertain — seems to me wholly natural and congenial; I suspect it is the one scientists and statisticians first think of for these techniques, only later attaching a different kind of significance to them on the basis of what I take to be misguided objectivist conceptions of statistical probability.

Final remarks

This much said in favour of the explication I have given to the notion of the statistical evidence available for a judgment of probability —

Statistical Probabilities

and the account I have given of how statistical methods for estimating probabilities can be used to determine numerical values of probability relative to such evidence — I may conclude this chapter by considering several difficulties with what is, no doubt, a somewhat novel account of statistical methods and the role of statistics in science. First of all, I must admit that the notion of the statistical evidence which 'can in practice be gathered by the entire human race as a whole', which I have repeatedly appealed to, is neither realistic, nor completely clear. In Chapter III I was at pains to give an exact and realistic account of the available specificatory evidence by reference to extant technological procedures, but the parallel explication for the notion of statistical evidence has been somewhat more sketchy, relying only on the distinction between propositions decidable in principle and those decidable in practice. Inevitably a number of issues were glossed over with such a sketchy treatment; for example, at several points in explaining the idea of the number of experiments which 'could in practice be ascertained by the entire human race' I referred to the number of persons who *could* in practice perform an experiment within a given time. One might well ask for further elucidation of the notion of 'could' in question here: would an untrained person who could — in practice — be trained to perform an experiment, but in reality remained untrained, count as one such person? This of course is just one of the issues which would have to be resolved in an exact account of the notion of possibility in practice I have relied upon.

Moreover, the slight elucidation I did give to this notion was unrealistic in certain important respects. I spoke of the possibility — admittedly ludicrous — of the entire human race tossing coins for fifty-two working weeks, but it is not clear whether there is any real sense in which this is 'possible in practice': at the very least some group of people would, in practice, have to work in other areas to provide food to sustain those performing these experiments, and this alone would reduce the number of trials which could be performed. To be realistic, the number of people who can perform a certain experiment is fixed by economic and political constraints — for example, the level of university funding in a society — and such considerations must be taken into account in determining the total number of experiments which can in practice be carried out in a given time period.

Happily none of these complications affect the substance of my proposal — no matter how one eventually explains the notion of 'possible in practice', the number of experiments which can in practice be performed by the entire human race will vastly exceed the number it is convenient to perform, for virtually every relevant kind of experiment. This is all that is required for my argument concerning the role of statistical methods of estimation in determining numerical probabilities, and for this reason the fine details of an account of the notion of 'possibility in practice' do not really bear on problems in probability theory.

A final, and more serious, criticism of my proposal is that the explication I have given to the notion of 'the available statistical evidence' does not even resemble the ordinary usage of that term. This seems to me fair comment: what scientists, statisticians, probability theorists and, I suppose, the ordinary layman mean by the term 'available statistical evidence', or 'available statistics', is the statistical evidence which has actually been gathered and disseminated in published form, not some vast body of statistical data which could, in some perhaps philosophically significant sense, be gathered. Moreover, the point is not terminological, for I dare say I would be entitled to coin a special term to indicate this vast body of evidence, and then use it in working out a version of the l.r.t. In fact, the real objection to my position is that it seems quite mistaken to attribute to scientists (or anyone else) the belief that the correct (ideal, unique, or preferential) probability for a certain phenomenon is that relative to such a vast body of statistical evidence; I should think prior to my discussing the matter in this way, no one else has ever considered such a proposition, much less believed in it.

But — and this will serve to tie up this discussion with that of previous sections of the chapter — we saw earlier in the chapter that the beliefs of scientists and statisticians on statistical probability were a tangled morass of sound intuitions and confused conclusions. It is my belief that *the only way* to make philosophically consistent and coherent sense of the different strands that we have seen twisted in other views on statistical probability — both explicitly stated by philosophers and implicitly believed by scientists and statisticians — is the one I have given above, and this seems to me to be the primary argument in favour of my account of the use of statistical evidence in science.

To substantiate this claim — though I hope it already appears somewhat plausible in the light of arguments given earlier in the chapter — it will be useful to conclude this chapter with a summary of my views on the role of statistical evidence in scientific discourse on probability, with particular reference to the questions on the meaning, methodology for application and objectivity of probability judgments that have been our central concern throughout the book so far.

Central to the concept of a probability estimate as it occurs in science is the idea that estimates based on small samples are always provisional. However, it seems to me indisputable that probability statements based on observations of frequencies in small samples are regarded as provisional by scientists only because it is *possible* to gather more than that small amount. A proposition ascribing a numerical value to a magnitude is regarded as an estimate if, and only if, we envision that there could obtain conditions which, if known, would justify us in rejecting the value ascribed to the magnitude. With the probability statements, one of the crucial kinds of conditions which we envision as requiring revision of an estimate based on a small sample is knowledge of greater amounts of statistical evidence. The proper way to systematize this process of revision is, to my mind, the explanation I have given in this chapter; specifically, the revision of probability statements based on knowledge of greater amounts of evidence is to be explained as revision to elliptical statements of probability relative to the ever-increasing bodies of evidence we envision as known, according to the precept of always using the total amount of evidence known as the basis for such ordinary elliptical statements of probability.

Contrary to the criticism that the l.r.t. leads to a subjectivist conception of probability, it is possible within this explanatory framework to give an objective basis for judgments of probability based on statistical evidence: an objective judgment is one that incorporates all the statistical evidence it is *possible* to obtain. But — and this brings us to the very heart of what is elusive in the notion of statistical probability — there is no limit to the amount of statistical evidence it is in principle possible to obtain; thus the notion of a single body of statistical evidence which is the maximum it is possible to obtain, and which would thus constitute an objective, or ideal, basis for the judgment of probability, seems to elude us. However, to conceive the matter this way is to ignore the practical purposes to which probability judgments are put and the constraints imposed by such practical needs: to be of practical use, probability judgments must be made within certain finite time-spans by a group of finite beings with a specific finite number of members during that time-span, i.e. the human race. The limitations imposed by the practical purposes to which probability judgments are put means that the concept of possibility that is required for the context underlined above is that of possibility in practice, not possibility in principle. This is what allows us to fix a finite limit on the amount of statistical evidence which can be used at a given time as the basis for an ordinary statement of probability, and the probability value relative to the maximum amount of evidence which can in practice be gathered can be regarded as the objectively correct value for the purpose of action.

Unfortunately it is all too easy to overlook the fact that any judgment of probability which is to be applied in practice within a given time can only be based on an amount of statistical evidence that can — in practice — be gathered within that time, which is what permits us to single out one relational value which is objectively correct (i.e. the one relative to the total amount which can so be gathered). In fact a good deal of this chapter has been devoted to examining the reason for this: while the amount of statistical evidence which can in practice be ascertained by the entire human race as a whole within a finite time is a limited finite amount, the amount of statistical evidence which can in principle be gathered by finite beings is unlimited. Since — as I have stressed throughout the book — such evidence is a crucial part of the means by which we recognize the truth of ordinary probability statements (the other parts being specificatory evidence and logical relations of partial entailment), it is all too easy for scientists and statisticians to regard an ordinary probability statement made tacitly relative to *any finite body* of statistical evidence e_i as potentially mistaken — and thus not, objectively speaking, correct — even if it is made relative to the maximum amount of evidence which can in practice be gathered by the human race as a whole in a given time. The amount of statistical evidence which can in principle be ascertained is unlimited, and because we implicitly adhere to the practical precept of using the total known evidence as the basis for our ordinary (elliptical) probability statements, the scientist or statistician can always imagine himself possessed by a body of evidence e_j greater than e_i, which then requires revision to the ordinary elliptical statement made relative to e_i. This of course is the process of reasoning elaborately examined throughout this chapter (and, for specificatory evidence, the previous chapter).

What I hope has emerged from this chapter (and what I have tried particularly to bring out in this summary) is that such reasoning confuses fundamental matters on the meaning and conditions of application for probability judgments: statistical evidence with no limit on the

Statistical Probabilities

number of trials in question is part of the means by which *in principle* we recognize the truth of ordinary probability statements and, if the anti-realist theory of meaning I have favoured is accepted, should be thought of as determining part of the *meaning* of our concept of probability. Such a theory, I believe, is provided by the l.r.t., which explains statements of probability as being, by their very meaning, statements on relations between hypotheses concerning the future and bodies of evidence. Such evidence always includes a statistical part, which may of course refer to any finite number of trials.

However, the conditions which fix the meaning of a concept — the conditions by which we can in principle recognize the truth of ordinary statements involving that concept — must not be confused with the conditions under which we can on specific occasions, at different times, actually recognize the truth of particular ordinary statements involving the concept. In the case of probability statements, the latter conditions are what I have called the conditions for applying statements of probability in practice and they must be a proper subset of the former. The question of just which proper subset of the conditions by which in principle we can recognize the truth of probability statements should be used in practice on any given occasion — just how much evidence should be taken into consideration — is what I (and other l.r. theorists) regard as a problem in the methodology of probability theory. Specifically, it is a question of what relational probability is the most desirable for the purpose of action. In proposing that the practical application of our concept of probability should be made on the basis of the very large, but limited, finite body of statistical evidence which can in practice be ascertained by the entire human race at a given time, I have hoped to give a methodological precept which objectively determines the numerical probability value most desirable for the purpose of action. At the same time, I have hoped to keep matters relating to the meaning of probability statements separate from those concerning its application. These matters, as I have said, I believe to have been seriously confused in other philosophical accounts of the relation of probability and statistics, as well as in popular beliefs of scientists and statisticians.

VI
THE PRINCIPLE OF INDIFFERENCE AND THE CLASSICAL THEORY OF PROBABILITY

My concern throughout the book so far has been to elaborate and defend the l.r.t., particularly in regard to problems posed by scientific discourse on probabilities. In this and the final chapter, I will be concerned with more historical issues, specifically the classical theory of probability and the principle of indifference. What I hope to show is that a definition of probability quite similar to the l.r.t. underlies the classical conception of probability, particularly its reliance on the notorious principle of indifference. Of course affinities between the classical theory of probability and the modern logical relation theory have already been noted by other writers; Carnap, for example, cites numerous passages from classical writers to support his general contention that the explicandum they had in mind is his concept of probability$_1$. But the position I wish to maintain is considerably stronger than this and it depends on a detailed analysis of the principle of indifference. What I wish to show is that the principle of indifference *itself* embodies an early and rudimentary version of the definition of probability as a relation between evidence and hypothesis, one in which probability is defined as the comparative concept of evidential support. Whether one should go further and characterize the relational definition encapsulated in the principle as a purely logical relation is a somewhat more complicated matter, which I will consider explicitly near the end of the next chapter. Before doing so it will be necessary to come to a full understanding of the relationship between the l.r.t. as a theory of quantitative probability and the principle of indifference. A number of the points which emerge from the examination of this relationship will bear directly on issues raised

The Principle of Indifference

earlier — particularly concerning the choice of measure function for a system of inductive probability — and so the discussion in these chapters will have considerable relevance to my earlier treatment of the l.r.t.

However, the principle of indifference still exercises considerable fascination for probability theorists and my main concern in these chapters will be to resolve the controversies surrounding it. By analysing it as a form of relational definition of probability, I hope to show that well-known objections to the principle are either natural (but not insoluble) objections to the definition encapsulated in it, or objections to the characteristic manner in which this definition was applied to yield the 'unique' judgments of probability needed for the purpose of action.

THE PRINCIPLE'S HISTORY

At first sight it might appear strange to construe the principle as an instance of the definition of probability as a relation of evidential support. Certainly its usual formulation to the effect that alternatives are equally likely if, and only if, there is no reason to choose between them does not, on the face of it, look like a definition of probability. But, as has been widely recognized by philosophers, one perfectly proper way to provide a semantics for a concept is to state identity conditions for that concept. Thus in just the way that, say, Frege's definition of number was constituted by the statement of the conditions under which classes† were equal in number, the principle of indifference in effect amounts to a semantic definition of probability, in so far as it fixes the conditions under which different alternatives are equal in probability.

Let me hasten to add that I do not believe that those who previously advocated the principle intended it as a definition of probability; indeed if such an interpretation of the principle already existed, there would be little point in arguing for it here. Rather I believe that both advocates and critics of the principle have failed to note its definitional character and in consequence failed to appreciate what are the real issues involved in the controversies surrounding it. Certainly such a situation would not be without precedent in the history of

---

† Or rather for him 'concepts', in his extensional sense of that expression.

science; until the definitional and empirical components of Newton's Third Law of Motion were clearly separated and identified by Mach, one could not properly evaluate various objections to Newton's introduction of the concepts of 'force' and 'mass' in his theory. Once the definitional and empirical components of the Third Law were separated, it became clear that critics of Newton were correct if they maintained that inertial mass (and thus, by the Second Law, force as well) was not a concept that could be given a meaning independently of the Third Law, but were incorrect in denying him the right to introduce an operationally defined concept, which, moreover, had important testable consequences.

Such an analogy is particularly appropriate to my view of the principle of indifference, since I believe that it, like Newton's Third Law, combines definitional and non-definitional components in a manner that is bound to cause confusion until each is properly sorted out. In this and the next chapter I will try to do just that; however, before going into the details of this analysis, we should begin with a quick look at some of the variety of views to be found in the literature concerning the principle. An immediate — and important — problem is that there seems to be no agreement on what exactly constitutes the principle of indifference. I suppose that nowadays both critics and defenders of the principle would accept that it states that alternatives are equally likely if, and only if, there is no reason to choose between them,† but there is considerable latitude in the way this is interpreted. For example, Keynes, whose discussion of the principle is perhaps the best known in the field, gave it the following formulation:

> The Principle of Indifference asserts that if there is no *known* reason for predicating of our subject one rather than another of several alternatives, then relatively to such knowledge the assertions of each of these alternatives have an *equal* probability. (1921, p. 42)

Now it might be thought that reference to *known* reasons for preference and judgments of probability *relative* to such knowledge is peculiar to Keynes's treatment of the principle, but a careful look at the formulations given to the principle more recently shows that knowledge (or as it has become customary to say, 'evidence') plays

†In point of fact, I know of no writer who includes 'only if' in his formulation of the principle but, as we will see, this is probably something of an oversight as the necessary conditions for judgments of equal probability are far less problematic than the sufficient conditions.

The Principle of Indifference

some role in most discussions of it. Kneale for instance (1949, p. 173) remarks: 'According to the principle we may call alternatives equally probable if we do not know that the available evidence provides a reason for preferring any one to any other.' Thus, although Keynes regarded knowledge, i.e. awareness of some available evidence, as that relative to which the principle warranted judgments of equal probability, Kneale thinks that the judgments of equal probability determined by the principle are based on *not* knowing something about the available evidence.

In fact Kneale's discussion has become something of a focal point for writers attempting to explain just what evidence, or knowledge, is required for application of the principle. Blackburn (1973, pp. 116-21) devotes five pages to a discussion of Kneale's views of the principle and concludes that his conception of 'ignorance of the properties of the available evidence' is 'itself very unclear'. He attempts to avoid 'any trouble' caused by Kneale's formulation of the principle by expressing it in the form of an entailment between preposition

      (5)   Nothing that I know, nor rationally believe, nor should have discovered, favours A rather than B

and (6)   It is unreasonable for me to have more confidence in A than B.

It seems fairly clear that Blackburn thinks the total available evidence, in either the objective or inter-subjective sense explained in Chapter II, should be considered before employing the principle. If so, Blackburn has considerable weight of authority, for Bernoulli, who first proposed the principle, seems to have held that it could only properly be applied in relation to the total available evidence. In the same section of *Ars Conjectandi* in which he enunciated the principle, he states what Keynes (1921, p. 313) calls his second maxim, that in determining probabilities:

> Non sufficit expendere unum alterumve argumentum, sed conquirenda sunt omnis, quae cognitionem nostram venire possunt, atque ullo modo ad probationem rei facere videntur. [It is not sufficient to weigh just one piece of evidence, but all of the evidence is to be sought out which can enter into our knowledge and seems in anyway to relate to the demonstration of the matter.]

It seems clear, particularly from the occurrence of the verb 'possunt', that Bernoulli would have regarded judgments of probability arrived at by use of the principle as correct only if the total available evidence, in the objective sense of what *can* be known in a situation, gave no reason for preference.

In contrast, Mackie criticizes a reformulation by Mellor of Kneale's treatment of the principle and then offers yet another formulation of what is involved in the principle: having argued (1973, p. 162) that (some form of) the principle is valid for judgments of what he calls simple probability, he goes on to ask if the judgments of simple probability warranted by the principle should 'be treated as relative to the information that is *available* rather than to the information that someone has'. He replies: 'A simple probability indicates what in our present state of knowledge and ignorance it is reasonable to believe,' adding that, accordingly, the principle's 'function is merely to indicate what it is reasonable to believe in light of whatever information we now have.' (pp. 201-2)

Thus while most writers agree that evidence (or 'knowledge') must be considered when deciding if there is, or is not, reason for preference among alternatives, there is no clear agreement on just what evidence must be considered when applying the principle. This is a problem I will return to later. At the moment, however, we should gloss over these differences and instead consider a number of the arguments that have been given for and against the principle. We might begin with an example of the kind of uncritical acceptance of the principle that has aroused such vehement opposition to it.

Among twentieth-century writers of prominence, Jeffreys has been the principle's most unflinching advocate, arguing that it is analytic in virtue of the meaning of 'probability'. Thus we find:

> If there is no reason to believe one hypothesis rather than another, the probabilities are equal. In terms of our fundamental notions of the nature of inductive inference, *to say that the probabilities are equal is a precise way of saying that we have no ground for choosing between the alternatives*. All hypotheses that are sufficiently definitely stated to give any difference between the probabilities of their consequences will be compared with the data by the principle of inverse probability; but if we do not take the prior probabilities equal we are expressing confidence in one rather than another before the data are available, and this must be done only from definite reason. To take the prior probabilities different in the

The Principle of Indifference

absence of observational reason for doing so would be an expression of sheer prejudice. The rule that we should take them equal is not a statement of any belief about the actual composition of the world, nor is it an inference from previous experience; it is merely a formal way of expressing ignorance . . . It is not a new rule in the present theory because it is an immediate application of Convention 1 [that 'We assign the larger number on given data to the more probable proposition (and therefore equal numbers to equally probable propositions)']. (1961, pp. 33-4 and p. 19)

The reader may be excused for failing to see exactly how the principle of indifference follows directly from Jeffreys' Convention 1, as the convention presupposes that we have already determined certain propositions to be equally probable — and that is exactly what the principle is intended to provide a criterion for. Be that as it may, it is clear that Jeffreys sees the principle as following directly from the meaning of the term 'probable', and to my mind this claim is not altogether implausible. The impression that the principle borders on the analytic is felt most strongly if we try to think of a counter-example to it, that is, two propositions that we hold to be equally probable, despite having reason to prefer one to the other. The difficulty of finding such a counter-example readily convinces us that, as Keynes puts it,

the principle certainly remains as a negative criterion; two propositions cannot be equally probable, so long as there is any grounds for discriminating between them. [This and all subsequent quotations from Keynes come from his 1921, Chapter IV, unless otherwise stated.]†

On the other hand, there are those, particularly of a frequentist persuasion, who, far from accepting the principle as analytic, wholeheartedly reject it — and not without certain justification. Von Mises, for example (1957, p. 75), cites the famous argument that by using the principle of indifference one can arrive at the seemingly absurd result that any proposition of which we know nothing is half probable,

---

† Keynes's negative criterion, which I believe none would dispute, is simply the 'only if' clause referred to on p. 222. As I indicated then, this statement of a necessary condition for judgments of equal probability is largely unproblematic.

because by hypothesis, we have no reason to choose between it and its negation. He then goes on to argue in reply to Keynes's attempt to resolve this and related difficulties that: 'it does not occur to him to draw the simple conclusion that if we know nothing about a thing, we cannot say anything about its probability.'

Between the extremes of outright acceptance and outright rejection, we find numerous writers who think that the principle is unacceptable in its traditional form, but believe it can be reformulated in a satisfactory manner. The details of the reformulations proposed vary considerably; for the moment we will restrict ourselves to those of Kneale, Keynes and Carnap.

Beginning in the vein of the remark 'Ex nihilo nihil' made by Ellis in 1842, Kneale says, 'Probability statements may be modest assertions, but even they cannot be justified by mere ignorance.' (1949, p. 147) Kneale then attempts to modify the principle so as to base judgments of equal probability on 'the knowledge of absence' rather than 'the absence of knowledge':

> I have argued that we are entitled to treat alternatives as equiprobable if, but only if, we know that the available evidence does not provide a reason for preferring any one to any other. According to the principle of indifference we may call alternatives equiprobable if we do not know that the available evidence provides a reason for preferring any one to any other. Instead of knowledge of absence Laplace and those who agree with him accept absence of knowledge as a sufficient ground for judgments of probability. This change accords with their subjectivism. For 'absence of knowledge' signifies only a fact about the mind, where as 'knowledge of absence' signifies not only a fact about a mind, but also a truth about something independent of that mind. The same point can be put in another way by distinguishing two senses of the word 'indifferent'. According to the principle of indifference alternatives are equally probable if I am indifferent in my attitudes towards them. According to the theory I have put forward it is necessary that the alternatives themselves should be indifferent i.e. without difference in a certain respect. (ibid.)

The charge of subjectivism levelled by Kneale at the principle is of course a common complaint put forward by many others. For the moment the merits of this objection need not detain us – we note it only for the purpose of conveying something of the range of objec-

The Principle of Indifference

tions to the principle.

Within this range we find writers who raise other objections to the principle but do not find its alleged subjectivism problematic. Keynes, for example, acknowledges that unless certain precautions are taken, the principle leads to outright contradictions; however, once the principle's application has been restricted in such a way as to avoid these contradictions, Keynes thinks the principle wholly acceptable. He begins his famous chapter on the principle by saying: 'The rule as it stands may lead to paradoxical and even contradictory conclusions. I propose to criticise it in detail and then discover whether any valid modification of it is discoverable.'

A particularly simple version of the contradictions he has in mind is an example concerning the colour of a given book:

> Thus if a and $\bar{a}$ are contradictories, about the subject of which we have no outside knowledge, it is inferred the probability of each is ½. In the same way the probabilities of two other propositions, b and c, having the same subject as a may be each ½ ... If, for instance, having no evidence relevant to the colour, we could conclude that ½ is the probability of 'This book is red', we would conclude equally that the probability of each of the propositions 'This book is black' and 'This book is blue' is also ½. So that we are faced with the impossible case of three exclusive alternatives all as likely as not.

After leading us through a maze of similar contradictions, engendered in large part, as we shall see later, by dividing up a given problem into different sets of mutually exclusive and exhaustive alternatives, Keynes proposes, for non-geometrical probabilities, that the principle only be applied to those cases where the alternatives are 'ultimate'. For geometrical probabilities, his restrictions for avoiding difficulties are more complicated, but, he assures us, if 'we are careful to enunciate the alternatives in a form to which the principle can be applied unambiguously we shall be ... able to reach conclusions in geometrical probability which are unambiguously valid'.

We should note that Keynes never explicitly characterizes the logical status of his resurrected principle of indifference. Despite the existence in Part II of the *Treatise* of an elaborate classificatory system of definitions, axioms and theorems for the fundamental principles of probability theory, the principle evades classification. Unlike Jeffreys, who justifies it twice over by stating it to be at once a direct application of a fundamental convention and also an analytic consequence of the terms involved, Keynes only characterizes it as 'the most important' rule 'by means of which the probabilities of different arguments can be compared.'

Carnap's Interpretation

This situation was complicated — and not altogether resolved — by Carnap's pioneering work in inductive logic, in which the principle, in some form or other, played an ongoing role. Unfortunately, as with much else in inductive logic, Carnap's interpretation of the principle changed over time, with important questions associated with it unresolved at his death. I think it is fair to say that Carnap always regarded the principle as determining measure functions, but just which, and how many functions, seemed to vary over time. In his first two works on inductive logic, *The Logical Foundations of Probability* and *The Continuum of Inductive Methods*, Carnap construed the principle as a rudimentary form of the m^+ and m^* measure function on atomic sentences of a language for inductive inference; however, he recognized that in the rudimentary form in which it was first put forward, the principle was not consistent and could only be rendered so by certain conventions. Later (e.g. Schilpp, 1963, Carnap and Jeffrey, 1973, and Jeffrey, 1980), he regarded the 'valid core' of the principle as fixing a set of invariance conditions for adequate measure functions. The measure functions which conformed to these invariance conditions were the ones he called 'symmetric' and he regarded them as the most plausible basis for an elementary inductive logic. However, he also realized that there were many cases which could not be dealt with in terms of symmetric measure functions and assigned these to the study of a logic for co-ordinate languages (Carnap and Jeffrey, 1973, p. 119). In his final publication (Jeffrey, 1980, p. 71) he could only note that many issues in regard to such languages 'are today not yet sufficiently clear and need further investigation'.

Carnap's later interpretation of the principle as stating 'invariance conditions' for measure functions — and thus determining the class of symmetric measure functions — can be seen as a generalization of his earlier work, in which he tried to unravel the ambiguities and inconsistencies surrounding the principle in terms of the m^* and m^+ measure functions. Thus it seems appropriate then to begin our analysis of his interpretation(s) of the principle by examining his derivation of these functions from the principle.

The Principle of Indifference

In Carnap's original formulation of a system of inductive logic, the degree of confirmation — $c(h,e)$, or probability$_1$ — assigned to a hypothesis h on the basis of evidence e is determined by the ratio of the measure of the evidence and the hypothesis to the measure of the evidence alone, i.e. $c(h,e) = \frac{m(e,h)}{m(e)}$. Thus to fix a confirmation function we need only determine a measure function for the atomic sentences of our language. In keeping with his range conception of probability, Carnap stipulates that the measure $m(j)$ for a sentence j is the measure assigned to the range of j. The range of a sentence j is the set of state descriptions in which j holds, with a state description defined as an assignment of one from each set of exclusive and exhaustive primitive predicates (and their negations) to each individual constant of the language. Thus with a language with one primitive predicate P and two individual constants a and b, there are four state descriptions: $Pa. Pb$, $Pa. {\sim}Pb$, ${\sim}Pa. Pb$, and ${\sim}Pa. {\sim}Pb$. Since the measure assigned to a range, i.e. set of state descriptions, is the sum of the measures of all the constituent state descriptions, the determination of a measure for a sentence j depends on determining a measure for state descriptions. As we obtain a confirmation function directly from measures on atomic sentences, the problem of finding a confirmation function for h and e is eventually reduced to the question of finding a measure function for the individual state descriptions of the language.

To resolve this question, Carnap initially cited one of the longstanding controversies surrounding the principle of indifference: whether individual distribution (constitutions) or statistical distributions (ratios) are to be assigned equal probabilities in the absence of relevant information. To understand this controversy, and Carnap's treatment of it, think of an urn of which we know nothing except that it contains two balls, each white or not-white. By the principle of indifference we might argue that, in the absence of any reason for preference, ball a is as likely to be white as not-white and the same for ball b. This renders us four distinct possibilities, each equally likely:

Ball a	Ball b
W	W
W	~W
~W	W
~W	~W

Here we hold each individual distribution or constitution equally likely.

The Principle of Indifference

Alternatively, in the absence of any relevant information, we might reason that the overall statistical distributions (ratios) of two not-whites, one not-white and one white, and two whites are each equally likely. This contradicts our previous result, in that the combination of two white balls would now have a probability of 1 in 3, rather than 1 in 4. Carnap correctly remarks that, as the debate stands, neither side is right, for either way of assigning probabilities can be shown to be internally inconsistent, unless substantially qualified.

Consider what happens if we find out that there are exactly two distinct ways a ball in the urn can be non-white, either by being black or red. By assuming individual distributions to be equally likely, we would then conclude that there are nine distinct and equally likely possibilities:

Ball a	Ball b
B	B
B	W
B	R
W	W
W	B
W	R
R	B
R	W
R	R

Here, by holding individual distributions to be equally likely, we reach the conclusion that there is a 1 in 9 chance of both balls being white, whereas by holding individual distributions equally likely and considering only the two predicates 'white' and 'not-white' we arrive at a figure of 1 in 4. Obviously the probability of there being two white balls varies considerably depending on which set of predicates are used for the basis of determining the equally likely individual distributions. This line of argument, which is simply one instance of the contradictions engendered by the principle of indifference, can easily be used to show that, with our 3 colours, each of the 6 statistical distributions (e.g. 2 reds, 1 red 1 black ... etc.) is equally likely.

Carnap concludes that such difficulties can only be met by using consistently one set of exhaustive and mutually exclusive predicates to describe a given situation. Not unnaturally, he favours using those sets of exclusive and exhaustive predicates that explicitly involve all

The Principle of Indifference

the relevant primitive predicates of the language — the set of 'W', 'R', and 'B' in our example. In Carnap's system the matter is expressed in terms of Q-divisions; unfortunately the definition 'Q-divisions' for languages with any finite number of primitive predicates is fairly complicated and change over time (cf. Schilpp, 1963, p. 974), and it would be inappropriate to explain here the details of this complicated definition. However, in a language with one set of exclusive and exhaustive predicates, it is quite easy to see Carnap's intention here — particularly as explained after 1963 — and so throughout this discussion it will be convenient to use our language with 'W', 'R' and 'B' as the primitive predicates. In our language with primitive predicates 'W', 'R', and 'B', the set of (molecular) predicates $\{M_1, M_2\}$ where $M_1 = W$ and $M_1 = R \vee B$, form a 'division', and these two predicates of course are the troublesome predicates 'white' and 'not-white' from above. But the set of predicates $\{Q_1, Q_2, Q_3\}$ where $Q_1 = W$, $Q_1 = R$, $Q_3 = B$ also form a division and since this division involves explicitly all the primitive predicates of the language, it is what Carnap would call a Q-division. Carnap diagnoses the problem we have just considered as arising from an application of the principle of indifference to different divisions, one formed by the predicates M_1 and M_2, the other formed by Q_1, Q_2 and Q_3. He stipulates that the problem is to be resolved by applying the principle only to Q-divisions formed by the predicates $Q_1, Q_2,$ and Q_3.

But this still leaves us with the question of whether, by the principle of indifference, we should assign equal probabilities to individual distributions under the Q-division or to statistical distributions under the Q-division. In Carnap's system, individual distributions under the Q-division constitute state descriptions. Similarly, statistical distributions under the Q-division correspond to Carnap's 'structure descriptions'. Thus we find:

The controversy [surrounding the principle of indifference] concerned the question as to which of the following rules should be accepted:

(A)   Individual distributions have equal m [measure] values

(B)   Statistical distributions have equal m [measure] values.

Now it can easily be shown that either rule leads to contradiction if taken in the given unrestricted form and hence applied to all divisions.

However, each of the two rules becomes consistent if restricted to any one division. It seems natural to take here for each system the strongest division possible in the system, which is that formed by the Q's. The individual distributions for all the individuals of the system with respect to the Q's are the state descriptions. The corresponding statistical descriptions... [are] structure descriptions... Thus the two modified rules are as follows:

> (A')   State descriptions have equal m values [measures]
>
> (B')   Structure descriptions have equal m values [measures]

(1952, p. 39)

Carnap then remarks that rules (A') and (B') are the most natural rules for a measure function to determine logical probabilities; (A') determines measures for each state description by holding all state descriptions equal and taking, as one must, the sum of the measure of all state descriptions to be 1. (B') also determines measures for all state descriptions, but in a slightly less direct manner — each statistical distribution, or structure description, is assigned an equal measure, e.g. in our example of balls that can be red, black or white only the measure of 1/6 would be given to each structure description '2 white balls', '1 white ball, 1 red', '2 black balls', etc. To determine measures for the state descriptions of this example, we must, according to Carnap, apportion out the measures for each structure description equally among the state descriptions that constitute the structure description. (To use Carnap's terminology, we divide the measures of the structure descriptions by the number of isomorphic state descriptions.) That is to say, the state description '*Wa. Wb*' receives a measure of 1/6 as that is the only state description by which the structure description '2 white balls' can be achieved. The state description '*Wa. Rb*' is given a measure of 1/12, as it is one of two state descriptions that leads to the structure description of 1 white 1 red ball, the other being '*Ra. Wb.*'

The important point to note is that the probability of drawing a second white ball after a first one will be very different depending on

The Principle of Indifference

whether one bases the measure function (and thus confirmation function) on (A') rather than (B'). Taking h as 'Wb' and e as 'Wa', we see that a measure function m^+ based on A' yields $m^+(e) = 1/3$ (e holds in 3 of 9 state descriptions, each given an equal measure by (A')); similarly $m^+(e.h) = 1/9$. Thus, as the confirmation function c^+ follows directly from the measure function m^+, we have $c^+(h,e) = 1/3$.

But using rule (B') to establish a measure function m^*, we see that $m^*(e) = 1/3$. As $m^*(e.h) = 1/6$, we have $c^*(h,e) = 1/2$, using rule (B') for our measure function. In general, rule (A') leads to assignments of probability wherein the probability of a hypothesis h on evidence e is independent of the content of the evidence e but the confirmation function c^* based on (B') leads to probability assignments wherein the probability of a hypothesis h stating the occurrence of a property increases in virtue of the evidence of previous instances of that property.

This fact allows Carnap to adjudicate between his two improved versions of the principle of indifference, rules (A') and (B'). Carnap notes (1952, p. 40, and 1962, p. 565) that many 'prominent' writers have 'accepted' the principle of indifference in the form of (A'), among them Keynes and Wittgenstein. He also notes that the derived confirmation function c^+ is 'simple, natural' and 'at first glance quite plausible'. However, as the c^+ determines probability values for hypotheses on evidence irrespective of the content of the evidence,

> the choice of c^+ as the degree of confirmation would be tantamount to the principle never to let our past experience influence our expectations for the future. This would obviously be in striking contradiction to the basic principle of all inductive reasoning.

But using the principle of indifference in form (B') leads to the measure function m^* and the confirmation function of c^*; the confirmation function c^* has just the properties desired for inductive reasoning, and so the m^* measure function is, for Carnap, the acceptable form of the principle of indifference:

> The preceding considerations show that the following argument, admittedly not a strong one, can be offered in favour of m^*. Of the two m functions which are most simple and suggest themselves as the most natural ones, m^* is the only one which is not entirely inadequate. (1962, p. 565)

The essential point here is that at this stage in the development of his thought, Carnap saw the principle as the basis for two measure and confirmation functions used to explicate his quantitative concept of probability; one fairly standard interpretation of the principle yielded an apparently plausible, but unsatisfactory, measure function, while another well-known interpretation led to an adequate measure function and confirmation function.

Lest the reader become convinced by this interpretation of the principle of indifference, let me point out that this proposal, rather than vindicating the assignment of equal measures to structure (or statistical) descriptions at the expense of equal measures to state (or individual) descriptions, actually relies on the assumption, at certain crucial points, that state descriptions are to be given equal measures. That is, with Carnap's m^* function, each state description that is an instance of a given structure description is assigned an equal measure — the measure for each state description is the measure for the structure description of which it is an instance, divided by the number of isomorphic state descriptions. But once we have abandoned the idea that we can use the principle of indifference to justify assigning equal measures to *all* state descriptions, it becomes difficult to see the reason for assigning equal measures to all state descriptions that fall under a given structure description.

Perhaps because of dissatisfaction with such a derivation of the m^* measure function, Carnap, as we noted before, modified his interpretation of the principle in his later work. Rather than fixing the two functions m^+ and m^*, the principle was later interpreted by him to set invariance conditions which were met by the class of symmetric measure functions. Symmetry in respect of individuals was fixed by the following axiom:

A7 The value $c(h,e)$ remains unchanged under any finite permutation of individuals. (1963, p. 975)

From our point of view, this is the most important invariance axiom. Roughly speaking, it states that inductive probabilities do not vary with the identity of the individuals of the language; e.g. nothing in the above example would change if we took h as '*Wa*' and e as '*Wb*'. The intuitive connection of this axiom to the principle of indifference seems clear — we have no reason to treat a hypothesis such as '*Wa*' differently from one such as '*Wb*' and so must assign them equal probabilities in similar situations. Combined with a few other axioms and the principle of instantial relevance — that we learn from experience — this axiom yielded the λ class of measure functions excluding $\lambda = 0$ and $\lambda = \infty$

The Principle of Indifference

(The former, as we will see, does not allow us to assign probabilities on the null relevant evidence and so is excluded as 'irregular'; the latter is $m^\dagger$ and so violates the principle of instantial relevance.)

Thus, in effect, in his later work Carnap generalized his earlier interpretation of the principle: in the earlier work he identified the $m^\dagger$ and m^* functions as the consistent forms of the principle, with the former excluded as violating the principle of instantial relevance; in his later work he saw all the λ measure functions, save $\lambda = 0$, as consistent forms of the principle, again with $m^\dagger$ ($\lambda = \infty$) ruled out by the principle of instantial relevance. Although far from implausible, Carnap's interpretation of the principle as a form of measure function seems to me mistaken, and I hope to show this by offering my own alternative analysis of it.

Rather than seeing the principle as a measure function for determining a priori numerical probabilities, I see it is a rudimentary form of the definition of probability as the comparative relation of evidential support. Just how (and why) it has become almost exclusively associated with the determination of numerical a priori probabilities — of which Carnap's treatment of it is perhaps the most elaborate version — is a complex matter and one that can only be unravelled after we have come to see the definitional component incorporated in the principle.

THE PRINCIPLE AND IDENTITY CONDITIONS FOR JUDGMENTS OF PROBABILITY

To appreciate the definitional character of the principle, it is necessary to realize that we may never speak of there being 'no reason to prefer' one alternative to another *simpliciter*, but, rather, only in relation to some body of evidence do we speak of there being no reason to choose between them. This much in fact should be clear from the discussion at pp. 222-4 concerning the manner in which evidence, known or available, figures in various formulations of the principle. Despite the different formulations we observed, each writer implicitly accepted the idea that only relative to some evidence, known or available, could we say there was no reason to prefer one alternative to another. And this of course seems wholly correct; in regard to epistemic matters — which alone concern us here — it is only some body of relevant evidence that can provide or constitute a reason in favour of a particular hypothesis. More exactly, we may say that only some body of evidence which supports a hypothesis more than its negation is a reason in favour of accepting that hypothesis. Conversely, evidence which supports the negation of a hypothesis more than the hypothesis itself constitutes, or provides, a reason against that hypothesis.

This characterization of 'reason for' a hypothesis, in terms of a body of evidence supporting that hypothesis, can be extended to explain the idiom of having a reason to prefer one hypothesis to another. Just as a body of supporting evidence is all that can constitute a reason for or against a hypothesis, only some body of evidence which supports a hypothesis q_1 more than q_2 can constitute a reason for preferring q_1 to q_2. This can easily be generalized to the sets of mutually exclusive and exhaustive alternative hypotheses $q_1 \ldots q_n$ that provide the primary application for the principle of indifference: a reason for preferring q_1 to any of $q_2 \ldots q_n$ is, simply, some body of evidence which supports q_1 more than it supports any of $q_2 \ldots q_n$.

Although it is thus only some body of evidence supporting a hypothesis q_1 more than $q_2 \ldots q_n$ which constitutes a reason for preferring q_1, we would not ordinarily say we have reason to prefer q_1 to each of $q_2 \ldots q_n$ just because some *one* body of evidence supports q_1 in this manner. Such evidence would constitute *a* reason for preferring q_1 to $q_2 \ldots q_n$, but a consideration of other relevant factors is necessary before we could conclude that, on balance, there is reason to prefer q_1 to $q_2 \ldots q_n$. Thus, for example, if the total evidence e we know strongly supports q_2, but contains a part e_1 which supports q_1 more than each of $q_2 \ldots q_n$, it would be thoroughly misleading to say we had reason to prefer q_1 to each of $q_2 \ldots q_n$: e_1 does constitute a reason for preferring q_1, but the additional evidence contained in e gives us, on balance, reason for preferring q_2.

But what, in general, are the 'other relevant factors' which must be considered before we can conclude we have 'reason to prefer' a certain hypothesis, when one body of evidence already supports that hypothesis more than any alternative? The example just cited indicates that it is other evidence relevant to the alternatives which must be surveyed before we decide which hypothesis we have reason to prefer. But is it, as the example indicates, only other parts of the evidence *known* to us that must be considered? What of relevant parts of the evidence which are easily available but not, as of yet, known to us — are we right in saying there is reason to prefer q_2 to q_1 and $q_3 \ldots q_n$, if the evidence we know supports q_2 more than each of these, but the total available

The Principle of Indifference

evidence favours, say, q_3?

These questions bring us back to the topic already discussed on pp. 222-4 — the exact nature or extent of the evidence to be considered before applying the principle. Without entering yet into a detailed analysis of this matter, one point is clear: virtually all writers on the principle share the assumption that some one body of evidence must be considered in its entirety before we can decide whether there is, or is not, reason for preference between competing alternatives. With Blackburn and Mackie, it is fairly clear that, respectively, the total available evidence and the total evidence known to a particular person at a particular time, should be considered before applying the principle. With Keynes (and for that matter Kneale), it is less clear just what single body of evidence is to be considered in its entirety, but there can be little doubt that Keynes, at least, believed that the principle could only be applied relative to one body of evidence taken in its entirety. Thus, for example we find him reasoning in the following way:

> This distinction enables us to formulate the Principle of Indifference at any rate more precisely. There must be no relevant evidence relating to one alternative, unless there is corresponding evidence relating to the other; our evidence, that is to say, must be symmetrical with regard to the alternatives and must be applicable to each in the same manner.

Whatever the nature of the evidence Keynes has in mind here, i.e. whether it is the total available or simply the amount known by a particular person at a particular time, it is clear that some body of evidence in its entirety must be surveyed before applying the principle. Only if the information contained in a body of evidence were reviewed in its entirety would we be in a position to decide that there was no relevant evidence relating to one alternative, save where it is balanced by relevant evidence for the other alternatives — if we considered only part of a body of evidence, it might be that some other part of the evidence was favourable to an alternative without similar evidence in favour of the others.

Since there is substantial agreement that some body of evidence must be reviewed in its entirety before judging that there is reason for preference among competing alternatives — and, in any case, this is the most natural way to interpret the idiom of 'reason for preference' — it will be convenient to have a vague term to refer to the body of evidence on which the principle is applied, without prejudicing the question of just what body this is. Thus throughout the remainder of this chapter and the next, I will use the vague term 'extant' evidence whenever I wish to indicate the body of evidence, which, taken in its entirety, serves as a basis for a judgment of equal probability in accordance with the principle. I will employ more precise distinctions, for example between the total evidence known and the total evidence available in, say, an objective sense, only when such distinctions are particularly germane.

Granted that it is by considering the extant evidence in its entirety that we decide whether there is, or is not, reason for preference among alternative hypotheses — what, then, is the precise relationship between this evidence and the hypotheses in virtue of which it does, or does not, give reason for preference? The considerations adduced on p. 236 suffice to answer this. Just as any body of evidence, taken in isolation, constitutes a reason for preferring one hypothesis to others if, and only if, it supports that hypothesis more strongly than the others, it is the greater evidential support of the extant evidence in its entirety for that hypothesis that would constitute reason for preferring it to the others.

Characterized in this way, it then becomes apparent that the idiom of 'reason to prefer' which figures so prominently in the principle of indifference is nothing other than an intuitive expression of what Carnap has called the comparative concept of evidential support — with it understood that the evidence occurring in these comparisons is the extant evidence taken in its totality. The concept of evidential support at issue is clearly comparative, for when we judge there to be reason for preference among hypotheses, we are simply judging the extant evidence to give unequal degrees of support to those hypotheses. The basic point, which is in my opinion essential to unravelling the controversies surrounding the principle, is that the truth conditions for the idiom of having 'reason to prefer' one hypothesis to another are those in which the extant evidence, taken in its totality, provides a greater degree of support to that hypothesis than to the other. Conversely, when we speak of there being no reason to prefer one hypothesis to another, we only mean that the extant evidence supports each hypothesis equally well. This analysis applies as well to the problematic case — to be discussed in detail later — wherein the extant evidence provides no information relevant to the hypotheses in question. In such cases the ascription of equal probability values to the hypotheses by the principle is again based on relations of evidential support — here

The Principle of Indifference

the extant evidence does not provide more support for one hypothesis rather than another, for the evidence provides no support for any of the hypotheses.

To put it more generally, the principle of indifference simply specifies the identity conditions for judgments of probability in terms of comparative relations of evidential support, where the evidence used in the comparisons is the total amount extant. From this interpretation of the principle, it is a short step — and one we will take shortly — to the conclusion that the principle of indifference is primarily definitional in character, for, as we noted before, any statement fixing identity conditions for a concept thereby fixes a particular meaning for it.

Keynes's Analysis

First, however, let me note that my interpretation of the principle of indifference as fixing identity conditions for probability judgments in terms of comparative relation of evidential support closely parallels Keynes' own trenchant analysis of a 'reason for preference'. Beginning a line of argument that includes, near its end, the passage from the *Treatise* most recently cited, Keynes says:

> The principle states that there must be no known reason for preferring one set of alternatives to any other. What does this mean? What are reasons, and how are we to know whether they do or do not justify us in preferring one alternative to another? I do not know any discussion of Probability in which this question has been so much as asked. If, for example, we are considering the probability of drawing a black ball from an urn containing balls which are black and white, we assume that the difference of colour between the balls is not reason for preferring either alternative. But how do we know this, unless by a judgment that, on the evidence in hand, our knowledge of the colour of the balls is irrelevant to the probability in question. We know of some respects in which the alternatives differ, but we judge that a knowledge of these differences is not relevant ... Before, then, we can begin to apply the Principle of Indifference, we must have a number of direct judgments to the effect that the probabilities under consideration are unaffected by inclusion in the evidence of certain particular details. We have no right to say of any known difference between the two alternatives that it is no reason for preferring one of them,

The Principle of Indifference

unless we have judged that a knowledge of this difference is irrelevant to the probability in question.

Keynes then goes on to define more exactly what is meant by 'irrelevance' and, by contrast, 'relevance'. Although the theory of relevance can be quite complex we need only consider here Keynes's 'simplest definition of irrelevance', which still forms the basis of the theory of relevance:

> h_1 is irrelevant to x on evidence h, if the probability of x on hh_1 is the same as its probability on evidence h.

Evidence h_2 is relevant to x if, and only if, it is not irrelevant. We should note that in this account, as in others, irrelevance, and thus relevance, is defined in terms of judgments of equal probability, namely h_1 is irrelevant to x on h if, and only if, the probability $x/h_1 h = x/h$. Since for Keynes the equal (or unequal) probabilities of hypotheses on evidence represent the equal (or unequal) degrees of confirmation or evidential support for those hypotheses, we may also express his definition of irrelevance (and relevance) using Carnap's symbolism and notation for confirmation: evidence e_1 is irrelevant to a hypothesis h on e if, and only if, $c(h, e.\ e_1) = c(h, e)$.

Keynes proceeds to use these concepts to elucidate the principle of indifference:

> This distinction enables us to formulate the Principle of Indifference at any rate more precisely. There must be no relevant evidence relating to one alternative, unless there is corresponding evidence relating to the other; our relevant evidence, that is to say, must be symmetrical with regard to the alternatives, and must be applicable to each in the same manner. This is the rule at which the Principle of indifference somewhat obscurely aims. We must first determine what parts of our evidence are relevant on the whole by a series of judgements of relevance, not easily reduced to rule, of the type described above. If this relevant evidence is of the same form for both alternatives, then the Principle authorises a judgement of indifference [i.e. a judgment of equal probability].

The interesting feature about this line of argument is that Keynes, very much in contrast to Carnap and Carnap's interpretation of him, does not use the principle of indifference to define a measure function and corresponding confirmation function which would determine the

The Principle of Indifference

degree of probability of some hypothesis h on evidence e; rather, Keynes requires the existence of judgments similar to those determined by a confirmation function, as a precondition for the employment of the principle of indifference. That is to say, Keynes's 'judgments of relevance' and judgments that the evidence is 'symmetrical with regard to the alternatives' and 'applicable to each in the same manner', which are the prerequisites for employing the principle of indifference, are all judgments as to the degree and means by which evidence supports, or confirms, the hypotheses in question. As such, these are judgments that in a rigorous quantitative system, such as Carnap's, would be determined by the confirmation function. Whereas Carnap determined a measure function and confirmation function by using the principle of indifference, Keynes requires for use of the principle a series of judgments similar to those determined by a confirmation function, save that the judgments of relevance, irrelevance, symmetry and applicability that Keynes requires are primarily comparative, rather than quantitative judgments of confirmation. For example, a judgment that h_1 is relevant to x on h is a judgment that hh_1 supports x to a greater or lesser, but not equal, degree as h itself supports x.

How then should we characterize the logical status of the principle of indifference in Keynes's account, if it is not used to determine judgments of confirmation or evidential support, but, rather, presupposes them? Keynes in summarizing his views on the principle provides us with the following answer:

> In the first place we have stated the Principle of Indifference in a more accurate form by displaying its necessary dependency upon judgments of relevance and so bringing out the hidden element of direct judgment or intuition, which it has always involved. It has been shown that the Principle lays down a rule by which direct judgments of relevance and irrelevance can lead to judgments of preference and indifference [judgments of unequal and equal probability].

What Keynes has accurately perceived here is that the principle simply equates the truth conditions for judgments of equal and unequal probability with judgments of relevance and irrelevance of evidence on the hypotheses. Like Keynes's less exactly defined, but similarly important judgments of applicability and symmetry of evidence, these judgments concern the greater, lesser or equal degree of which various pieces of evidence support the hypotheses we are concerned with. Accordingly Keynes's account of the principle turns out to be remarkably similar to that just given, namely that the principle does nothing more than fix comparative judgments — or as we now say, relations — of evidential support as the truth conditions for judgments of probability.

A Definition of Probability

With this conclusion in mind we are now in a position, I think, to understand the longstanding appeal of the principle and its great historical importance. This is most easily done if we begin by considering the principle in so far as it specifies identity conditions for judgments of probability in terms of comparative relations of evidential support. The additional fact that we use the total extant evidence in making these comparisons is best left as a separate matter for later discussions, when, as promised, I shall return to the question of the exact amount of evidence used in these comparisons.

As we noted before, statements of identity conditions for a concept fix the sense of that concept, for they express the conditions in virtue of which we repeatedly apply that concept. Hence any assertion which fixes identity conditions for a concept will serve as at least the rudiments of a semantic definition of the concept. In so far, then, as the principle of indifference specifies the identity conditions for judgments of probability between hypotheses in terms of comparative relations of evidential support for those hypotheses, it serves as a rudimentary form of the definition of probability as the comparative concept of evidential support. Considering the widespread appeal of the definition of probability as a relation of evidential support and the well-known preference of earlier writers for comparative probability judgments, it is hardly surprising that an even rudimentary form of the definition of probability as the comparative concept of evidential support would play a central role in the history of probability. The degree of conviction with which the principle was once accepted can thus be traced to its status as a form of a highly attractive definition of probability.

Of course it should be stressed that no advocate of the principle explicitly put it forward with the aim of defining probability as the comparative concept of evidential support. Indeed in the classical theory of probability the principle was only used as an adjunct to the definition of probability as the ratio of favourable cases to possible cases, where the cases were equiprobable (or 'equipossible', as was sometimes said in a rather unsuccessful attempt to mask an obvious circularity). But as we have seen specifically with the passage from Jeffreys's *Theory of Probability*, much of the principle's appeal stemmed from an appearance of analyticity, and this suggests that the principle was often conceived as a direct consequence of some definition of probability. Having seen that the principle fixes identity conditions for probability judgments in terms of comparative relations of evidential support, we need only recall that statements that fix identity conditions for a concept determine the sense of that concept to see that the principle actually *is* a form of the definition of probability as the comparative concept of evidential support.

To put this same point another way, my claim is that the principle fixes identity conditions for probability judgments in terms of comparative relations of evidential support and, whether or not it is recognized at the time, any statement fixing identity conditions for a concept fixes a particular sense for that concept. As I remarked before, my claim here is analogous to Mach's claim about Newton's Third Law — Newton did not regard the Third Law as a definition of inertial mass; rather, he took that concept to be clear enough and thought of the Third Law as a purely empirical statement. What Mach realized was that, among other things, the Third Law provided an operational criterion for equality and inequality of inertial mass and so acted implicitly as a definition. In just the same way, the principle, by fixing identity conditions for judgments of probability, implicitly constitutes a definition of probability.

APPLYING THE PRINCIPLE IN PRACTICE

Now, this interpretation of the principle of indifference can easily be objected to on the grounds that, as it stands, it provides no account of the primary application actually given to the principle — the determination of unique quantitative probability values. Interpreting the principle as a version of the definition of probability as the comparative concept of evidential support seems, at first glance, to be at variance with this practice in two important respects. First of all, the definition of probability as the comparative concept of evidential support should lead to probability assignments of the form of nonquantitative comparative judgments on the greater, lesser or equal degree of probability between various hypotheses. Secondly, a definition of probability as the comparative concept of evidential support warrants numerous different orderings of a given set of hypotheses in respect of comparative degrees of probability, for such orderings are relative to the body of evidence chosen, e.g. the probability of h_1 and h_2 relative to e might be the same, but relative to different evidence $e'h_1$ might be more probable than h_2. But this variability of the comparative probability of hypotheses seems a far cry from the actual application usually given to the principle, namely the determination of unique numerical probabilities.

The first difficulty is easily dealt with: almost invariably the principle was applied to sets of mutually exclusive and exhaustive alternatives and in such cases (and only such cases) comparative judgments of probability can be turned into quantitative judgments. By the fact that the n alternatives are exhaustive, we deduce that the sum of their separate probabilities is 1. If we then make the comparative judgment that each of the n exclusive alternatives are equally likely, we can directly conclude that the probability of each is $1/n$. Thus the application of the principle in arriving at numerical results can easily be explained in terms of comparative judgments of probability, applied to members of an exclusive and exhaustive set of alternatives.

There remains the apparent difficulty that in defining probability as the comparative relation of evidential support, the principle of indifference would lead to different relational probabilities rather than the unique probabilities traditionally arrived at. It should be clear that the definition of probability as a relation of evidential support, whether we use a quantitative or comparative concept, will yield unique results only if it is supplemented by some criterion for selecting a unique body of evidence. As we have seen at length elsewhere, the most common and natural method for selecting a preferred body of evidence is that prescribed by the requirement of total evidence. In so far as the total available evidence is the body of evidence that is used in applying the definition of probability as the comparative concept of evidential support to given situations, this definition will yield unique orderings in respect of comparative degrees of probability. It then follows that this definition will yield unique numerical probabilities in those situations in which our comparative judgment is that each of a set of mutually exclusive and exhaustive alternatives is equally likely in relation to the total available evidence.

Now, on one natural interpretation of the principle of indifference

The Principle of Indifference

— which I attributed to Blackburn as well as to Bernoulli — the absence of reason for preference, on which it determines equal probabilities, depends on the total evidence available (in a strong sense) not supporting any alternative more than another. Since the principle encapsulates the definition of probability as the comparative concept of evidential support, applying it to cases where the total available evidence gives no reason for preference yields unique — and numerical — probabilities.

For exactly the same reasons the principle will lead to unique probabilities — either quantitative or in respect of comparative ordering — if it is employed on the basis of all the information known to a particular person at a particular time, as for example, Mackie interpreted it. The total evidence known to any person at a given time is just as much a single, unique, body of evidence as the total evidence 'available', in some strong sense (indeed we noted in Chapter III a possible sense of 'available' evidence, in which the total available evidence was simply the total known evidence). For different people, of course, the total evidence known at a given time will be different, but not so for one and the same person. Thus if a person applied the definition of probability expressed in the principle on the basis of his current knowledge, he would always be led to what *for him* would be unique orderings for hypotheses in respect of comparative degrees of probability. When he found a set of mutually exclusive and exhaustive hypotheses which were equally well supported by the totality of his current knowledge, this definition would allow him to assign unique and equal numerical probabilities to each hypothesis.

The same considerations apply of course if any one body of evidence is taken in its entirety as the basis for applying the principle. Thus, even if, as we found with Keynes, the principle is enunciated in a form in which its employment is made relative to bodies of evidence given no further characterization (such as the total available, etc.), it will yield the appropriate unique results. Employed in relation to any one body of evidence in its entirety, the definition encapsulated in the principle will yield a unique comparative ordering of probability, and, then, in the case where a set of mutually exclusive and exhaustive hypotheses are found equally likely, it will yield a unique numerical probability.

Indeed, because the principle of indifference will yield unique numerical probabilities if it is employed in relation to any single body of evidence taken in its entirety (whether it be the total available, in a strong sense, the total actually known, or any other body), the different formulations of it considered at the start of this chapter come to very much the same thing. In all formulations, the principle of indifference combines the two distinct components necessary for determining the unique probabilities we require for the purpose of action: on the one hand, the principle incorporates the definition of probability as the comparative concept of evidential support, for, by use of the idiom of reason for preference, it specifies identity conditions for judgments of probability in terms of relations of evidential support; on the other hand, since some one body of evidence in its entirety is always understood as the basis for judging that there is no reason for preference, the relational definition encapsulated in the principle invariably has the unique application to actual situations needed for the purpose of action.

Characterized in this way, the principle is seen to function in just the same manner as modern relational definitions of probability when such definitions are applied on the basis of a methodological rule giving them unique application. In specifying identity conditions for judgments of probability, the principle encapsulates a relational definition of probability; the principle's employment in practice has yielded unique probabilities because it is characteristically employed in relation to a single body of evidence taken in its totality. Such a view of the principle is necessary, I believe, for a proper understanding of the principle and its role in the history of probability theory. Although the principle is largely definitional in character, this has not been properly appreciated, as the definition of probability as the comparative concept of evidential support it encapsulates seems at variance with the unique and numerical probabilities so often determined by the principle. Thus, not surprisingly, we find even such a sophisticated writer as Carnap treating the principle as the basis for a measure function for a quantitative conception of probability. On the alternative analysis I have given, the unique numerical results determined by the principle are arrived at through the combination of the comparative and relational definition encapsulated in the principle and the characteristic application of it on the basis of one body of evidence in its totality.

THE CLASSICAL THEORY OF PROBABILITY

Let me conclude this chapter by explaining how the analysis I have just given of the principle accords with the definition of probability explicitly offered by the principle's first and most ardent advocates,

The Principle of Indifference

the classical theorists. The definition of probability they explicitly offered was that probability was the ratio of favourable cases to possible cases, provided that each case was equiprobable or equipossible; the principle of indifference was simply thought to provide a criterion for determining equiprobable or equipossible cases.

Now, construing the principle itself as a definition of probability yields the anomaly that the classical writers had in mind two distinct definitions of probability, but the anomaly is only apparent. The two different definitions in question are in no way incompatible — indeed the two definitions answer roughly to what we now distinguish as an uninterpreted axiomatic definition of the concept of probability and a semantic definition for the concept. If we understand 'equipossible cases' as a primitive undefined term, the classical definition of probability as the ratio of favourable to equipossible cases constitutes an uninterpreted axiomatic definition of probability; the principle of indifference, which even in classical writings was understood as fixing a sense for the concept of equipossible cases, can then be regarded as the semantic rule which gives a suitable interpretation to the basic undefined term of the axiom system.

Carnap, despite his criticisms of the principle and, in my opinion, misappropriation of it to provide a measure function or class of measure functions, admirably sets the stage for this characterization of the relationship between the principle of indifference and the definition of probability as the ratio of favourable to equipossible cases:

> At the first look, the classical theory seems to be much stronger than the modern axiom systems; in other words stronger than a mere theory of regular c-function. And we find indeed many stronger theorems stated by classical authors. However, a closer examination shows that proofs for these stronger theorems make use, explicitly or implicitly, of the principle of indifference. The classical theory claims to give a definition for probability, based on the concept of equipossible cases. The only rule given for the application of the latter concept is the principle of indifference, since we know today that this principle leads to a contradiction, there is in fact no definition for the concept of equipossibility. In order to base the classical theory on a consistent foundation, we may proceed in the following way. We regard it, not as an interpreted theory as it was intended, but as an uninterpreted axiom system with 'equipossible cases' as undefined, primitive term without interpretation. Then we take the

classical definition of 'probability' based on 'equipossible'. Thus this definition is here an uninterpreted axiomatic definition. (1962, p. 343)

In fact the classical definition of probability as the ratio of favourable to equipossible cases is distinctly similar to the modern axiomatic definition of probability as the measure of an attribute space (favourable cases) in a sample space (possible cases), and one can hardly deny that the classical authors as mathematicians pursued the consequences of such an axiomatic definition of probability with great mathematical insight.

Now of course any axiomatic definition of probability requires supplementation by a semantic definition which is today given explicitly by rules of interpretation for the undefined terms of the axiom system. We can hardly expect the classical writers to have given a semantic definition of probability by explicitly formulating rules of interpretation in the modern style for all the terms of their axiom system. However, as 'equipossible cases' was the fundamental term of the axiom system of the classical writers, it might well be that the semantic definition classical theorists had in mind became expressed in the rule for interpreting this fundamental term, which was of course the principle of indifference. And indeed this is just what we have found already in this chapter — the principle of indifference in fixing identity conditions for judgments of probability actually embodies the highly plausible semantic definition of probability as the comparative concept of evidential support.

In this light the concept of probability articulated by the classical theorists should not be thought of as outdated, in the way it commonly is today; rather the concept of probability they articulated is a close approximation to a highly plausible and thoroughly modern one. Their theory presented an astonishingly fruitful axiomatic definition of probability in terms of the ratio of favourable to equipossible cases, and moreover, with the principle of indifference, they supplied, in a rudimentary form, the highly plausible semantic definition of probability as the comparative relation of evidential support to supplement their axiomatic definition.

VII
OBJECTIONS TO THE PRINCIPLE OF INDIFFERENCE

Objections to the principle of indifference have been so numerous and diverse that it seems best to treat them in a separate chapter. My general position is that all these objections are explicable — and also soluble — on the basis of the interpretation given to it in the last chapter; in particular I believe virtually all objections to it either involve natural misgivings over the role played by the null relevant evidence in a relational definition of probability, or familiar doubts on the objectivity of probability judgments made on the basis of such a relational definition.

However, before examining objections to the principle from this perspective, we should consider, again, Carnap's first interpretation of the principle as equivalent to one or the other of the two most natural measure functions on atomic sentences of a language, the m^+ and m^* functions. Although I regard this analysis as mistaken, it provides a convenient point of departure for our later discussions of the null relevant evidence. My primary objection to this analysis is precisely the contention that the principle itself constitutes either the m^+ and m^* measure functions and thus the c^+ and c^* confirmation functions. As we saw in our discussion of Keynes's treatment of the principle, judgments about comparative degrees of evidential support (e.g. judgments of relevance and irrelevance) are required before the principle can be applied. The principle, as Keynes realized, only equates equal probability with equal evidential support and so can only be applied to yield probability values when we have already made comparative judgments about degrees of evidential support. As Carnap's confirmation functions lay down rules for correctly judging quantitative degrees of evidential support, the principle could be used after such quantitative judgments were made, for it is easy enough to deduce comparative judgments from quantitative ones. But this is a very different matter from treating the principle *itself* as a quantitative measure or confirmation function: rather than leading immediately to quantitative judgments of evidential support, the principle requires a series of comparative judgments of evidential support before it can even be applied.

Moreover, as indicated before, I find Carnap's derivation of the m^* and c^* spurious, because, despite the apparent use of the principle as applied to structure descriptions rather than state descriptions, it requires a secondary application of the principle to each state description falling under a particular structure description to lead to the m^* function. Thus it is particularly clear that the m^* and c^* functions cannot be regarded as forms of the principle as originally put forward, but only correspond to a very special application of it designed to suit Carnap's system. (I will later explain in more detail why this 'special application' of the principle was so important to Carnap's system (see pp. 264ff).)

Similarly, on serious reflection, Carnap's ascription of the m^+ and c^+ functions to Keynes and others who wrote on the principle is not very plausible. As Carnap himself remarks, these functions are 'tantamount to the principle never to let our past influence our expectations of the future'. Such a principle can hardly be attributed seriously to the author of *The Economic Consequences of Peace*. More generally, we must remember that most advocates of the principle emphasized that judgments of equal probability were only justified if experience gave no reason to choose between the hypotheses in question. Given that 'experience' can only have taken place in the past, it is clear that proponents of the principle believed that the past should influence our expectations for the future. Thus, as with the m^* and c^* functions, the m^+ and c^+ functions are not forms of the principle as traditionally understood, but, rather, are derived by an application of it within Carnap's own system.

Carnap's later treatment of the principle as having a valid core which expresses certain invariance conditions seems to me no more plausible an analysis, or interpretation, of the principle as traditionally understood. Here the principle may be thought of as determining a certain class of measure functions – what Carnap calls symmetric measure functions – but, as Carnap himself acknowledged, this severely weakens the principle as originally conceived. Indeed this 'valid core' cannot even be used to determine unique judgments of equal probability, when there exists relevant evidence. By defining a wide (indeed infinite) class of measure functions the principle — or what remains of it — would not determine a single value of probability on the basis of a body of relevant evidence, but rather would determine different probability values corresponding to each measure function of the class.

In fact both Carnap's earlier and later interpretations of the principle involve, to my mind, a thorough misunderstanding of the relationship between a priori numerical measure functions on the atomic sentences of a language and the comparative relations of evidential support between the sentences of that language with which the principle is primarily concerned. To become clear about the relationship of the principle to the class of measure functions determined by Carnap's invariance conditions, it is necessary to distinguish two quite different ways in which the principle can be applied, specifically its application on the basis of evenly balanced relevant evidence versus its application on the basis of the null relevant evidence. To my knowledge, Lewis (1946, pp. 306ff) is the first writer to have made this distinction explicitly, but it is an obvious one and, as we will see later, was probably accepted tacitly by *most* writers on the principle. Carnap, however, was exclusively concerned with the principle's employment on the basis of the null relevant evidence and this, I believe, explains why he persistently misinterpreted the principle as fixing a priori numerical measure functions. The full elucidation of the connection between the principle application on the basis of the null relevant evidence and Carnap's λ system of measure functions is, however, a complex matter and will only be completed with our discussion of the paradoxes and contradictions associated with the principle, to be given in the next but one section.

NULL EVIDENCE AND EQUALLY BALANCED EVIDENCE

Since, on my view, it is only evidence which can provide reasons in favour of hypotheses, one possible circumstance in which the extant evidence would give no reason to choose between hypotheses is when that evidence is distinctly relevant to the matter in hand, but is equally balanced in respect of those hypotheses. The clearest examples of such evenly balanced relevant evidence are those in which we have information that the alternatives in question have in the past occurred, or will in the future occur, in equal proportions. To give a rough example, which I will examine more precisely later, imagine a coin which has been carefully examined and found to be exactly symmetrical in its weight distribution. Furthermore, extensive tests on it and similarly weighted coins have revealed a percentage of roughly 50 per cent heads in tosses by the kind of mechanism we are employing; we may also imagine we have extensive knowledge of the workings of our tossing mechanism. Here we obviously have evidence relevant to competing hypotheses about the toss of a coin — indeed no information could be more relevant — but our evidence is equally balanced between the two hypotheses, supporting the hypothesis of heads no more or less than it supports the hypothesis of tails.

In contrast, we have the more problematic circumstances in which our evidence may be said to give no reason for preference among alternatives because it is wholly irrelevant to each. This 'total absence of knowledge', so often referred to in the principle's history, is also one in which our evidence gives no reason for preference among the alternatives, as such reason can only be provided by a body of evidence relevant to the matter which supported one alternative more than another.

A key passage in Keynes, already cited twice, illustrates well the fact that two quite different circumstances can warrant use of the principle: 'There must be no relevant evidence relating to one alternative, unless there is corresponding evidence relating to the other ... This is the rule that the Principle of Indifference obscurely aims at.' Clearly either the null relevant evidence or a body of evidence which is relevant and evenly balanced in respect of the alternatives would fulfil this condition.

How at a general level are we to characterize the difference between the two kinds of circumstances in which the principle can be applied? In the previous chapter, I argued that the principle should be interpreted as a rudimentary form of the definition of probability as a comparative relation of evidential support, and in a somewhat truistic and superficial way we may say that the two different circumstances in which the principle can be applied reflect the fact that two quite different kinds of comparative relations of evidential support can constitute the identity conditions for judgments of probability. In cases where our evidence is relevant to the question at hand and equally

Objections to the Principle of Indifference

balanced, the identity condition for judgments of probability given by the principle is the relation of equal evidential support between sets of sentences $\{h,e\}$ and $\{h', e'\}$, when e is relevant to h and e' relevant to h'. When the evidence is the null relevant evidence, the identity condition for judgments of probability given by the principle is the comparative relation which obtains between the pair of sets $\{h,e\}$ and $\{h',e'\}$, where e is irrelevant to h and e' irrelevant to h':

But the matter seems to me more complicated than this, and characterizing the difference between the two circumstances in which the principle can be applied in this way begs a fundamental question: does a genuine relation of equal probability obtain between the pair $\{h,e\}$ and $\{h',e'\}$, where e is irrelevant to h and e' to h'? It is noteworthy, that this question would arise for anyone wishing to define probability in terms of comparative relations of evidential support, even if the principle of indifference had never been formulated. That is to say, if we wish to give a definition for the concept of probability in terms of comparative relations of evidential support, we are inevitably faced at some point with a decision as to what, if any, comparative probability holds between pairs of hypotheses and their null relevant evidence: an adequate definition of probability as the comparative relation of evidential support must provide a criterion for deciding what, if any, comparative probability relation obtains between *any* pairs of evidence and hypothesis, of which a pair of hypotheses and their null relevant evidence are of course one instance.

In fact we have two options here: on the one hand, we may wish to admit that such pairs can be compared in degree of probability and then there is little alternative but to say that each member of the pair is equal in respect of probability. It is clearly arbitrary to treat either member of the pair differently, as they are both instances of the same, i.e. the null, evidentiary relation, and so the decision that sets of hypotheses and their null relevant evidence can be compared in respect of probability must culminate with the judgment that they are all equal in this respect. This, I take it, is why numerous proponents of the principle have argued that the assignment of unequal a priori probabilities would be wholly arbitrary.

Of course at this juncture critics of the principle would be (and have been) quick to point out that the assignment of equal a priori probabilities is really no more justified than the assignment of unequal a priori probabilities: what we should do is not assign either. This seems to me a perfectly viable position, and one that corresponds to the second alternative I referred to above: namely that in giving a definition of probability in terms of the comparative relation of evidential support, we may simply decide that sets of hypotheses and their null relevant evidence are not comparable in degree of probability and then we would simply not assign a comparative degree of probability to $\{h,e\}$ in relation to $\{h',e'\}$, where e and e' are irrelevant. Such a decision seems to me quite plausible as, in effect, we simply decide to assign the null probability relation to pairs whose members exhibit the null relation of evidential support.

Once it is seen that an adequate definition of probability as a comparative relation of evidential support must provide an answer — in the affirmative or negative — to the question of whether a comparison in respect of probability can be made between different hypotheses coupled with their null relevant evidence, the assignment by the principle of equal probabilities in the absence of all relevant information can be understood in its proper light. The principle, on my view, is an instance of the definition of probability as a comparative relation of evidential support, and so we should hardly be surprised that it sanctions equal probabilities in the total absence of relevant information: one possible way for such a definition to deal with the case of two hypotheses, each taken with its null relevant evidence, is to stipulate that it exhibits the comparative relation of equal probability. However, such a stipulation is not the only possible decision and, as I indicated above, it seems to me far more plausible to maintain that there is a null degree of comparative probability between pairs consisting of hypotheses and their null relevant evidence, namely that we cannot speak of probabilities in the total absence of relevant information.

In any case, these considerations explain, to a large extent, why the principle appears at times almost analytic, at other times appearing highly suspect. In so far as it fixes comparative relations of evidential support, where the evidence is relevant and equally balanced, as identity conditions for judgments of probability, it will have the appearance of analyticity to be expected of an intuitively plausible definition of probability; in so far as it also fixes as identity conditions comparative relations of evidential support where the evidence is totally irrelevant to the alternative hypotheses, it will be as suspect as the assumption thus relied on — that sets of hypotheses and evidence irrelevant to them can be compared at all in respect of probability.

We may also note that many of the most common objections

to the principle are easily avoided if we do not use it to determine probabilities on the basis of the null relevant evidence. It is clear, to begin with, that restricting the principle's use to cases in which there exists relevant evidence overcomes the objection that the principle produces knowledge out of nothing, for it is only in the total absence of relevant evidence that we know nothing concerning a particular set of hypotheses. Similarly, such a move forestalls Von Mises' objection that if 'we know nothing about a thing, we cannot say anything about its probability', for restricting the principle to circumstances in which the evidence was relevant to the matter at hand insures that 'we know something about a thing' before we assessed its probability.

In addition, if recast to assign equal probabilities solely on the basis of equally balanced relevant evidence, the principle will actually be in a form advocated by many of its critics. Kneale claimed that the correct basis for probability judgments was not the 'absence of knowledge' but the 'knowledge of absence'. In a similar vein Reichenbach indicated (1949, p. 353) that he was prepared to accept a criterion of equiprobability if '... the equiprobability does not appear as following from the absence of reasons, but as a result of the existence of definite reasons'. Mellor also attempts a reconstruction of the principle along these lines (1971, p. 138) and from Keynes's remarks on the history of the principle, it would appear that Czuber attempted such a reformulation of the principle as early as the nineteenth century under the guise of the 'Principle of Compelling Reason'.

Now, the existence of relevant but evenly balanced evidence that I have indicated as the more satisfactory grounds for the principle of indifference's assignment of equal probabilities does constitute such a definite, or compelling, reason for holding alternatives equally probable. We have seen how a definite reason for assigning unequal probabilities could only be provided by relevant evidence that supported one hypothesis more than another, and so by similar reasoning it is clear that what is meant by definite reason for assigning equal probabilities would be the existence of relevant evidence that is equally balanced between hypotheses. Thus if the principle were used to determine equal probabilities solely on the basis of such evenly balanced relevant evidence, it would be in a form not merely acceptable to, but actually advocated by, most of its critics.

THE CONTRADICTIONS

Of course, the most important objection raised against the principle was that its application led to contradictory and absurd results. Significantly these contradictions only arise when the principle is applied in relation to the null relevant evidence and this seems to me to be a particularly strong argument in favour of restricting the principle's use to cases where there exists equally balanced relevant evidence. I should also add that I believe a careful analysis of the way in which the principle's a priori application engenders contradictions sheds a good deal of light on the nature of Carnap's λ system of measure functions, and, in the end, an analysis of these contradictions yields a convincing argument in favour of $\lambda = 0$.

To have a simple example of this kind of contradiction long associated with the principle, let us consider Keynes's discussion of the probability of a book having a certain colour. Keynes explicitly states that the example is one in which we have 'no evidence relevant to the colour' of the book in question, so it only remains to be seen that this contradiction could *not* have arisen if instead we had a body of evenly balanced relevant evidence. Now, the first step in the reasoning that leads to the contradiction is that having no reason to choose between 'This book is red' and its negation, we must assign each a probability of 1/2. This first step could be arrived at by an application of the principle of indifference in relation to an evenly balanced body of relevant evidence — for example, it might be known that red was used very nearly half the time by publishers, with the remaining publications divided evenly between a number of common colours such as blue, black, green, etc. If that were the evidence we had, we would have no reason to prefer red to not-red or vice versa, and so, by the principle of indifference, each would be half probable. But now we cannot take the next step which leads to the contradiction — that we have no reason to prefer the hypothesis 'This book is black' to its negation — for we do have a reason to prefer its negation, i.e. the predicate 'not-black' encompasses the more frequently used colour red.

It should be clear that similar considerations apply to the other contradictions to which the principle is known to lead: in the absence of any relevant evidence, we have no reason to choose between each member of a particular set of mutually exclusive and exhaustive hypotheses, but inconsistent results are obtained by applying the same

Objections to the Principle of Indifference

reasoning to a different set of mutually exclusive and exhaustive hypotheses pertaining to the same problem. However, if we take a body of equally balanced relevant evidence as the basis for our judgment that there is no reason to choose between one set of alternatives, this reasoning is blocked, as our evidence provides reason for preference among the members of the *other* sets of alternatives appropriate to the same problem. The alternatives under the second set will encompass varying numbers of alternatives from the first set, and, by hypothesis, the extant evidence gives equal reason to expect each of the alternatives from the first set.

The contradictions in regard to geometrical probabilities can be dealt with in a similar but slightly more complex way. As an example, let us consider Bertrand's paradox: here we are asked to determine the probability of a chord in a circle drawn at random exceeding the length of the side of an inscribed equilateral triangle. If we think of the chord as fixed by its angle from a tangent to the circle, the principle of indifference apparently yields the conclusion that the probability of the chord exceeding the length of the side of the triangle is 1/3: the chord will be longer than the side if, and only if, the angle from the tangent is in the range of 60-120°; having no reason to prefer the angles of 60°-120° to 0°-60° or 120°-180°, we conclude that each of these possibilities is equally likely. Alternatively we may think of the chord as fixed by the location of its mid-point. Viewed in this fashion the principle can yield the result that it is half probable that the chord will be longer than the side of the triangle: if, and only if, the mid-point of the chord is at a distance less than $\frac{r}{2}$ from the centre will the chord be longer, and since there is no reason for the chord's mid-point to be less than $\frac{r}{2}$ from the centre, rather than more, each of these possibilities is equally likely. But, to give us a third application of the principle of this problem, it should be clear that if the chord is longer than the side of the triangle if, and only if, its mid-point is less than $\frac{r}{2}$ from the centre of the circle, a concentric circle of radius $\frac{r}{2}$ encompasses the area in which mid-points of longer chords fall. Since the area of this concentric circle is a quarter that of the original circle, and since there is no reason to expect the mid-point to fall within any particular area, the principle of indifference here yields the result that the probability of the chord being longer than the side of the triangle is 1/4.

The problem here, as Keynes saw, is that the principle of indifference is applied to choices between three different infinite sets of possibilities, and it is necessary to decide on one particular set as the appropriate one if we are to resolve the paradox. This, as Kneale's later and more detailed analysis of the difficulty suggests (1949, p. 186), is easy enough if we know the specific means by which the chord is to be drawn. If we know that the location of its mid-point is determined by, say, the fall of a raindrop, it seems most appropriate to measure the probability of the chord exceeding the side in length by reference to the area in which the mid-point lies and, if we take all areas as equally likely, our result is 1/4. Alternatively, if we know that the chord is drawn along the line of a pointer that is spun around an axis on the edge of the circle, it is most appropriate to measure the probability value by reference to the angle formed by the chord to a tangent, and, if we hold each angle equally likely, our result is 1/3. Other mechanisms for drawing the chord would make the distance of the mid-point from the centre the appropriate factor to be considered.

The important thing to note here is that this line of a solution to the paradox requires us to have knowledge of the method by which the chord is actually drawn; once we have such knowledge we have passed from our state of total ignorance and have begun to acquire evidence which is relevant to the problem at hand. Thus, as with non-geometric probabilities, the contradictions engendered by the principle will not arise if we evaluate the problem in question on the basis of relevant evidence, rather than evidence which is wholly irrelevant.

This perhaps becomes clearer if we consider that our evidence concerning the mechanism by which the chord is drawn is not, in itself, sufficient to determine the unique probability value we desire. For example, given that we know the chord to be drawn by spinning a pointer aligned with the edge of the circle, we only know that the probability of the chord exceeding the side in length depends on the probability of the pointer forming various angles with its axis. Only if we take all angles equally likely do we arrive at the result of 1/3.

Here of course we might try appealing to the principle of indifference: knowing nothing about the nature of the spinning mechanism, we might assume every angle equally likely, as there is no reason to prefer any particular angle. But this is nothing more or less than an application of the principle of indifference to a problem of geometrical probabilities in the absence of relevant evidence and, as Bertrand's paradox shows in a particularly elegant and appealing way, such applications lead to contradictory results. As Keynes puts it, the basic problem with applying the principle to geometrical prob-

Objections to the Principle of Indifference

abilities is that

> In general, if x and $f(x)$ are both continuous variables, varying always in the same or in the opposite sense, and x must lie between a and b, then the probability that x lies between c and d, where $a < c < d < b$, seems to be $\frac{d-c}{b-a}$ and the probability that $f(x)$ lies between $f(c)$ and $f(d)$ to be $\frac{f(d)-f(c)}{f(b)-f(a)}$. These expressions, which represent the probabilities of necessarily concordant conclusions, are not, as they ought to be, equal.

So, although we have evidence relevant to the selection of a chord, i.e. knowledge that a spinning mechanism is used, and thus can avoid Bertrand's paradox, we will need further evidence about the nature of the spinning mechanism to avoid arriving at other contradictory conclusions.

In point of fact, most serious analyses of Bertrand's paradox eventually call on further relevant evidence to establish the equal probabilities required for a numerical answer to the original problem. Kneale, for example, maintains, by use of a celebrated argument of Poincaré, that only a few further plausible assumptions, such as the relative size of the areas covered by each possibility, are required for the ultimate solution. Mellor contends in reply (1971, p. 142) that these assumptions are actually quite sweeping. In any event, both writers agree that the paradox requires for the solution further empirical evidence which will be highly relevant to the question at hand. Moreover, in so far as we are able, on the basis of such relevant evidence, to reach the conclusion that a certain set of alternatives are equally likely, it will only be because this evidence is equally balanced in favour of each alternative. Thus in considering geometrical probabilities we again find that the principle only leads to contradictions when used in relation to the null relevant evidence rather than evenly balance relevant evidence.

The Contradictions and the Choice of Predicates

Once it is recognized that the contradictions associated with the principle only arise when it is applied on the basis of the null relevant evidence, it is possible to give a general account of their origin. Earlier I argued that once we made the decision that sets of hypotheses and their null relevant evidence could be compared in respect of probability, we had to judge them equal in order to avoid *arbitrary* treatment of essentially similar sets. This is just what causes the trouble since the same hypothesis (e.g. 'This is white') coupled with its null relevant evidence can be compared with quite different hypotheses ('This is not white' or 'This is red', etc.) and their null relevant evidence, and must be judged equally likely in relation to each, leading to contradiction.

If this analysis of the origins of the contradictions associated with the principle is correct, we may expect any solution to them which does not involve abandoning the principle's application on the basis of the null relevant evidence to be arbitrary: since it was just the need to avoid arbitrary treatment of similar instances of the null relation of evidential support which engendered the contradictions, any proposal to treat some of these instances differently will be arbitrary. This is just what we find with the proposals that have been put forward to resolve the contradictions without wholly abandoning the principle's a priori application, which almost invariably take the form of specifying a unique set of predicates to characterize a given problem. Keynes's recommendation that the principle only be applied to 'ultimate' alternatives and Carnap's suggestion that its employment be restricted to the Q-division are the best-known examples of such an approach to the contradictions; since the latter proposal is closely connected to Carnap's construction of the λ continuum of measure function it is of particular interest to us.

As we saw in the previous chapter, for a simple example of a language with one family of predicates ('W', 'R', 'B') and two individual constants ('a' and 'b'), Carnap's Q-division determines the three Q predicates $Q_1 = R$ $Q_2 = W$ and $Q_3 = B$. Carnap held it to be a matter of controversy whether, in applying the principle to the Q-division, we held individual or statistical distributions equally probable, with sound inductive reasoning favouring the latter. Our concern for the moment, however, is the selection of the Q-division and, for the sake of simplicity, I will begin by assuming the principle is to be applied to individual distributions under whatever division is chosen, only later returning to its application to statistical distributions. As we saw, an application of the principle to individual distributions under the Q-division leads to equal probabilities for each state description, for an individual distribution under the Q-division is a state description. But an alternative division was available in our example, with the so-called molecular predicates $M_1 = W$ and $M_2 = R \vee B$, or, more simply, W and $\sim W$. Using the principles to assign equal probabilities to individual distributions under this division led to quite different probability assignments and, to avoid contradiction, we are required by Carnap

Objections to the Principle of Indifference

to choose the more 'natural' Q-division. In particular this meant we were to hold the hypothesis 'Wa' less likely than '$\sim Wa$', for the latter holds in six state descriptions ('$Ra. Wb$', '$Ba. Bb$'...), while the former only holds in three ('$Wa. Wb$', '$Wa. Rb$', '$Wa. Bb$').

But can the greater degree of probability assigned to '$\sim Wa$' be justified in the absence of all relevant evidence? If, by the principle's dictum that we are to treat alternatives as equally likely if, and only if, there is no reason to choose between them, the unequal probability values assigned to 'Wa' and '$\sim Wa$' would require a reason to be known in favour of '$\sim Wa$', but, in the absence of any relevant evidence, there can be no such reason. Only relevant evidence can provide a reason for preference.

Now it has been claimed, by Keynes and Blackburn (Blackburn, 1973, p. 122), that in such a case we do have knowledge that provides a reason for preference between 'Wa' and '$\sim Wa$' — namely the very fact that '$\sim Wa$' involves the assignment of two primitive predicates to a and thus holds in six individual distributions under the Q-division, whereas 'Wa' involves the assignment of one and thus only holds in three individual distributions under the Q-division. That such relevant information could resolve the contradiction fully accords with the point made already, that the contradictions engendered by the principle only arise in relation to the null relevant evidence; however, if we claim that this knowledge provides reason for preference, we must abandon any pretence that our probability values are determined in the total absence of relevant evidence. We now are assigning probability values on the basis of the evidence, deemed relevant, of the number of primitive predicates covered by a hypothesis — which of course is proportional to the number of individual distributions the hypothesis holds in under the Q-division. Given that we deem the number of primitive predicates involved as relevant to the hypothesis in question, and thus deem relevant the number of individual distributions under the Q-division, the assignment of unequal probabilities to 'Wa' and '$\sim Wa$' is not done in the total absence of relevant evidence, but, rather, is done on the basis of relevant evidence favourable to one hypothesis.

Put this way, I hope it begins to appear somewhat doubtful that the number of primitive predicates, and hence individual distributions under the Q-division, *is* evidence relevant to the probability of hypotheses of our language. As far as I can see, in saying this we have not offered an argument of any kind, but have only stipulated that we intend to regard the number of individual distributions under the

Q-division as relevant evidence. What independent rationale can be given for regarding this as relevant evidence? Can we not just as easily regard the number of individual distributions under the division formed by the predicates M_1 and M_2 as relevant evidence, which decides the matter. We may feel like saying that hypotheses covering more distributions under the Q-division can happen in more ways; after all '$\sim Wa$' can occur as 'Ra' or 'Ba'. But only by regarding the matter from, so to speak, the perspective of the Q-division can such hypotheses happen 'in more ways'; it is equally true that '$\sim Wa$', like 'Wa', happens in only one way, namely by a not being white.

Again one might be tempted to reply that hypotheses like '$\sim Wa$' can *really* happen in more ways than ones like 'Wa', because there are more state descriptions in which '$\sim Wa$' holds and the number of state descriptions in which a hypothesis holds is the important fact. But now we have come full circle: a state description is simply an individual distribution under the Q-division, and so by claiming that the number of state descriptions in which a hypothesis holds *is* the relevant evidence, we simply restate our previous claim that the number of individual distributions under the Q-division is the relevant evidence. And again I ask why is this evidence, as opposed to evidence of the number of individual distributions under some other division, the relevant evidence which decides the matter?

Now no doubt there is some intuitive plausibility to regarding the number of individual distributions under the Q-division as the correct way to view such problems. But the reason for this is not hard to uncover: when we consider the simple gambling devices used to illustrate probability theory – coins, dice, roulette wheels, etc. – we are aware that alternatives under the appropriate Q-division are, usually, equally likely. In the case of coin-tossing, our family of primitive predicates is 'heads' and 'tails' and, as there are no other primitive predicates, each is a Q-predicate. With a die our family is 'one', 'two' ... 'six' and each of these would be a Q-predicate. Thus in holding 'heads' and 'tails' equally likely, as well as each face of the die equally likely, we hold individual distributions under the Q-division equally likely. But in doing so, we are really relying on a body of past experience concerning similar objects, for, on the whole, we have observed coins to come up with equal frequency for heads and tails, and similarly so for each face of a die. Thus our ground for judging individual distribution under the Q-division to be equally likely in such cases is past observation of the equal proportion among the alternatives; conversely, it is the observed disproportion of instances of predicate such as 'one' and 'not-one' (which form a molecular division) that leads us to regard individual distributions under this division as unequal in probability.

But these considerations only undermine the position argued for by Keynes and Blackburn, namely that the number of individual distributions under the Q-division is *in itself* relevant evidence which can be employed to block the contradictions. Their suggestion was that when there is no 'external' evidence, as Keynes calls it, relating to a particular problem, we could use the evidence of the number of alternatives under the Q-division — which is 'ultimate' — as reason for preferring one alternative to another, when our alternatives were defined by molecular predicates. Since we only judge the number of alternatives under the Q-division as relevant evidence because of additional information and their past equal proportionately, we in fact have no grounds for treating the number of alternatives under this division as in and of itself the relevant evidence which decides the matter.

In any event, my argument here does not materially affect the main point I wish to make about the contradictions: it was acknowledged that the contradictions would not occur if we used the principle of indifference in relation to relevant evidence. The discussion in the above four paragraphs only concerns what we may legitimately appeal to as relevant evidence. Now, in point of fact, Carnap, whose solution to the contradictions we were considering, does not, and could not, regard the information of the number of state descriptions in which a hypothesis holds as *evidence* relevant to that hypothesis. Rather, the number of state descriptions in which a hypothesis holds determines its range, and it is other sentences having different ranges that constitute evidence for the hypothesis. How then can he justify as other than arbitrary the choice of the Q-division as the unique division to which the principle of indifference is to be applied? The probability values that result are different for certain different hypotheses and if we think of the probability values as reflecting degrees of rational credence, such assignments apparently reflect different degrees of rational credence to be accorded various hypotheses. But it is difficult to see how, in the absence of any evidence relevant to two competing hypotheses, we can rationally have more credence in one than the other, and so such probability assignments will be arbitrary.

The arbitrary character of any restrictions imposed to give a consistent application of the principle in relation to the null relevant evidence is most clear when we consider geometrical probabilities. We have

Objections to the Principle of Indifference

seen that any inconsistency is avoided in a wholly natural way if we assign equal probabilities on the basis of equally balanced relevant evidence, such as, for Bertrand's paradox, knowledge of the method used for drawing the chord and knowledge of the proportions yielded by this method. But what are we to do in relation to the null relevant evidence? To ask this of course is just to ask which of the three methods of determining probabilities used in Bertrand's paradox is to be chosen as the correct one in a state of total ignorance. The force of Bertrand's paradox is that any choice must be wholly arbitrary — this, I take it, is what Borel and Poincaré meant when, as Keynes puts it, they found the choice of any particular procedure for determining geometric probabilities with the principle simply a matter of 'convention'. Unlike non-geometrical probabilities for which certain restrictions to avoid contradictions (such as Carnap's proposal to use only the Q-division) appear at first glance plausible (for the reasons just discussed), geometrical probabilities are amenable only to restrictions that are all patently arbitrary.

The upshot of this discussion, then, is that the principle can be given a consistent application on the basis of the null relevant evidence, but only at the cost of introducing the restriction that it be applied to one set of exclusive and exhaustive predicates for each problem; however, in the absence of all information, there can be no justification for choosing one set of predicates, rather than another, to determine probabilities and so the results of applying the principle in this way will be arbitrary. To some extent this conclusion is obvious — compare, for example, Ayer (1972, p. 35) — and merely restates longstanding doubts over the a priori probabilities determined by the principle. However, there is one important consequence of this discussion which bears directly on a central issue raised in earlier chapters, and we should explicitly take note of it now: all the measure functions seriously proposed by Carnap as explicata for a quantitative concept of confirmation, namely the integer values of the λ system from 1 upwards, are simply derived by an a priori application of the principle to statistical distributions under divisions with k predicates, for $k = 1, 2, 3, \ldots$ If it is true that the choice of the division to be used to determine probabilities in the absence of knowledge is arbitrary, then the choice of a measure function from $\lambda = 1, 2 \ldots$ will be arbitrary, as there is no difference between choosing a particular integer value k of λ and applying the principle to statistical distribution for a division with k predicates.

Choice of a λ Value

This point is most easily seen if we abandon the terminology Carnap first used in developing his system of inductive logic — that of molecular divisions and Q-divisions — in favour of his later formulations of the system in terms of families of predicates. A family of predicates in a set of mutually exclusive and exhaustive predicates applicable to a given problem — namely 'red', 'white' and 'black' form one family in our example, and 'white' (with its negation 'not-white' understood) forms another.

The problem of which division to use for a given problem in the absence of all relevant evidence becomes, in this terminology, the problem of which family of predicates to use. Above I argued that applying the principle of indifference to one set, or family, of predicates to the exclusion of another is arbitrary, but what is important at present is the connection of this problem to the choice of a λ value in Carnap's system. As indicated above, the link between these two apparently distinct questions comes via Carnap's m^* function, which assigns equal measures to statistical distributions; as he himself recognized, different integer values of λ correspond to assignments of equal a priori probabilities to statistical distribution for a family with k predicates. (For example, in Jeffrey, 1980, p. 116, he explicitly characterized the m^* function as 'the general rule assigning to any family of k attributes the value $\lambda = k$'.)

Despite their common origin, Carnap always maintained the measure function based on different values of λ constituted genuinely different 'inductive methods'. The criteria he gave for choosing between the different methods varied over time — initially (1952, p. 55), he listed 'performance, economy, aesthetic satisfaction and others', later extending this to include more complicated logical factors such as 'similarity influence' and 'distance' between attributes. Perhaps the only common thread throughout his discussion of the choice of value for λ was his belief that different values of λ expressed different weights attached to logical versus empirical factors. As we saw, with $\lambda = 0$ empirical factors alone determined probability values, and so this function could not be used in the absence of all relevant evidence; with $\lambda = \infty$ the logical factor alone determined probability values and so these values would not change with changing experience; in between, the effect of the logical factor in relation to the empirical factor varied as λ increased in value.

But is there anything in our intuitive concept of induction — anything in the way we ordinarily determine inductive probabilities —

which corresponds to such a scale in which logical and empirical facts intermingle to varying degrees? At various points (e.g. Jeffrey, 1980, pp. 111-15) Carnap suggests that different individuals — with different personalities — would attach different weights to the two factors and so use different λ values for the same family of predicates. The difference could be attributed to their different 'inductive inertia'. Besides raising serious questions on the objectivity of probability judgments — which Carnap acknowledges (ibid., p. 114) and which I will discuss later — Carnap's claim that there are different personality types with different degrees of inductive 'inertia' seems far-fetched. I find it difficult to imagine two individuals — scientists, gamblers or any others — agreeing on observational data, yet disagreeing on the inductive probabilities to be inferred from that data, because of a different weight ascribed to a logical factor of the language they speak. To do so, one must imagine them discussing the number k of primitive predicates of the language applicable to a given problem, then shaking their heads in regret that they can reach no agreement over how much significance to attach to this number in connection with the matter at hand.

In one respect Carnap's position here is correct: if posed with the question of how we are to choose a λ value, we are at a loss to see how the matter is to be decided. There simply are no considerations which could resolve the difference between two individuals who choose different λ values, but to my mind this only shows that there is no genuine continuum of inductive methods among which choice is possible. We simply have no intuitions on how much weight to attach to 'logical factors' in comparison to empirical factors and so any choice of a λ value will be arbitrary. In fact, I think, this is because we intuitively attach no weight to Carnap's alleged logical factor. This indicates that $\lambda = 0$ is the most plausible choice of measure function, a point I will return to shortly.

By now, however, such a conclusion should not surprise us: it is just the conclusion we reached independently on the basis of our discussion of the application of the principle of indifference in the total absence of relevant information. To begin with we saw that the assignment of equal a priori probabilities by the principle to individual distributions could be made consistent by stipulating that it be applied to just one set of predicates for a given problem, but that the probability distribution so determined was arbitrary. We then saw that the different integer λ values resulted from applying the principle to statistical distributions with k predicates. Since different integer λ values arise in this way, the problem of justifying the assignment of equal a priori probabilities to one set of predicates (rather than another) recurs as the problem of justifying the choice of any particular λ value; thus any choice of a given integer value of λ will be arbitrary in the same way that any choice of one set of predicates had to be.

This conclusion can easily be generalized to all real numbered values of λ, though it is not clear how seriously Carnap took non-integer λ values (see Jeffrey, 1980, pp. 1-2). On my view, the only basis for Carnap's allegedly different inductive methods is this: while the assignment of equal a priori probabilities to statistical distributions yields a measure of probability for a predicate which increases with observation of positive instances of that predicate, the value of that increase for a given number of observations varies *inversely* with the number of alternative predicates applicable to a given problem. To construct his continuum, Carnap simply found a general mathematical way to characterize the effect on these two factors — the observations made and the number of predicates used — in determining the probability of a given phenomenon. This is his formula (1952, p. 33):

$$c\ (h_{ij}\,c_i) = \frac{s_i + \lambda/k}{s + \lambda},$$

which, of course, permits non-integer values of λ. Carnap explained this formula as a method by which 'to standardize by convention the weight of the empirical factor s_i/s_j [so that] then the weight of the logical factor $1/k$ determines the value' of confirmation (p. 27). My only difference with Carnap is in the interpretation of the so-called logical factor $1/k$. To me, this is just a convenient way of representing the inverse effect of the number of predicates employed on the increase in probability due to observation of positive instances, when we assign equal a priori probabilities to structure descriptions; for Carnap, $1/k$ is a genuine factor affecting inductive inference.

This way of expressing the difference between our positions, however, disguises the radical nature of my objection to Carnap's enterprise: I also maintain that the decision to assign equal a priori probabilities to one set of predicates rather than another is arbitrary and so the correlate choice of λ value must also be arbitrary. Put generally — and in a way that makes its connection to the principle of indifference wholly explicit — we may say Carnap's entire conception of a continuum of inductive methods based on a variable weighting of logical and empirical factors is nothing other than a *fiction* generated by using the principle of indifference to assign equal a priori probabilities to structure descriptions involving families with varying number of predicates; characterized in this way there should be no temptation to see the choice of λ value as reflecting a balance of factors relevant to inductive inference, rather than a recurrence of the old problem of just what sets of predicates we are to assign equal a priori probabilities to on the basis of the principle of indifference.†

Thus to summarize our findings so far on a priori probabilities: given that the principle is a form of the definition of probability as the comparative relation of evidential support, and that the only non-arbitrary way to include instances of the null relation of evidential support in this definition is to hold any pair of hypotheses coupled with their null relevant evidence equal in probability (regardless of the predicates used in expressing the hypothesis), any consistent assignment of equal a priori probabilities must involve arbitrary stipulations. Prior to Carnap's work these stipulations took the form of arbitrary restrictions on the set of predicates to be used for a given problem and were fairly widely recognized as such; in Carnap's work the stipulation took the form of a choice of a λ value > 0 and the choice of this value for a given problem can be no less arbitrary.

Of course there still remains λ = 0 as a measure function, which I argued for on more or less independent grounds earlier. Since the λ = 0 measure function does not determine probabilities in the absence of relevant information, its selection corresponds to the second pos-

---

†I might also add — as a point of historical interest — that Carnap probably initially construed the λ continuum as reflecting a balance of factors genuinely relevant to inductive inference because of his (misguided) belief in the 'descriptive completeness' of languages for inductive reasoning. If a single set of k predicates can be identified once and for all as the correct basis for all inductive inferences in a language — including those on qualitatively difference phenomena — then different λ values can only be construed as representing different weights attached to the logical fact that k predicates are in use. Originally Carnap did hope to identify such a unique set of predicates — the Q-predicates in a language fulfilling the requirement of descriptive completeness. Of course it is not possible to determine once and for all such a single set of predicates for all inductive inference, and this is why Carnap abandoned the requirement. With the realization that different families with different k members of predicates are necessary for inductive inference, there should be no reason to construe different λ values as anything other than what they are — reflections of the differences in the assignment of probability values due to use of families with different members (k) of predicates.

Objections to the Principle of Indifference

sibility I discussed in regard to the problem of null evidence — we may simply decide that no comparison in respect of degree of probability can be made between pairs of hypotheses and their null relevant evidence, i.e. that no assignment of probability can be made in the absence of all relevant information. The discussion of this section provides an additional (and powerful) argument in favour of this option: as the contradictions long associated with the principle show, probabilities determined in the absence of all relevant information will vary with the number of predicates we use in a particular case. While it is possible to disguise this variability by representing it as an effect of some logical factor in inductive reasoning, the original difficulty of justifying the choice of one set of predicates, rather than another, recurs as the problem of justifying the choice of a value for λ, weighing the logical factor. Conversely, if we determine probabilities *solely* on the basis of evenly balanced relevant evidence, there is no dependency of the values so determined on the logical factor of the number of predicates used and thus no need to make arbitrary choice in this regard. In Carnap's λ system, this is accomplished by adopting $\lambda = 0$ as our measure function.

Indeed, on reflection the $\lambda = 0$ measure function appears ideally suited as a reconstruction of the method by which we affect the comparison between evidence and hypotheses in respect of evidential support when applying the principle. Earlier I remarked that independently of its problematic use to determine equal probabilities in the absence of all relevant evidence, the principle also identified equal probability with the equal evidential support supplied by evenly balanced relevant evidence. The most natural examples of such evenly balanced evidence (as we have already seen and will have occasion to note again) are cases in which statistical evidence exists as to the equal proportionately of the alternatives in question. In such cases it is highly plausible to think that the equal probabilities assigned by the principle are based on the equal evidential support given to the competing hypotheses by the extant evidence on the basis of the $\lambda = 0$ measure function.

It is natural to object here that if we apply the principle only to cases where evenly balanced relevant evidence exists, we give up the most important feature of the principle. That is to say, historically much of the interest surrounding the principle has depended on its capacity to assign a priori probabilities, and of course the discovery of an unassailable means to assign a prior probabilities would be not unlike the discovery of the proverbial philosopher's stone. But to hold that the principle's main interest and appeal stems from its determination of a priori probabilities — which was Carnap's view — is to get the matter the wrong way round. Once we see the principle as offering a definition of probability in terms of comparative relations of evidential support and realize how plausible this is in those cases where the evidentiary relations to be compared are those between hypotheses and their relevant evidence, we can see the comparison in the cases where the evidence is irrelevant as a possible, but neither necessary, nor particularly desirable, extension of this plausible definition to include extremely problematic cases.

A Historical Remark

The impression that the principle's determination of 'a priori' probabilities is not so much an essential feature of it, but rather an extension of the definition of probability encapsulated in it to cover the problematic cases involving null relevant evidence, is amply supported by examination of the writings of the principle's staunchest advocates. In fact most advocates of the principle, as opposed to its critics, intended it to be used *primarily* to determine equal probabilities on the unproblematic basis of relevant but equally balanced evidence; moreover, they would appear to have had in mind something very much like the $\lambda = 0$ measure function when 'balancing' the extant evidence between competing alternatives.

First let us consider Bernoulli's second maxim, already discussed, namely that we are to take all the relevant evidence that we can in a given situation. Such a maxim was hardly called for if it were envisioned that the total evidence possible would, in most cases of interest, turn out to be the null relevant evidence. Given the expectation that we shall usually have to deal with the null relevant evidence, we need not be exhorted to consider the total relevant evidence possible, for there is no such evidence to be considered in part of *in toto*. Thus Bernoulli's maxim is only really appropriate in the context of the expectation that the total evidence will, on the whole, be relevant.

Again, consider the kinds of situations to which the principle traditionally was applied: these were games of chance involving dice, roulette wheels, cards, etc. Of course, coins and dice have been tossed for a very long time; the physical properties that are deemed relevant are simple measurable magnitudes of weight and size, while the statistical results, if carefully gathered, can be easily evaluated. (Many philosophical studies of probability actually cite lengthy trials of coin tossing.) Moreover, even in the absence of any seriously gathered statistics, it is widely believed that the actual proportions which have occurred in tossing ordinary coins or dice (as well as spins of roulette wheels and distributions of shuffled cards) are roughly equal for each ordinary alternative, e.g. 'heads' or 'black'. It seems clear that just such a belief served as the basis for the judgments of equal probability made by the principle of indifference in these cases. We have no reason to prefer heads to tails in a coin in ordinary circulation, because such coins are believed, on the whole, to have produced heads in one out of every two trials; similarly so for the other games. And, as we have seen at length already, the assignment of equal probabilities in such circumstances is based on the existence of relevant but evenly balanced evidence, and can be plausibly thought of as measured by the $\lambda = 0$ measure function.

Such examples, then, seem to indicate that in fairness to advocates of the principle, we should consider it as primarily intended to offer the plausible definition of probability as the comparative concept of evidential support, where the evidence employed is relevant to the hypotheses in question, and thus treat the assignment of a priori probabilities as an extension of this definition to other, more problematic, cases.

SUBJECTIVISM AND THE PRINCIPLE OF INDIFFERENCE

The only serious objection to the principle of indifference that remains to be considered is the common complaint that it leads to a subjectivist conception of probability. Although not wholly unrelated to the problems we have been discussing in regard to a priori probabilities, the primary basis for this objection lies elsewhere; indeed it is best understood in the context of the discussion of subjectivism and the l.r.t. given in earlier chapters. Specifically, in Chapters I and III, I tried to explain how a definition of probability in terms of relations of evidential support could lead to a subjectivist conception of probability; we saw that one way such a definition could lead to subjectivism was if it were applied to determine unique probabilities on the basis of different amounts of evidence known to different individuals. This is what I called subjectivism in the application of a definition of probability and it could only be prevented by formulating the methodological precept guiding our application of the theory – the requirement of total evidence – in a strong, objective fashion.

Now, on the account given in the previous chapter, the principle of indifference not only constitutes a relational definition of probability, but also determines a 'unique' comparative ordering of probability – and so, often, unique numerical values. Despite certain differences in detail, all writers on the principle interpreted it so that on any one occasion it was to be applied in relation to just one body of evidence in its totality; so interpreted, the principle led to the unique probabilities needed for the purpose of action in precisely the same manner in which any relational definition of probability would yield unique probabilities when supplemented by the requirement of total evidence. Accordingly, just as any application of the l.r.t. on the basis of the total evidence known to a particular individual at a particular time led to a subjective conception of probability, any interpretation of the principle which held that it should be applied in relation to the evidence known to a particular person at a particular time would lead to a subjectivist conception of probability. In both cases a relational definition of probability is applied on the basis of the evidence subjectively known by an individual.

In fact, as we saw in the previous chapter, there are various views on whether the principle is correctly applied in relation to the total evidence known to a particular person, rather than, say, the total evidence that a rational person could know. Indeed because of the different views on this matter we were, at the start of the previous chapter, in difficulty in finding a uniform formulation of it. But there is no doubt some writers, for example, quite recently Mackie, have interpreted the principle in such a way as to sanction its application in relation to the total evidence known to a given individual at a particular time. Such an interpretation inevitably leads 'subjective' assignments of probability values, for the values will vary depending on the different bodies of evidence known to different individuals.

But as we have also noted, various writers, e.g. Blackburn and Bernoulli, interpreted the principle so that it could only be applied on the basis of the total evidence available, in a strong sense. If such an interpretation of the principle is accepted, it will not lead to the kind of subjectivism just discussed; on their interpretation, the principle is only properly applied in relation to the totality of evidence one could or should have known in a given situation, and the evidence we could have known or should have known are both totalities fixed quite independently of what evidence is actually known by particular people in a situation. Thus if we determine probabilities by applying the principle on the basis of such totalities of evidence, the results of applying it will *not* vary from person to person. This parallels the way in which a sufficiently strong formulation of the requirement of total evidence prevented subjectivism in the application of the l.r.t.

Now, I am not primarily interested in arguing for, say, Mackie's interpretation of the principle, and so convicting it of a form of subjectivism, or arguing for the Blackburn-Bernoulli interpretation and vindicating it. Rather, I am only interested in uncovering the reason why the principle has seemed for some to lead to an objectionably subjectivist conception of probability and not so for others. The basic reason for this is that the principle of indifference is amenable to *different* interpretations in regard to the question of just what evidence must be considered before applying it; in particular, these interpretations differ as to whether this body of evidence is the totality known to the person who wishes to apply it or a larger totality incorporating 'available' evidence not necessarily known to the person in question. On the former interpretation, the principle leads to that kind of subjectivism we diagnosed as arising when we attempt to give unique application to theories which define probability as a relation of evidential support. On the latter interpretation, found in Bernoulli and Blackburn, this variety of subjectivism is entirely avoided.

Subjectivism in the Theory Proper

Subjectivism in the application of a theory of probability is not the only kind of subjectivism possible; in Chapter I we also noted that relational definitions of probability would lead to a subjectivist conception of probability if the probability values assigned to sets of evidence and hypothesis were made to depend on particular individuals' beliefs about the relationship between the evidence and hypothesis — this is what I termed subjectivism in the theory proper. In a theory in which probability is defined as a comparative relation of evidential support, sets of evidence and hypothesis are not assigned numerical probabilities one by one, but only comparative probabilities in relation to other sets of evidence and hypothesis. In recent times probability theorists have devoted considerably less attention to the comparative concept of probability than to the quantitative concept; however, even since Keynes, Koopman has offered a theory of probability as a comparative relation of confirmation (1940, pp. 269-92), and Carnap himself devoted considerable attention to giving the outlines of such a theory (1962, Chapter VII). It seems fairly clear that the comparative relation Koopman tried to elucidate was one based on subjective beliefs, while Carnap envisioned one which made the comparative probabilities assigned to pairs of evidence and hypothesis depend only on objective logical relations between the evidence and hypothesis of each member of the pair.

What of the definition of probability as the comparative concept of evidential support which I have claimed is implicit in the principle of indifference? Are the equal probabilities sanctioned by the principle when the extant evidence gives no reason for preference based on purely logical relations between that evidence and the hypotheses in question? Well, the principle of indifference, as I interpret it, only presents in a rudimentary way a semantics for the concept of probability; among other reasons why this definition must be regarded as rudimentary is that the classical theorists did not explain clearly and exactly the phrase 'reason for preference'. We have seen how 'reason for preference' among competing hypotheses can only be supplied by some body of evidence which supports one hypothesis more than another, but in the absence of an explanation by classical theorists of the crucial idiom of 'reason for preference', we can only conjecture what they would have regarded as the grounds for saying a body of evidence did or did not support one hypothesis more than another. Was it purely logical considerations, say, of the range of evidence and hypothesis that made the evidence support one hypothesis more than another, and thereby, provide a reason for preferring it? Or might someone rightly hold that a body of evidence supported one hypothesis more than other, thereby making it 'preferable', just because it looked that way to him? It seems plausible to think that the classical theorists did not hold the latter view, but alternatively it would seem a gross anachronism to ascribe to them the former.

The difficulty with the principle is that the definition of probability it encapsulates is given in such a rudimentary way — and expressed in such a vague intuitive idiom — that the kind of elaboration required in a relational theory of probability (proper) to avoid such subjectivism just was not provided, and so it must be a matter of some speculation as to whether the principle leads in this way to a subjectivist conception of probability. However, I do think our earlier discussion of the principle's application on the basis of evenly balanced relevant evidence,

Objections to the Principle of Indifference

versus its application on the basis of the null relevant evidence, provides some fuel for this speculation, and I will conclude this chapter by pursuing this question in some detail.

Subjectivism and the Choice of λ-Value

As I indicated above, classical writers were primarily concerned with cases in which equal probabilities were assigned on the basis of evenly balanced relevant evidence; moreover, such evidence almost invariably involved information on the past equal proportionately of the alternative in question. This, as I remarked before, would suggest that classical theorists had the $\lambda = 0$ measure function in mind (in at least some vague way) when they made comparisons between hypotheses in respect of the evidential support provided by the extant evidence. If this measure function is employed as the basis for such comparisons, the principle will not lead to the kind of subjective we are now concerned with: as I explained in Chapter III, relational probabilities determined on the basis of $\lambda = 0$ could be regarded as wholly objective.

The issue becomes more complicated when we consider the principle's use to determine equal a priori probabilities in the absence of all relevant evidence. In one way, the assignment of a priori probabilities might not appear to involve 'subjective' judgments, for, in my view, the determinations of equal a priori probabilities follows directly from the decision to compare in respect of probability sets of hypotheses and their null relevant evidence. As I stressed before, once such a decision is made, the need to treat similar sets in a similar (i.e. not arbitrarily different) fashion, leads to the assignment of equal a priori probabilities; viewed in this light the assignment of equal a priori probabilities does not depend on the subjective matter of a particular individual's beliefs.

But as our lengthy examination of the contradictions engendered by the principle's a priori application revealed, the matter is not so simple. To give the principle a consistent application in the absence of all relevant information, some one set of predicates must be singled out as the correct basis for determining probabilities, and, as I tried to show, any such selection must be arbitrary. Moreover — and this is the important point at present — where one individual might (arbitrarily) choose one set of predicates to apply to a given problem in the absence of all information, another might choose a different set. In such cases, the a priori probabilities determined would vary from individual to individual, and so would be subjective in character.

Since the principle does sanction equal a priori probabilities — as well as equal probabilities based on the existence of evenly balanced relevant evidence — it can quite properly be criticized as leading in this way to a subjectivist conception of probability.

This of course provides yet another reason for thinking that the definition of probability encapsulated in the principle can be put in a satisfactory form if, but only if, it is restricted to cases where there exists relevant evidence. This is a point I have made before repeatedly and so need not elaborate on now; however, the connection between Carnap's λ system and the a priori application of the principle to statistical distributions for families of k predicates is so close that we cannot avoid noting how criticisms of the principle as subjectivist in character relate to his system of inductive logic. As we saw before, choice of a λ value to apply to a given problem was tantamount to choice of a specific number of predicates to be used in the assignment of equal a priori probabilities. If the choice of predicates for this purpose is arbitrary, as I have claimed it is, so then is the choice of λ value; similarly, if the probability values determined by a selection of predicates is only subjectively valid, the probability determined by choice of λ value > 0 will only be subjectively valid.

In fact, Carnap eventually had to admit as much: having begun his investigations with the claim that the l.r.t. provided an objective account of probability (1962, Section 12), he eventually had to characterize it as 'a (modified) subjectivist point of view', precisely because he could find no justification for choosing one of an infinity of λ values bounded by certain limits (Jeffrey, 1980, pp. 111-12). Although he describes the matter quite differently, there seems to me no doubt that the origin of this 'modified subjectivism' is precisely the same as that for which we just found the principle of indifference rightly criticised — the arbitrariness of any consistent distribution of probability in the absence of all relevant information.

Again we should note that no such problems attend the $\lambda = 0$ measure function and, as I first claimed in Chapter III and reiterated above, this function provides a genuinely objective measure of evidential support. It was of course for this reason that I recommended that it be adopted as the basis for a reconstruction of a concept of probability appropriate for scientific discourse within the terms of the l.r.t. As I remarked then, the l.r.t. yielded a wholly objectivist conception of probability if (and to my mind, only if) $\lambda = 0$ were adopted as a measure function and the requirement of total evidence

Objections to the Principle of Indifference

designed to give the l.r.t. unique application were given a suitably objective formulation. We now see — and this may be an appropriate note on which to conclude — that the very issues which, as we saw in earlier chapters, most directly affect the objectivity and subjectivity of probability judgment, actually have a long and complicated history: they are part and parcel of the longstanding controversies over the principle of indifference, as the discussion in this section indicates. On the interpretation I have given of the principle, this should not surprise us. As an early, and therefore rudimentary, version of the definition of probability as a relation of evidential support, it could be expected to have been a focus of attention for just those issues on the objectivity and subjectivity of probability judgments with which I have been concerned throughout this book.

BIBLIOGRAPHY

Ayer, A.J. (1972), *Probability and Evidence*, London, Macmillan.
Ayers, M.R. (1968), *The Refutation of Determinism*, London, Methuen.
Benenson, F.C. (1977), 'Randomness and the frequency definition of probability', *Synthese*, vol. 36, 1977, pp. 207-33.
Blackburn, S. (1973), *Reason and Prediction*, Cambridge University Press.
Braithwaite, R.B. (1953), *Scientific Explanation*, Cambridge University Press.
Carnap, R. (1945), 'Two concepts of probability', *Philosophy and Phenomenological Research*, no. 5, 1945.
Carnap, R. (1952), *The Continuum of Inductive Methods*, University of Chicago Press.
Carnap, R. (1962), *The Logical Foundations of Probability Theory*, 2nd ed., University of Chicago Press.
Carnap, R. (1963), *The Philosophy of Rudolf Carnap*, ed. P.A. Schlipp, La Salle, Illinois, Open Court.
Carnap, R. and Jeffrey, R.C. (eds.) (1971), *Studies in Inductive Logic*, I, Berkeley and Los Angeles, University of California Press.
Dummett, M. (1978), *Truth and Other Enigmas*, London, Duckworth.
Hacking, I. (1965), *The Logic of Statistical Inference*, Cambridge University Press.
Hempel, C.G. (1965), *Aspects of Scientific Explanation*, New York, Free Press.
Jeffrey, R.C. (ed.) (1980), *Studies in Inductive Logic*, II, Berkeley and Los Angeles, University of California Press.
Jeffreys, H. (1961), *Theory of Probability*, 3rd ed., Oxford, Clarendon Press.
Keynes, J.M. (1921), *A Treatise on Probability*, London, Macmillan.
Kneale, W. (1949), *Probability and Induction*, Oxford, Clarendon Press.
Koopman, B.C. (1940), 'The axioms and algebra of intuitive probability', *American Mathematical Series 2*, no. 41, 1940, pp. 269-92.

Bibliography

Kyburg, H. (1961), *Probability and The Logic of Rational Belief*, Middleton, Conn., Wesleyan University Press.
Kyburg, H. (1970), 'More on maximal specificity', *Philosophy of Science*, vol. 37, 1970.
Levi, I. (1980), *The Enterprise of Knowledge*, Cambridge, Mass., MIT Press.
Lewis, C.I. (1946), *An Analysis of Knowledge and Valuation*, La Salle, Ill., Open Court.
Lucas, T.R. (1970), *The Concept of Probability*, Oxford, Clarendon Press.
Mackie, J.L. (1969), 'The relevance criterion of confirmation', *British Journal of the Philosophy of Science*, no. 20, pp. 27-40.
Mackie, J.L. (1973), *Probability, Truth and Paradox*, Oxford, Clarendon Press.
Mellor, H. (1971), *The Matter of Chance*, Cambridge University Press.
Neyman, J. (1952), *Lectures on Mathematical Statistics and Probability*, 2nd edn, Washington, Department of Agriculture.
Pagels, H.R. (1982), *The Cosmic Code*, New York, Simon & Schuster.
Popper, K.R. (1959), 'The propensity interpretation of probability', *British Journal for the Philosophy of Science*, no. 10, pp. 25-42.
Popper, K.R. (1968), *The Logic of Scientific Discovery*, 2nd edn, London, Hutchinson.
Ramsey, F.P. (1926), 'Truth and probability', *The Foundations of Mathematics*, ed. Braithwaite, 1931, London, Routledge & Kegan Paul.
Reichenbach, H. (1949), *The Theory of Probability*, 2nd edn, Berkeley, University of California Press.
Salmon, W.C. (1967), *The Foundations of Scientific Inference*, University of Pittsburgh Press.
Schilpp, P.A. (ed.) (1963), *The Philosophy of Rudolf Carnap*, La Salle, Ill., Open Court.
Swinburne, R. (1973), *An Introduction to Confirmation Theory*, London, Methuen.
Von Mises, R. (1957), *Probability, Statistics and Truth*, 2nd edn, New York, Unwin.
Wright, C.J.G. (1980), *Wittgenstein on the Foundations of Mathematics*, London, Duckworth.

INDEX

anti-realist theory of meaning: and objective theories, 55, 56-9, 70-1, 154, 156, 161, 175-6; and probability statements, 5, 6, 14-22, 26-7, 31-2, 37-8, 43, 56, 57-8, 66, 218-19
application: of l.r.t., 78, 194-6, 202, 207, 218-19: methodology of, of l.r.t., 27, 30, 34-9, 100, 219; of principle of indifference, 243-6
Aristotle's 'Sea Battle Tomorrow', 139
Ayer, A.J., 24, 39-43, 95-6, 264
Ayers, M., 80

belief, degrees of, 45; *see also* credence
Bernoulli, J.; Law of Large Numbers, 6, 179, 182, 213-14; principle of indifference, 223-4, 270, 272-3
Bertrand's paradox, 257-9, 264
binomial law, 6, 155, 177-87, 213-14
Blackburn, S., 43, 54, 116-18, 136, 142-8; and principle of indifference, 223, 237, 261, 263, 272-3
Borel, E., 117, 264
Braithwaite, R.B., 2, 7, 55, 153-61, 167-8

Carnap, R.; and binomial law, 179-81; and evidence, 23, 77-8, 108; and frequency theory, 47; and inductive logic, 14, 228-9, 265-8, 276; and l.r.t., 14, 27, 68, 76-8, 152, 276; measure functions, 76, 105-13, 176n, 228-9, 231-5, 249-51, 265-9, 276; principle of indifference, 228-35, 247-8, 249-51, 260-70, 274, 276; and two concepts of probability, 11, 46, 68-75, 103, 151, 167
Chebyshev inequality, 155, 177-87, 212-13
Chi Square test, 9, 151n
classical theory of probability, 220, 242, 246-8, 274
confidence intervals, Neyman-Pearson, 67, 161-6
confirmation functions, Carnap's, 229, 233-4, 241-2, 249-51, 264-9
confirmation theory, 71-5
confirmation of universal hypothesis, 8
credal probability, 45
credence: degree of, 60-2, 63n, 65, 68-9, 74-5, 263; rational, 68-71, 263; *see also* belief
Czuber, E., 255

Index

decidability: in principle and practice, 26-7, 30, 37, 87-93, 100-1, 131-2, 147-8, 189-95, 198-205, 207-8, 215-19; and probability theory, 2, 7, 31, 56, 89-93, 114; and statistical probability, 189-95
determinism, 51, 142-4
Dummett, M., 2-3, 5, 21, 55-6, 57-8, 166n, 175n

effectiveness of concepts of probability, 52-4, 56, 57-8, 65-6
effective procedures, 17, 56-9, 66, 81-90, 129, 166n, 206
epistemic probability, 7, 45, 50, 68-70, 74, 181, 183
estimation, theory of, in frequency theory, 47-8, 53, 60-5
evidence: and principle of indifference, 222-4, 226, 235-42, 244-5, 249-65, 268-71, 272-6; relativity of probability statements to, 12-37 *passim*, 90-1, 108-10, 114, 118-28, 133-41, 145-8, 180-1, 188, 211-14; specificatory available, 80-6, 90, 93-4, 106-7, 108, 120, 150; statistical, 80, 105-7, 108, 149-52, 166-75, 177-88, 191-204, 214-19 (available, 205-14, 216); total available, 23-43 *passim*, 49-50, 77-9, 84-6, 90, 94-102, 108, 148, 208-14; total known, 35, 77-9, 98-9, 102, 108, 191-5, 200

finite attainability, Reichenbach's, 198
Frege, G., 221
frequency theory, 2, 4, 11, 47-9, 51, 52-4, 60-5, 69n, 174-6; finite, 196-205; and realism, 54-6

Goodman's New Riddle of Induction, 41

Hacking, I., 11, 48, 142-3
Hintikka, J., 8, 85n
Hume's problem of induction, 41

identity conditions and principle of indifference, 235-43, 246
indifference, principle of, 220-1; application of, 243-6, 250, 251, 256, 260, 264, 266-7, 272-3; and classical theory of probability, 246-8; history of, 221-35; and identity conditions, 235-43; and l.r.t., 7, 106, 220-1, 274; objections to, 249-77
induction, straight rule of, 104-13, 171-2; in frequency theory, 52, 174-6, 198; *see also* measure functions
inductive logic, Carnap's, 228-9, 265-8, 276
inductive probability, 1, 8, 9, 25-6, 41-2, 68-9, 71, 75; estimating, 210-14; and science, 103-13, 179-81
intuitionism, 5, 21, 175n, 176, 193n

Jeffreys, H., 224-5, 227-8, 243

Kemeny, J., 103
Keynes, J.M., 13-14, 45; and principle of indifference, 222-3, 225-8, 237, 239-41, 250, 256-9, 261, 263
Kneale, W., 223-4, 226, 255, 259
Koopman, B.C., 273-4
Kyburg, H., 7, 45-6, 203n

Levi, I., 45-6
Lewis, C.I., 2, 7, 69n, 251
logical relation theory (l.r.t.), 1, 2-3, 8, 13-23, 63-6; application of, 78, 194-6, 202, 207, 218-19; and classical theory of probability, 220; and confirmation theory, 71-2, 74-5;

Index

evidence, *see* evidence; and induction, 41-2, 103-13; methodology of application, 27, 30, 34-9, 100, 219; and objectivity, 42-3, 56-7, 75-8, 83-4, 93-4, 98-102, 118-20, 132, 208-9, 276-7; and principle of indifference, 220-1, 274; and relevance, 9; and revision of probability statements, 113-15, 116-41, 145-7, 167-70, 172-3, 178-87; and statistical probability, 151-3, 166-70, 172-5, 178-87; and subjectivity, 13, 44-5, 46-7, 75-8, 93-4, 98-100, 102, 208, 276-7

Lucas, J.R., 78

Mackie, J.L., 11, 43, 224, 237
meaning of probability statements, 15-22 *passim*, 26-8, 31, 37-9, 91-2, 159-60, 189-90, 202-4, 218-19
measure functions, 8, 76-7, 104-13, 149, 173, 176, 186n; in principle of indifference, 228-9, 231-5, 249-51, 260, 264-70, 275-6; $\lambda = 0$, 8, 76, 104-14, 149-50, 173-4, 176, 178, 186, 210, 234-5, 256, 265-9, 275-8
Mellor, H.; and Neyman confidence coefficient, 67n, 163-4; objection to l.r.t., 24, 26n, 49-50, 117-18; and principle of indifference, 255, 259; propensity theory, 11, 48, 50-1, 55, 142-3
methodology of application of l.r.t., 27, 30, 34-9, 100, 219

Neyman, J., 105
Neyman-Pearson confidence intervals, 67, 161-6

objective theories of probability, 17, 23, 43-4, 47-51, 52-4, 59-67, 68-71; and anti-realism, 55, 56-9, 70-1, 154, 156, 161, 175-6; finite frequency theory, 196-205; and realism, 54-7, 58-9, 175; and rejection rules, 151-6, 161, 165-6; and revision of probability statements, 53, 54, 117-20, 130-1, 136-42, 151, 186-7, 188
objectivity: and l.r.t., 42-3, 56-7, 75-8, 83-4, 93-4, 98-102, 118-20, 132, 208-9, 276-7; of probability statements, 3-4, 8, 12-13, 43-4, 117-20, 142-3
operational definition of probability, 161-6

personalist probability, 7, 45
physical states, changes in, revising probability statements, 136-41
Popper, K.R., 48, 55, 71-5, 153
posits in Reichenbach's frequency theory, 62-3
positivism, 2, 153-4
probability: classical theory of, 220, 242, 246-8, 274; concepts of, 10-13, 19-20, 26, 27-8, 46-7, 52-4, 56-8, 68-72; and confirmation, 71-5; credal, 45; epistemic, 7, 45, 50, 68-70, 74, 181, 183; estimates of, 3-7, 39-40, 54, 60-8 *passim*, 113-18, 127-8, 152, 167-8, 184-9, 210-14, 217; finite frequency theory of, 195-206; frequency theory of, 11, 47-9, 51, 52-6, 60-5, 69n, 174-6; inductive, 25-6, 41-2, 68-9, 71, 75, 103-13, 179-81, 210-14; l.r.t., *see* l.r.t.; objective theories of, *see* objective theories; operational definition of, 161-4; personalist, 7, 45; and principle of indifference, 242-8, 252-5,

282

Index

261, 268-71, 274-6; propensity theory of, 11, 48, 49-50, 52, 53, 54-6; rational corpora theory of, 45-6; relational theory of, 49; statistical, *see* statistical; subjective theories of, 7, 43-4, 46-7, 75-8, 271-7
propensity theory, 2, 4, 11, 48, 49-51, 52, 53; and anti-realism, 55-6; and realism, 54-6
Putnam, H., 85n, 176n

Quine, W.V., 109n

Ramsey, F.P., 45, 46
randomness, 9, 46, 162n
rational corpora theory, 45-6
rational credence, 68-71, 263
realism: and objective theories, 54-7, 58-9, 175; and probability, 2, 3, 6, 13, 16-17, 23, 66; and revision of probability judgments, 129-32
Reichenbach, H.; finite frequency theory, 196-205; and frequency theory, 2, 47, 49, 53, 61-2, 174-6; and pragmatic justification of induction, 63n, 174-6; and principle of indifference, 255; and straight rule of induction, 105, 174-6, 198
rejection of probability statements, 151-61, 165, 171-3, 177-85, 212-13; *see also* revision of probability statements
relevance, 9, 72, 74, 150n; and principle of indifference, 234-5, 240-1, 249, 251-64 *passim*
revision of probability statements, 3-5, 70n; indefinitely extendible, 3-6, 114, 127-9, 144, 156, 167-8, 170-4, 182-8, 194; l.r.t. and, 113-15, 116-41, 145-7, 167-70, 172-3, 178-87; objective theories and, 53, 54, 117-20, 130-1, 136-42, 186-7, 188; realism and, 129-32;

statistical evidence and, 166-76, 177-88, 199-201: *see also* rejection of probability statements

Salmon, W.C., 35, 47-8, 49, 53, 174-6
single-case probability values, 23, 28-31, 32-4, 36, 39-40, 48-51
statistical probability, 3-4, 5-7, 68, 149, 214-19; availability of statistical evidence, 205-14, 216; confidence intervals and, 161-6, and decidability, 189-95; finite frequency theory and, 196-205; rejection rules and, 151-61, 165, 171-3, 177-85, 212-13; and revision of probability judgments, 166-78, 199-201
straight rule of induction, 104-13, 171-2; in frequency theory, 52, 174-6, 198; *see also* measure functions
subjectivist theory, 2, 7, 43-5, 46-7; and principle of indifference, 271-7
subjectivity: and l.r.t., 13, 43-5, 46, 75-8, 93-4, 98-100, 102, 208, 276-7; and principle of indifference, 226-7
Swinburne, R., 74, 120-2

time, revision of probability with, 25, 91, 93, 102n, 120-8, 133-41, 192-6
truth of probability statements: and l.r.t., 14-23, 26-7, 30-4, 90-2, 100-1, 124-6, 132, 189-90, 204, 218-19; and objective theories, 53, 56, 57-8, 59, 70, 117, 156, 159

uncertainty relations, Heisenberg's, 43-4

verification, 203-4
Von Mises, R., 47-8, 225-6, 255

Index

Waismann, F., 47, 105

Wittgenstein, L., 175

International Library of Philosophy

Editor: Ted Honderich

(Demy 8vo)

Allen, R.E. (Ed.), **Studies in Plato's Metaphysics** *464 pp. 1965.* **Plato's 'Euthyphro' and the Earlier Theory of Forms** *184 pp. 1970.*
Allen, R.E. and Furley, David J. (Eds.), **Studies in Presocratic Philosophy**
  Vol. 1: The Beginnings of Philosophy *326 pp. 1970.*
  Vol. 11: Eleatics and Pluralists *448 pp. 1975.*
Armstrong, D.M., **Perception and the Physical World** *208 pp. 1961.* **A Materialist Theory of the Mind** *376 pp. 1967.*
Bambrough, Renford (Ed.), **New Essays on Plato and Aristotle** *184 pp. 1965.*
Barry, Brian, **Political Argument** *382 pp. 1965.*
Becker, Lawrence C. **On Justifying Moral Judgments** *212 pp. 1973.*
† Benenson, F.C., **Probability, Objectivity and Evidence** *224 pp. 1984.*
† * Blum, Lawrence, **Friendship, Altruism and Morality** *256 pp. 1980.*
Bogen, James, **Wittgenstein's Philosophy of Language** *256 pp. 1972.*
Brentano, Franz, **The Foundation and Construction of Ethics** *398 pp. 1973.* **The Origin of our Knowledge of Right and Wrong** *184 pp. 1969.* **Psychology from an Empirical Standpoint** *436 pp. 1973.* **Sensory and Noetic Consciousness** *168 pp. 1981.*
Broad, C.D., **Lectures on Psychical Research** *462 pp. 1962.*
† Clarke, D.S., **Practical Inferences** *160 pp. 1985.*
Crombie, I.M., **An Examination of Plato's Doctrine**
  Vol. 1: Plato on Man and Society *408 pp. 1962.*
  Vol. 11: Plato on Knowledge and Reality *584 pp. 1963.*
† Davies, Martin, **Meaning, Quantification, Necessity** *294 pp. 1981.*
Dennett, D.C., **Content and Conciousness** *202 pp. 1969.*
Detmold, M.J., **The Unity of Law and Morality** *288 pp. 1984.*
Dretske, Fred I., **Seeing and Knowing** *270 pp. 1969.*
Ducasse, C.J., **Truth, Knowledge and Causation** *264 pp. 1969.*
Fann. K.T. (Ed.), **Symposium on J.L. Austin** *512 pp. 1969.*
Findlay, J.N., **Plato: The Written and Unwritten Doctrines** *498 pp. 1974.*
† Findlay, J.N., **Wittgenstein: A Critique** *240 pp. 1984.*
Flew, Anthony, **Hume's Philosophy of Belief** *296 pp. 1961.*
† Fogelin, Robert J., **Skepticism and Naturalism in Hume's Treatise** *192 pp. 1985.*
† Foster, John, **The Case for Idealism** *280 pp. 1982.*
Glover, Jonathan, **Responsibility** *212 pp. 1970.*
Goldman, Lucien, **The Hidden God** *424 pp. 1964.*
† Gray, John, **Mill on Liberty: A Defence** *160 pp. 1983.*
Hamlyn, D.W., **Sensation and Perception** *222 pp. 1961.*
† Honderich, Ted (Ed.), **Morality and Objectivity** *256 pp. 1985.*
† * Hornsby, Jennifer, **Actions** *152 pp. 1980.*
Husserl, Edmund, **Logical Investigations** *Vol. 1: 456 pp.*
  Vol. 11: 464 pp. 1970.